Black in the British Frame

The Black Experience in British Film and Television

STEPHEN BOURNE

CONTINUUM
London and New York

Continuum
The Tower Building
11 York Road
London SE1 7NX

370 Lexington Avenue
New York
NY 10017-6503

© Stephen Bourne 2001

First published in 2001

British Library Cataloguing-in-Publication Data
A catalogue record for this book is available from the British Library.

ISBN 0-8264-5741-X (hardback)
    0-8264-5539-5 (paperback)

Typeset by BookEns Ltd, Royston, Herts.
Printed and bound in Great Britain by Biddles Ltd,
Guildford and King's Lynn

Contents

Contents

List of Illustrations

Acknowledgements

I would like to thank David Barker (Continuum); Linda Bellos; Arthur and Kathleen Bourne; Carl Daniels (*Black Film Bulletin*); Dr Jim Fowler (Theatre Museum); Ray Funk; Laurence Gouldbourne (London Borough of Southwark Equalities Unit); Jeffrey Green; Noreen Harewood; Janice Healey (British Film Institute); Keith Howes; Peter Powell; Leon Robinson; Howard Rye; Ken Sephton; Menelik Shabazz (*Black Film-maker*); Marika Sherwood (Black and Asian Studies Association); Aaron Smith; Rita E. Smith (National Film Theatre); Robert Taylor; Simon Vaughan (Alexandra Palace Television Society); Val Wilmer and Dr Lola Young (Middlesex University).

For photographic stills reproduced in this book, unless otherwise stated, we thank Newton I. Aduaka, Royal Television Society, Alexandra Palace Television Society, Nadia Cattouse, Colin Richardson (*Gay Times*), Yvonne Salmon, Channel 4, Granada Television, BBC Photograph Library and BFI Stills, Posters and Designs.

Though every care has been taken, if, through inadvertence or failure to trace the present owners, we have included any copyright material without acknowledgement or permission, we offer our apologies to all concerned.

Preface

The following extracts have been edited and revised from a *Black Film Bulletin* interview with Stephen Bourne conducted by Onyekachi Wambu about the first edition of *Black in the British Frame*.

Black Film Bulletin (BFB): *Tell us something about your background.*

Stephen Bourne (SB): As a child in the 1960s I grew up in a racially mixed, working-class community on a council estate in Peckham and went to Oliver Goldsmith, a culturally diverse primary school on Peckham Road. On the other side of London lived Aunt Esther, a black woman born here before the First World War. I was ten years old in 1968 when racism hit me. Enoch Powell and his fictional disciple Alf Garnett, from BBC television's *Till Death Us Do Part*, surfaced. Powell made his infamous 'Rivers of Blood' speech. Garnett spouted racist abuse in British homes up and down the country. As a youngster I experienced all of this with anger and frustration and it didn't surprise me that, as a teenager in the early 1970s, I witnessed a rise in popularity of the National Front. As long as I live I will never forget the horror of watching – from my bedroom window – members of the National Front march along Peckham Road with police protection.

When I was growing up our local police stations – Peckham, Brixton, Carter Street in Walworth Road – had bad reputations. If we saw a policeman we didn't ask him the time, we just ran for it. In 1980 my fear and mistrust of the police was confirmed when I was stopped and searched by two officers near my home in Peckham. It didn't surprise me when, a year later, young – mostly black – people in Peckham and Brixton vented their anger and frustration with the police. I understood how they felt. Clearly, growing up in a racially mixed community, and having a black aunt, gave me insights that most white children in Britain did not get.

BFB: *Why did you write* Black in the British Frame?

SB: When I grew up there weren't that many books around about black British history. Next to nothing about black British film and television, unless it was sociological or theoretical. I found plenty of material about black *American* entertainers and jazz musicians. By the age of fourteen I had read books about Dorothy Dandridge, Sammy Davis Jr, Duke Ellington, Eartha Kitt, Lena Horne, Sidney Poitier, Paul Robeson and, my favourite, Ethel Waters. As a teenager I read every book I could find about black cinema, but they were written from an American perspective, by such writers as Ed Mapp, Thomas Cripps, Gary Null, Daniel J. Leab and Eileen Landay. For me, the most interesting was Donald Bogle. His work opened up a whole new way of thinking about black actors. For instance, in Bogle's work, Hattie McDaniel, who won an Oscar for portraying Mammy in *Gone with the Wind*, became a real person, a gifted but exploited actress. But, with the exception of Thomas Cripps, none of these writers truly gave black British cinema the recognition it deserved. The only British book I found on the subject was Peter Noble's pioneer study *The Negro in Films*, but that was published in 1948! Black British actors received scant attention and were heavily overshadowed by their American counterparts. For years African-Americans have enjoyed a certain amount of publicity and celebrity status in this country, whereas black British actors and entertainers have been ignored. This made my work all the more important, and difficult.

BFB: *Tell us something about your experiences of watching television and films in the 1960s and 1970s.*

SB: As a child I didn't do homework. I watched television, everything from *Blue Peter* to *Cathy Come Home*. I practically *lived* in the Peckham Odeon but, apart from Sidney Poitier and Jim Brown, there were no black heroes in films in the 1960s. In the early 1970s I saw Richard Roundtree in *Shaft*, Diana Ross in *Lady Sings the Blues* and blaxploitation films but nothing from Britain except the 'big screen' version of that terrible television sitcom, *Love Thy Neighbour*. After that, Horace Ove made *Pressure* outside the so-called mainstream, but it was poorly distributed. In 1974 I became a member of the National Film Theatre, and this helped to broaden my knowledge of cinema. Until then I had been restricted to the Peckham Odeon, and occasional trips to the West End. However, by the end of the 1970s the Peckham Odeon was in decline. In 1981 it became the Ace Cinema and partly survived by screening a double-bill of two popular Jamaican films: *The Harder They Come*, starring reggae singer Jimmy Cliff, and a hilarious comedy called *Smile Orange*. The Odeon management had finally caught on that a young, enthusiastic black audience lived in the local area and wanted to see these films. I made my final visit to the Odeon in 1982 to see this double-bill. The Peckham Odeon closed in 1983 and was demolished to make way for a job centre.

When I started reviewing films for various black journals in the mid-1980s I had one or two bad experiences. In 1987 the *Caribbean Times*, a weekly national newspaper, asked me to review Richard Attenborough's *Cry Freedom*, starring Denzel Washington as Steve Biko. A top PR company handled the publicity, and I called them to request a reservation for the press screening at the Odeon, Leicester Square. To my horror my request was denied. The press officer said the *Caribbean Times* wasn't on their 'approved' press list, and she hadn't heard of it, anyway. I calmly explained that the *Caribbean Times* was one of only two national black newspapers in Britain – the other was *The Voice* – but the press officer refused to give me a ticket. So I threatened to take the matter further. I told her that I'd ask the editor of the *Caribbean Times* to run a cover story, and make a complaint to Mr Attenborough. There was silence, followed by, 'Let me take your number and I'll call you back.' Within the hour the phone rang and a well-spoken gentleman apologized for the 'misunderstanding', and offered me two tickets for the press screening! You see, all they were interested in was ensuring that the likes of Derek Malcolm from the *Guardian* and Barry Norman from the BBC's *Film 87* were coming and had nice, comfortable seats. They couldn't give a toss about *Caribbean Times*, one of Britain's top black newspapers.

BFB: *Tell us about your aunt.*

SB: Early on I was motivated to co-author my first book, *Aunt Esther's Story*, with my black British aunt. This gave me an insight into the lives of black working-class Britons between the wars. I had already found information about the black middle classes of that period, such as Marcus Garvey, C. L. R. James and Dr Harold Moody. Aunt Esther was a working-class woman who spoke eloquently, and movingly, about her life. By talking to her I discovered many interesting facts, and some fascinating connections to the story I have told *in Black in the British Frame*. For instance, in the late 1930s, her father, a Guyanese labourer, worked as an extra in Paul Robeson's films. At the same time, Aunt Esther, who was a seamstress, made dresses for the singer Elisabeth Welch, who starred opposite Paul Robeson in two films. From Aunt Esther, I learned about the importance of oral history testament, which is a major feature of all my books, including *Black in the British Frame*.

BFB: *Can you explain your use of the term 'black'?*

SB: In *Black in the British Frame* my use of the term 'black' means people of African or Caribbean descent, usually African-Americans (USA) or African-Caribbeans (Britain). For the record, this book is not intended to be definitive, and the reader will find many gaps. For instance, I have not included comedy or documentaries. I wanted to include a chapter about children's television, where great progress has been made, and another about the impact black images in American film and television have had in this country, such as *Star Trek*, *Shaft* and *Roots*. The book reflects my passionate interest in popular drama and entertainment.

BFB: *Where did you start your research?*

SB: I started at the beginning of cinema and the start of television. Most people think that the first black actor in British television was Rudolph Walker in *Love Thy Neighbour*, which is rubbish. It's like saying the first black people to come to Britain came on the *Empire Windrush* in 1948, which isn't true either. Black people have been settling here since the 1500s. So I scanned every cast list in Denis Gifford's invaluable reference book *The British Film Catalogue 1895–1985* and every page of the *Radio Times* to find appearances by black actors. I spent long, tiring hours in libraries making a note of every black person I could find. Everyone from major figures like Paul Robeson, to bit players like Napoleon Florent. I started doing this in 1976, when I was still at school, and it became a labour of love.

BFB: *Why the focus on Edric Connor and Winifred Atwell?*

SB: They were Trinidadians who made a huge impact on popular culture in post-war Britain at a time when it was easier for African-Americans to have celebrity status here. Winifred Atwell topped the British 'pop' charts in 1954 and became a household name. Someone once told me that, in America, black people who didn't know what she looked like thought she was white because they hadn't heard of anyone from the Caribbean reaching that level of success in British popular music. She was a trailblazer. Edric Connor was very ambitious, and succeeded in most of the things he attempted: acting, singing, film-making.

BFB: *So Edric Connor was a renaissance man – agent, behind the camera, in front of it, singer, etc?*

SB: Yes. That's why I call him 'A Man For All Seasons'. But sometimes his ambitions were thwarted by the white establishment. He was a popular calypso singer, but trained in opera too. However, to his distress, he was not invited to perform at Covent Garden on the opera stage. African-American concert singers like Marian Anderson could perform here. *Porgy and Bess* with William Warfield and Leontyne Price was staged in London's West End in 1952. Edric was shut out because he was from the Caribbean. In the end it defeated him. By the 1970s, Edric and Winifred were forgotten. Books about theatre, television and popular music completely ignored them. This erasure, this invisibility, is what I wanted to redress.

BFB: *How important was Paul Robeson, during the time that he spent here, to the development of black British film? And has anybody else since equalled the things he achieved in film in this country?*

SB: Paul Robeson is the only black actor to have been given star status in British films. He was included in the top-ten box-office list of 1937, with Gracie Fields and George Formby, and that is a measure of his popularity, even though his films were not always worthy of him. Let's not forget he disowned *Sanders of the River*. Earl Cameron came along in the 1950s, but the British film industry would not promote an African-Caribbean actor in the post-war years. And the careers of black British actors, like Earl, Thomas Baptiste, Cy Grant and Errol John, suffered because African-Americans were brought over to play roles *they* should have had in films like *The L-Shaped Room* [Brock Peters], *The Hill* [Ossie Davis] and *To Sir, With Love* [Sidney Poitier]. This was still happening in the 1980s when Denzel Washington came here to star in *Cry Freedom* and *For Queen and Country*.

BFB: *Isaac Julien directed* Black and White in Colour, *a documentary about the history of black people in British television, which I believe you helped research?*

SB: I researched it with Therese Daniels. We spent two years on the project. It was funded by the BBC and British Film Institute. Then Isaac was asked to make the documentary. Sadly, a great deal of early television is lost. In the early days, before the existence of videotape, we didn't have the technology to record television. It was broadcast live. But I did locate a worn, torn negative of a recording of Jan Carew and Sylvia Wynter's television play *The Big Pride*, first shown in 1961. I then persuaded the National Film and Television Archive to acquire, restore and preserve it. They also made a new viewing copy. If I hadn't done this, an important work by two major African-Caribbean writers would have been lost for ever.

BFB: *What about the prospects for the future? Will we break this cycle of frustration?*

SB: We will break this cycle one day, but it will only happen gradually. In the meantime, it is a long, slow, sometimes painful process. There is a wall of silence around the history of our nation's black people. And, I'm sorry to say, the academic world plays a role in keeping this history a secret. For instance, *Black in the British Frame* is *not* a theoretical study and, because of this, it will be attacked or ignored by film and television theorists. This happened with my first book, *Brief Encounters: Lesbians and Gays in British Cinema 1930–71*. Of course I want to see my books on sale alongside academic texts in Dillons bookstore in Tottenham Court Road, but I'd be a lot happier if I could find them on my own doorstep, for instance, in my local W. H. Smith branches in Peckham and the Elephant and Castle!

To answer your question, in Britain, the broadsheets tend to ignore black history books in their book review sections, so those of us who write them have to find other ways to promote them. We have to use our imaginations. For instance, *Aunt Esther's Story* sold out its first print-run, but this was partly due to my spreading the word at community level, distributing flyers, giving talks during Black History Month, that kind of thing. It's exhausting, but necessary if the cycle of frustration is going to be broken. I will probably have to do the same with *Black in the British Frame*.

(*from Black Film Bulletin*, Winter 1997–Spring 1998, Vol. 5/6, Issue 4/1)

What the black actor has managed to give are moments – indelible moments, created, miraculously, beyond the confines of the script; hints of reality, smuggled like contraband into a maudlin tale, and with enough force, if unleashed, to shatter the tale to fragments.

James Baldwin, *The Devil Finds Work* (1976)

1

The Uncle Tom Show

During Queen Victoria's reign (1837–1901) the main contact white Britons had with people of African descent was either in sport (primarily boxing) or in entertainment. However, few black entertainers existed on stage, though, as historian Ziggi Alexander explains, whites appeared with regularity in blackface:

> Blackface minstrelsy was popular with British audiences even into the second half of the twentieth century. For black performers and music-hall goers, entertainment and amusement were not without cost. Paradoxically so, since for the artist it provided a source of scarce work, and seeing fellow black people on stage gave black audiences a sense of race pride. Yet both groups were also aware that harmful racial stereotypes were continuously reinforced. Although white professionals dominated minstrelsy, there was interest in seeing black performers on stage … Whilst music-hall provided work for the vast majority of black performers, others succeeded by different means. In 1903, the black American show *In Dahomey* was staged at the Shaftesbury Theatre. The company comprised one hundred members, with Bert Williams and George Walker in the principal parts. So successful was this break from the minstrel convention that on 23 June 1903, members of the cast were invited to perform at Buckingham Palace during the garden party held for the ninth birthday of the King's eldest grandson, Edward (later Prince of Wales).[1]

One of the first films seen in Britain featured blackface minstrels. *The Wandering Negro Minstrels* (1896) showed half-a-dozen of them busking on a London street. For just forty-five seconds they sing, dance and play banjos, tambourines and bones to the delight of passers-by. The minstrels were filmed by the brothers Auguste and Louis Lumière. The brothers and their Cinématographe are synonymous with the invention of cinema. Following a successful commercial debut at the Grand Café in Paris on 28 December 1895, they swiftly exploited their invention worldwide.

For several years, blackface minstrelsy continued to surface in a number of silent film comedies. In *The Lightfooted Darkey* (1899) a minstrel dances in a Derby racecourse setting. In *Stump Speech* (1900) a 'negro minstrel' makes a speech. *Sambo* (1902) featured Sam Dalton, a blackface comedian, smoking a cigar. And in *Nigger Courtship* (1903) a black couple, probably played by whites in blackface, 'spoon' and kiss.

In the early years of sound, blackface stars of the music halls began making guest appearances in films. They included G. H. Elliott, an American who made his London debut in 1902, and billed himself as 'The Chocolate Coloured Coon'. In 1934 he was seen in *Music Hall*. Elliott continued working in blackface until he died, at the age of seventy-nine, in 1962. However, in the Edwardian era, it was not unusual to find black comedians blacking up, and these included Bert Williams of the *In Dahomey* company, and Harry Scott, one half of the popular African-American double-act, Scott and Whaley. Adelaide Hall, an entertainer who often worked with Scott and Whaley, once explained:

> In the old days, black comedians like Bert Williams, who starred in the Ziegfeld shows, were expected to black up. If they appeared on stage without it, they were booed off! Josephine Baker blacked up at the start of her career. Florence Mills and Paul Robeson were among the first black entertainers to be accepted on stage without having to wear blackface. They successfully broke away from the tradition.[2]

Eddie Whaley was born in America's Deep South, but lost his parents at an early age. With no family to support him, he was employed as a houseboy by a white family who ill-treated him. Eventually he ran away and travelled north, where he survived by singing on the streets of New York. It was there he befriended the comedian Harry Scott, who originated from Cleveland, Ohio, and together they formed a cross-talking double-act. Calling themselves 'Cuthbert and Pussyfoot', Whaley was the straight man, and Scott appeared in blackface.

Accepting an invitation to tour England in 1909, Scott and Whaley made their first appearance at the Hippodrome, Sheffield, and their London debut followed in 1910 at the Empire, Leicester Square. They arrived in England with bookings for only eight weeks, but they were so successful they never returned to America, and became British subjects. For over thirty years Scott and Whaley were a popular variety act, performing in music halls all over the country, as well as Paris, Vienna, Frankfurt, Copenhagen and Australia. Apart from their successful cross-talking routine, Scott and Whaley also worked a songs-at-the-piano act. Whaley was vocalist, and Scott a good jazz pianist. An article in a 1936 edition of *Radio Review* claimed that Scott and Whaley

Scott and Whaley

were the first people to introduce ragtime and syncopation to England. At their first performance they were given the bird! At rehearsal the conductor looked at the score and said it was impossible to play, so Scott had to accompany on the piano himself. At the second house they reorganised their show and were a riotous success![3]

In 1933 Scott and Whaley became nationally famous with their regular appearances on BBC radio in the popular, long-running series *Kentucky Minstrels*. In 1934 they became the first black performers to star in a British film when the director John Baxter, famous for making low-budget films about Britain's lower classes, cast them in *Kentucky Minstrels*, inspired by their radio success. Scott and Whaley played a couple of unemployed minstrels, living in poverty. An impresario, played by C. Denier Warren (who co-authored the screenplay with Harry S. Pepper), comes to their rescue and presents them in the finale of his latest stage spectacular. An incomplete print of this film exists in the National Film and Television Archive. Sadly, the Minstrel Show finale – which also features (white) Debroy Somers and his band (in blackface) and the African-American vocalist Nina Mae McKinney singing 'I'm in Love with the Band' – is missing.

When the partnership ended in 1946, Whaley teamed up with comedian Chris Gill, but Scott and Whaley were reunited for one final appearance together at the Queen's Theatre in Poplar on 19 May 1947. Sadly, Scott died one month later on 22 June 1947. Afterwards, Whaley retired to Brighton, where he opened a hotel. A few years earlier, in 1939, his son, Eddie Whaley Jr, was born in Brighton. As a youngster he appeared with his father on BBC radio, and in 1947 director Michael Powell cast him in the film classic *Black Narcissus*. Eddie Jr gave a scene-stealing performance as Joseph Anthony who helps a group of nuns to open a school/hospital in the remote Himalayas. He remembers Powell as 'a tyrant on the set who screamed a lot'.[4] Until he died in 1960, Eddie Snr's hotel in Brighton became a popular holiday home for black entertainers in Britain, and Eddie Jr remembers meeting just about every black star who worked in Britain in the 1940s and 1950s, including Turner Layton, Leslie 'Hutch' Hutchinson, Ellis Jackson, Ray Ellington, Ike Hatch and Adelaide Hall.

The *Kentucky Minstrels* radio series that Scott and Whaley helped popularize for the BBC ended shortly after celebrating its one-hundredth performance in 1948. That same year, the BBC televised a Kentucky Minstrels show from Alexandra Palace. Meanwhile, the appeal of the music-hall entertainer G. H. Elliott continued right into the 1950s (in 1951 he supported the Ray Ellington Quartet at the Finsbury Empire), but the writing was on the wall. Blackface minstrels looked old-fashioned and outdated, especially with the rise in popularity in Britain of glamorous black entertainers like Trinidad's Winifred Atwell and America's Harry Belafonte. By the late 1950s it should have been impossible for a blackface minstrel show to find an audience on national television, but nothing could have been further from the truth, for that is exactly what happened.

First, a blackface minstrel show was included in the National Radio Show at the Earls Court exhibition hall in London. This was televised by the BBC on 2 September 1957 as *The 1957 Television Minstrels*. George Mitchell's Minstrels, the Television Toppers, Ike Hatch (the African-American entertainer from the original *Kentucky Minstrels* radio series) and G. H. Elliott (still going strong) filled an hour-long broadcast, and it was so successful that a series was devised and produced by George Inns. Launched on 14 June 1958, *The Black and White Minstrel Show* was an instant hit, and ran for twenty years.

Though popular with viewers, complaints about the new version of *The Black and White Minstrel Show* started almost as soon as it began, especially after it won a major award. In 1961 the BBC entered a recording of the programme in the first world television contest held at Montreux, Switzerland. After winning the top prize, the Golden Rose of Montreux, the black British magazine *Flamingo* responded by dismissing the series as 'a piece of outdated and degrading rubbish'.[5] The article also quoted several black commentators including the Trinidadian theatrical agent Pearl Connor. She complained, 'white performers with black faces look ridiculous and make me feel ashamed'. In the same article, Lloyd Squires, a black businessman from Brixton, said, 'I feel ashamed and disgusted ... Some friends have told me they switch off the moment the show starts.'

In 1967, writer Dennis Potter exposed an overtly racist joke in the show in a review he wrote for the *New Statesman*: 'Leslie Crowther [the show's resident comedian] caught the spirit of the thing last Saturday with a joke (yuk, yuk) about a coloured immigrant who is happy to stay ' "so long as the National Assistance Board is keeping me here for free".'[6] Potter's reference to Crowther's joke reveals that the show was used as a platform for racist propaganda at a time when Enoch Powell and his fictional disciple, Alf Garnett, were spouting racist abuse in homes up and down the country.

But with sixteen to eighteen million viewers tuning in every Saturday evening, the BBC had no intention of taking the series off. Year after year, throughout the 1960s and 1970s, white men blacked up to sing the praises of dear old Alabammy, surrounded by leggy (white) dancing girls, and the BBC responded to protests and petitions with wide-eyed innocence. For instance, George Inns, the producer of the series, protested, 'I have never had a letter from a coloured person complaining about the show ... I don't see how you can bring politics into it. This is an innocent programme, providing entertainment ... as for finding a coloured choir to better our singers, I don't think I'd be able to do so.'[7]

When the BBC finally pulled the plug in 1978 there was a huge sigh of relief from its critics, and an even bigger outcry from white viewers who had grown up with the Minstrels in music halls, and turned a blind eye to the accusations of racism. But what had accounted for its immense popularity? Sarita Malik offers the following explanation:

Part of the explanation was undoubtedly the pleasure many got from the programme, with its meticulously choreographed dance routines and popular songs and melodies. George Inns combined white dancers with black-faced singers and this was believed to be visually striking, particularly when colour television was introduced in 1967. ... The racist implications of the premise of the programme were yet to be widely acknowledged or publicly discussed. But it was this which largely led to the programme's eventual demise.

Many felt that a large part of 'minstrel humour' was based on caricaturing black people and depicting them as being both stupid and credulous. This image was felt to be insensitive and inappropriate in an increasingly multi-racial and multi-cultural Britain.[8]

NOTES

1   Ziggi Alexander, 'Black entertainers of the Edwardian Era', *Weekend Voice*, 17–21 December 1987.
2   Adelaide Hall, interview with Stephen Bourne, London, 21 July 1993.
3   'News about people', *Radio Review*, 4 April 1936.
4   Eddie Whaley Jr, letter to Stephen Bourne, 25 September 2000. See also Stephen Bourne, 'Scott and Whaley: two's company', *The Stage*, 18 January 2001.
5   'Bad taste BBC!', *Flamingo*, September 1961.
6   Dennis Potter, 'The Uncle Tom show', *New Statesman*, 5 May 1967.
7   'Bad Taste BBC!'
8   Sarita Malik, 'The Black and White Minstrel Show', in Horace Newcomb (ed.), *Encyclopedia of Television*, Vol. 1, A–F (Chicago and London: Fitzroy Dearborn, 1997), pp. 185–6.

2

Ernest Trimmingham

In Edwardian Britain, Duse Mohamed Ali, who claimed to be 'of Egyptian birth and Nubian descent',[1] was a London-based theatrical impresario and literary agent who offered advice to would-be authors and playwrights. One of his earliest clients was Ernest Trimmingham from Bermuda. Trimmingham's *The Lily of Bermuda* was staged by Ali, but it opened to poor reviews in Manchester in 1909. Subsequently, Trimmingham turned his attention to acting, while Ali became active in journalism, working as a reporter for the *African Times and Orient Review*.

Trimmingham was successful in finding work as an actor, and he should be regarded as Britain's first black film actor until others of African descent are identified. However, the African–American singer Pete Hampton is the likeliest candidate for the first black actor or entertainer to appear in a British film. A former member of the Williams and Walker company, he came to London as a member of the cast of *In Dahomey* in 1903. With his wife, Laura Bowman, he enjoyed popularity with a stage act in Europe from 1903 to 1914. They also became recording pioneers.[2] In London in 1904, Hampton participated in his first recording session and, later that year, he recorded 'Hannah! Won't You Open That Door?'. According to Denis Gifford's *The British Film Catalogue 1895–1985*, in March 1909 Hampton made a film appearance for the Warwick Cinephone Films company, performing 'Hannah!' in synchronization with a gramophone record. This was an early experiment in matching sound to film, but doesn't appear to have survived. Hampton returned to America with his wife just before the First World War. He died in 1915.

So far, it has been possible to identify several appearances by Trimmingham in silent films. Released in 1912, *The Adventures of Dick Turpin: The King of Highwaymen* featured Trimmingham as a character called Beetles alongside Percy Moran's Turpin. The plot of this adventure involved Turpin, a countryman, stealing a cow, turning highwayman, robbing a mail coach and being chased by Bow Street Runners. Produced by the British and Colonial Kinematograph Company, the Dick Turpin series was a popular success, and this first entry received an enthusiastic review in *The Bioscope*, which described it as an 'excellent picture ... which has many of the merits of the wholesome, virile Western drama with the added charm to the Englishman of its antique native setting. *Dick Turpin* is a film which thoroughly deserves popularity.'[3] Interestingly, though it was unusual for a black actor to play a featured role in a film at that time, because most black characters were played by whites in blackface, there is no mention of Trimmingham or his character in *The Bioscope* review. Consequently, it has been impossible to establish who or what 'Beetles' is. Later that year, Trimmingham surfaced with Moran again in the third instalment, *The Adventures of Dick Turpin – 200 Guineas Reward, Dead or Alive*. In the romantic drama *Her Bachelor Guardian*, also released in 1912, he was listed in the cast as 'Negro'.

In 1919 Trimmingham made his most interesting film appearance, as Pete in *Jack, Sam and Pete*. The influence of Hollywood was very much in evidence in this adventure film, for it is one of the few British-made Westerns. Directed by Percy Moran, using the professional name Jack Daring, the plot involved a trio of cowboys who save a kidnapped child from a gang seeking hidden jewels. Moran also appeared in the film as Jack, and Eddie Willey completed the line-up as Sam. The film

Ernest Trimmingham in *Jack, Sam and Pete* (1919)

was based on the Edwardian children's adventure stories by S. Clarke-Hook. *The Bioscope* described the film as a 'stirring representation of sensational schoolboy literature. A cowboy drama in a British setting.'[4] Once again, there is no reference made in the review to Trimmingham being black. Neither has it been possible to establish if his character, Pete, was black in Clarke-Hook's original stories. Though black cowboys existed in America's Wild West, the presence of a black cowboy in a *British* Western in 1919 is, to say the least, unusual!

Trimmingham appears to have made his last film appearance in *Where the Rainbow Ends* (1921), a fantasy based on a stage play in which a group of children find a magic carpet and save their shipwrecked parents from a dragon. Trimmingham was featured as the Genie. Though he continued working as a professional actor in Britain for another twenty years, his name cannot be found in any other film cast list, including those starring Paul Robeson in the 1930s, which included numerous black players based in Britain.

On stage, Trimmingham acted in a number of West End stage productions and one of his last recorded appearances was in *Room V* at the Garrick Theatre in 1941. Shortly after his arrival here from Bermuda in 1939, Earl Cameron encountered Britain's pioneer film actor:

> We called him 'Trim', but I didn't know him personally and it couldn't have been his real name. The Trimmingham family in Bermuda were wealthy white people who had been there since before my time. The name Trimmingham was everywhere in Bermuda. They owned a lot of property, so Ernest must have taken his stage name from them.[5]

Trimmingham's death certificate confirms that he died on 2 February 1942, aged sixty-one, at 216 Clapham Road, Stockwell, SW9. Further investigation establishes that he was buried in the Variety Artist's Section of Streatham Park cemetery in south London. A visit to the cemetery reveals that he lies in an unmarked grave behind the memorial to the comedy actor Will Hay (1888–1949), one of Britain's most popular film stars of the 1930s.

NOTES

1   Jeffrey Green, *Black Edwardians: Black People in Britain 1901–1914* (London: Frank Cass, 1998), p. 80.
2   Rainer E. Lotz, 'Hampton and Bowman', in *Black People: Entertainers of African Descent in Europe, and Germany* (Germany: Birgit Lotz Verlag, 1997).
3   *The Bioscope*, 16 May 1912.
4   *Ibid.* 4 December 1919.
5   Earl Cameron, interview with Stephen Bourne, London, 17 March 1997.

3

Lonely Road

Paul Robeson on Stage and Screen in Britain, 1922–40

In the late 1930s the African-American actor and singer Paul Robeson was one of Britain's most popular film personalities. Between 1935 and 1940 he starred in six feature films, and was given top billing in all of them. On four occasions he was billed solo above the title. His success with British film audiences can be measured by his appearances in the popularity lists published by the *Motion Picture Herald* from the box-office returns of his films. These lists had twenty-five positions. In 1936 Robeson was placed twenty-second (Gracie Fields was first). In 1937 he had made it to tenth position behind (1) Gracie Fields, (2) George Formby, (3) Jessie Matthews, (4) Will Hay, (5) Jack Buchanan, (6) George Arliss, (7) Tom Walls and Charles Laughton (tie), (8) Anna Neagle and (9) Jack Hulbert. In 1938 he was eleventh (George Formby was first) and in 1939 he was listed as a 'runner-up' (an unnumbered position). In 1940, on the strength of just one film release (*The Proud Valley*), he moved up to twentieth position. However, in spite of his popularity in British films, in 1986 Robeson was missing from two major tributes to British cinema. John Kobal's *Portraits of the British Cinema*, a photographic collection of over one hundred stars of the British screen, failed to include Paul Robeson. When Kobal responded to a letter of complaint about this omission, he admitted he had made a mistake: 'it was too bad that he was left out. I wish I had a better excuse than oversight, but that is what it was.'[1] Robeson was also left out of the National Portrait Gallery's 'Stars of the British Screen' exhibition. Its curator, Robin Gibson, explained:

Although we took expert advice and tried to achieve a reasonable balance among the stars represented, there were, of course, a number of regrettable omissions, but we had to fix a limit for reasons of space. In retrospect, I feel you are certainly right about Paul Robeson, since his principal cinematic achievements were made in this country. I am only sorry it is too late to remedy the omission.[2]

These omissions show how easy it is for a black artist to be forgotten, even one of Paul Robeson's stature, and especially those who have contributed to the performing arts in Britain.

Paul Robeson may have been one of the most popular stage and screen actors of the 1930s, but he probably suffered more disappointments than any other leading actor of his generation. Black characters in American films of the period rarely moved beyond Al Jolson in blackface, or the dim-witted buffoons played by black actors like Stepin' Fetchit. For Paul Robeson, an intelligent and progressive actor, there were hardly any opportunities to play challenging roles, a situation he complained about in 1933: 'Hollywood can only visualise the plantation type of Negro ... it is absurd to use that type to express the modern Negro as it would be to express modern England in terms of an Elizabethan ballad.'[3] Though the characters he played in his British films were generally more dignified than those on offer to him in Hollywood, Robeson often found himself in conflict with a film industry that glorified and romanticized the British Empire and colonialism. This was the case with his first film, *Sanders of the River*, which he hated, though it put him on the map as far as commercial cinema was concerned. Even so, in all of his films, whatever their merits, Robeson succeeded in bringing intelligence, strength and compassion to his characters. Though most critics have agreed that his British films are not worthy of him, it cannot be denied that they helped to make him a world star. In 1970 David Shipman wrote movingly of Robeson in *The Great Movie Stars: The Golden Years*:

> He was one of the century's great artists ... He was successful, but he found the going tough. He had intelligence and fame; was in demand as a concert and recording artist, worked in films and on the stage; but remained always a loner in show business ... As a great singer, he was clearly qualified to be a solo artist, but his very greatness calls into question the neglect of Robeson by Hollywood ... The point is that no singer before or since ever caught the public imagination as Robeson did ... no singer before had seemed so real, so unencumbered by artifice, so warm, so sincere: his rich, bass-baritone, whether he sang aria or spiritual, 'spoke' to millions. Today we are accustomed to the singer who 'acts' his lyric; Robeson was virtually the first modern singer, in that the emotion conveyed was as true as the voice.
>
> He acted in the same way: powerful, direct, entirely natural. His few film performances were delightful ... His films were mainly poor, and they were *not* important in the Civil Rights movement which, inevitably, he espoused – nor important in any way except for his presence in them.[4]

In 1920 Robeson made his acting debut in *Simon the Cyrenian*, the story of the black man who was Jesus's cross-bearer. This one-act play was staged at the Harlem branch of the Young Women's Christian Association by an amateur group called the Colored Players' Guild. Robeson was a law student at the time, and had no interest in acting professionally. However, two years later he was persuaded to return to the stage. In 1922 he made his professional debut in Mary Hoyt Wiborg's *Taboo* in New York, playing a wandering minstrel who dreams of his former life in Africa. A British production, renamed *Voodoo*, followed. Starring Mrs Patrick Campbell, it opened on 17 July 1922 at Blackpool's Opera House, but flopped. It didn't reach London, but in a BBC radio interview Robeson spoke about the discovery of his singing voice during the opening performance. The end of the first act required him to whistle, but Robeson couldn't whistle, so he substituted a spiritual, 'Go Down Moses':

> I was startled to hear Mrs Pat whispering off-stage, for all the theatre to hear, 'Sing another song!' So I sang another spiritual. In all my supposedly heavy dramatic scenes, Mrs Pat would nudge me, and off I'd go – singing! – the audience seemed to love it! I got very nice reviews from it and found out that I was a singer, the first time *I* knew.[5]

His London stage debut followed at the Ambassadors Theatre in Eugene O'Neill's *The Emperor Jones* (1925). According to the *Sunday Times* (13 September 1925), he received 'a great ovation at the close. It was a wonderful performance.' In *Paul Robeson: Negro* (1930), Eslanda Goode Robeson, also known as 'Essie', described the impact London had on her young husband in the mid-1920s:

> There were few inconveniences for him ... He did not have to live in a segregated district; he leased a charming flat in Chelsea near his friends; he dined at the Ivy, a delightful restaurant with marvellous food, directly across from the theatre; he ate at many other restaurants in town with white or coloured friends without fear of the discrimination which all Negroes encounter in America. He was a welcome guest in hotels at the seaside places where he spent many week-ends. This was important for his general well-being ... So here in England, where everyone was kind and cordial and reasonable, Paul was happy. 'I think I'd like to live here,' he said; 'some day I will.'[6]

The Robeson's eventually settled in London, and in 1928 he enjoyed great success with his appearance as Joe in the musical *Show Boat* at the Theatre Royal, Drury Lane. Edith Day, who played Magnolia, later recalled her first impression of Robeson during rehearsals:

Jerome Kern, who wrote the music for *Show Boat*, came in with a splendid-looking Negro, whom he introduced as the actor engaged to play Joe. The young Negro straddled a chair and pushed his hat on to the back of his head, while Kern went to the piano and played a tune none of the company had ever heard before. That was how they were introduced to 'Ol' Man River' and to Paul Robeson – and there was not a dry eye in the place by the time that wonderful voice died away at the end of the poignant song.[7]

Following his screen debut in America in Oscar Micheaux's silent melodrama *Body and Soul* (1925), Paul and Eslanda took part in *Borderline* (1930), an experimental British film made on location in Switzerland. It was written and directed by Kenneth MacPherson, a member of an avant-garde group associated with the film journal *Close-Up*. Without sound or dialogue, the cinematic style of *Borderline* is influenced by the Russian director Sergei Eisenstein. It's a film about loneliness, rejection, racism and homoeroticism.

In 1925 Amanda Ira Aldridge, the London-born daughter of the African-American tragedian, Ira Aldridge (1807–67), befriended the Robesons and presented Paul with the earrings her father had worn when he played Shakespeare's Othello.[8] She hoped that Paul would play the role one day. Five years later her wish came true, when Robeson was cast opposite Peggy Ashcroft as Desdemona. He turned to Aldridge for diction and voice training. Ira Aldridge had been the first great African-American actor, and his career, which spanned an awesome period of four decades, took him all over the Continent and Russia. He made his professional stage debut at the Royal Coburg Theatre (later known as the Old Vic), in London in 1825, and played Othello in several productions, including an acclaimed version at the Haymarket in 1865. Unfortunately, the 1930 production of *Othello* at the Savoy Theatre was hampered by an inadequate director (Maurice Browne) and a disappointing performance by Robeson. Jamaican-born actress Pauline Henriques testifies to this:

I always had a tremendous admiration for him because he had such a wonderful voice – there was not another like it. He also had a tremendous presence, charisma. But I was disappointed with his performance of Othello, because, although he had tremendous size and presence augmented by his gorgeous voice, he was, in my opinion, quite wooden. He carried the part with presence, but that wasn't really enough. When you are as deeply immersed in the theatre as I was, you want something different and I found lacks in Robeson's portrayal of a man torn apart by jealousy.[9]

Robeson returned to the Savoy Theatre later that year for an engagement that included a concert of 'Negro Music' followed by the first act of *The Emperor Jones*. He then returned to the Ambassadors Theatre in 1931 for another Eugene O'Neill play, *The Hairy Ape*. However, his most successful London stage appearance took place in 1933 at the Embassy Theatre (later moving to the Piccadilly Theatre) when he appeared in O'Neill's *All God's Chillun, Got Wings*, a powerful study of an interracial marriage. The critics raved about Robeson and his leading lady, Flora Robson:

> The first night was an intoxicating experience. The stars were named as a major new team. 'Mr Robeson [has] the simplicity that gives pathos its depth and the dignity that saves it from historical declamation,' claimed *The Times* ... Flora would remain friends with the Robesons ... Many years later she was to see the dress rehearsal for Paul's famous *Othello*, in Boston. In the scene where Brabantio speaks of Desdemona's running 'from her guardage to the sooty bosom/Of such a thing as thou' she noticed that Paul hung his head and bit his lip. Paul had often maintained to Flora that black actors should always show humility. She was unable to see him after the rehearsal but managed to speak to Essie. She told her she felt he shouldn't give in like that. 'So he should be defiant,' said Essie. Flora replied, 'No. He is a general. He should be dignified. You cannot hurt people who have dignity.' Paul told Flora later that her suggestion had not only changed his playing of that scene, but it had changed his whole performance.[10]

When the producer Alexander Korda began working on his screen version of Edgar Wallace's *Sanders of the River*, released in 1935, he offered the role of Bosambo to Robeson. According to one of Robeson's biographers, Marie Seton, the original screenplay presented his character

> with both credibility and dignity and Robeson became engrossed in developing this character ... It seemed to him that if he could portray an African chief on the screen with cultural accuracy, then he was making a contribution to the understanding of the tribal culture which he considered was a part of his own heritage. The more he had studied Africa, the more strongly he felt that he was essentially an African.[11]

However, Robeson's association with Korda was not a happy one. During the editing process extra scenes were added, without Robeson's knowledge or approval, glorifying the British Empire and colonialism. Robeson was embarrassed by the version of the film that Korda released to the public, and subsequently disowned it, explaining:

> the twist in the picture which was favourable to English imperialism was accomplished during the cutting of the picture after it was filmed. I had no

idea that it would have such a turn *after* I had acted in it. Moreover, when it was shown at its premiere in London and I saw what it was, I was called to the stage and in protest refused to perform. Since that time I have refused to play in three films offered me by that same producer.[12]

Sanders of the River is a hymn to colonialism, and embarrassing to watch. The paternalistic Commissioner Sanders (Leslie Banks) is responsible for managing the N'Gombi district in Nigeria, and he refers to the Africans who live there as his 'black children'. Paul Robeson's first appearance in the film is shocking. Naked, except for a leopard skin covering his private parts, he enters Sanders's office in a stooping position, and humbly addresses his 'lord and master'. In this scene we discover that he is a Liberian convict and a prison escapee. In addition, he is devious and a liar, but wins the trust of Sanders, who allows him to become the leader of a village, an appointment which gains him respectability.

At this point it is interesting to look at how Robeson and his wife viewed Africa when they settled in Britain. The following extract is taken from Eslanda's book *African Journey* (1946):

> In America one heard little or nothing about Africa. I hadn't realized that, consciously, until we went to live in England. There was rarely even a news item about Africa in American newspapers or magazines. Americans were not interested in Africa economically ... politically, or culturally. Practically nothing was or is taught in American schools about Africa ... In England, on the other hand, there is news of Africa everywhere: in the press, in the schools, in the films, in conversation.[13]

Eslanda also describes her feelings about the Africans she befriended during her visit to the country in the mid-1930s, and her embarrassment with *Sanders*:

> These Africans, these 'primitives', make me feel humble and respectful. I blush with shame for the mental picture my fellow Negroes in America have of our African brothers: wild black savages in leopard skins, waving spears and eating raw meat. And we, with films like *Sanders of the River*, are unwittingly helping to perpetuate this misconception.[14]

When Robeson filmed *Sanders of the River*, he befriended many African extras on the set, but he was not prepared for their reaction to him, even before the film was released. Flora Robson later recalled:

> he wore a leopard skin and he was ticked off by a Prince of the Ashanti who was up at Oxford and said 'What do you wear a leopard skin for?' So Paul

said 'Well, what do *you* wear in Africa? Tweeds?' And the Prince said 'Yes. We do.' They didn't like him. They thought as an educated man he shouldn't play these primitive parts.[15]

But the contact he made with Africans on the sets of his films had a lasting impact on him, as Paul Robeson Jr explains:

> During his film career he met many Africans on the set of films like *Sanders of the River*. Among the extras of *Sanders* was Jomo Kenyatta, the famous burning spear, who then became the first President of Kenya. So culturally he was drawn to the Africans on the set. He found his own African roots, you might say, and became radicalized by the African anti-colonial fighters of that time like Jomo Kenyatta.[16]

At the time of its release, *Sanders of the River* met with a hostile reception from various black critics. In 1937 the Nigerian scholar Dr Nnamdi Azikiwe complained:

> Whoever sees this picture will be shocked at the exaggeration of African mentality, so far as superstitious beliefs are concerned, not to speak of the knavery and chicanery of some African chiefs. I feel that what is being paraded in the world today as art or literature is nothing short of propaganda.[17]

The 'Special Film Correspondent' for *The Keys*, the journal of the League of Coloured Peoples, described *Sanders* as

> just the kind of film which will appeal to the average English audience in a Jubilee year. It portrays the good old myth of the strong, silent white man quelling hordes of angry savages with his scowl, and peacefully and altruistically ruling his thousands of ignorant black children by the sheer strength of his personality; a myth which is unfortunately exploded as soon as he is gone. For ... the tribes begin to misbehave once more, and are only re-civilized when Sanders returns with a machine gun ... Mr Robeson's glorious voice is well recorded; it is less commonly realized that he is one of our finest living actors. As Bosambo he is completely wasted.[18]

However, Robeson's most outspoken black critic was Marcus Garvey, the Jamaican nationalist leader who is credited with inspiring black consciousness on an international scale. In the late 1930s, while residing in London, Garvey denounced Robeson's films. He strongly objected to the roles Robeson portrayed and, when he left Britain in 1935 to film *Show Boat* in Hollywood, Garvey declared: 'He is gone there to make another slanderous picture against the Negro.' In the American journal, *Black Man*, Garvey condemned Robeson's film image:

Paul Robeson is a good actor. There is no doubt that he is one of the front liners of the profession, but featured as he is as a Negro he is doing his race a great deal of harm. The Producers have been using Paul Robeson ... to put over a vile and vicious propaganda against the Negro. It is true that in some of the plays Robeson is used as the hero, but even in that the propaganda is more pronounced. ... The promoters are skilful in putting over their propaganda. The wonder is that Paul Robeson cannot see that he is being used to the dishonour and discredit of his race. We again affirm the belief that he is one of the best actors of our present age, but he is not as useful to the Negro as Roland Hayes, who conquered Europe and America by the culture of his voice. Robeson is pleasing England by the gross slander and libel of the Negro.[19]

In 1937 Garvey complained to the British Moving Picture Board about Robeson's films and attacked them in a pamphlet entitled *A Grand Speech of Honorable Marcus Garvey at Kingsway Hall, London, Denouncing the Moving Picture Propaganda to Discredit the Negro*, which he described as 'a criticism of Paul Robeson in pictures'. Explains Rupert Lewis in *Marcus Garvey: Anti-Colonial Champion* (1987):

Garvey felt that Black creative artists should not only identify with the struggle of their own people but that their work should be a direct contribution to this struggle. Overall, Paul Robeson did not fail that test for he was a political fighter who used his 'art' to combat racism.[20]

In response to these criticisms, Robeson expressed his own feelings about his relationship with the British and American film industries. In 1938 he admitted he had 'cut himself off' from the commercial film industry:

because I am no longer willing to identify myself with an organization that has no regard for reality – an organization that attempts to nullify public intelligence, falsify life and entirely ignores the many dynamic forces at work in the world today.[21]

That same year, he also reflected on *Sanders of the River* and the effect it had had on him:

'Sanders of the River' ... attracted me because the material that London Films brought back from Africa seemed to me good honest pictures of

African folk ways ... But in the completed version, 'Sanders of the River' resolved itself into a piece of flag-waving, in which I wasn't interested. As far as I was concerned it was a total loss. But I didn't realize how seriously people might take the film until I went back to New York. There I was met by a deputation who wanted to know how the hell I had come to play in a film which stood for everything they rightly thought I opposed. That deputation began to make me see things more clearly. I hadn't seen the film. I was that interested. After talking to them I did go and see it, and I began to realize what they'd been getting at.[22]

In 1935 there was talk of Robeson making a film in Russia for Sergei Eisenstein (*Black Majesty*), but this came to nothing. However, he did succeed in appearing on the London stage in two plays with political themes: *Basilik* (1935), at the Arts Theatre, about an African chief who resists white rule, and *Stevedore* (1935), at the Embassy, about racial and trade-union conflict. But it was C. L. R. James's *Toussaint L'Ouverture* (1936) that provided him with one of his most interesting roles. Presented by the Stage Society at the Westminster Theatre, James's 'dramatized biography' told the story of a general who rose from slavery to become the independent ruler of San Domingo before he was captured by the French to die of starvation in prison in 1803. C. L. R. James was a writer who came to Britain from Trinidad in 1932, and was passionate about the independence of the Caribbean. James's masterwork as a historian was *The Black Jacobins*, a study of L'Ouverture, published two years after the stage play.

Though settled in Britain, Robeson returned to America for the film versions of two of his stage successes: *The Emperor Jones* (1933), produced independently in New York, and *Show Boat* (1936), for Universal. Opportunities to work in Hollywood were almost non-existent, but in 1937 he contributed to one of Greta Garbo's most famous films. She requested that his recordings of spirituals be played on the set of MGM's *Camille* to put her in the proper mood for her now-famous death scene. In Britain, in spite of *Sanders of the River*, he continued acting in films until the outbreak of the Second World War.

For *Song of Freedom* (1936), directed by J. Elder Wills, he insisted on a clause in his contract which gave him the right to approve the final editing of the production. In the film, Robeson plays John Zinga, a London-born dock worker who acknowledges Africa as his ancestral home and dreams of visiting the continent. In a highly improbable and melodramatic plot, he is discovered by an impresario who helps transform him into an internationally acclaimed opera singer. When an anthropologist informs Zinga that he is the direct descendant of an African kingship, he travels to the West Coast of Africa to meet his people. But to his dismay he finds that they are mostly superstitious and poverty-stricken savages. He had tried, and almost succeeded, in acting in a film that departed from the traditional racist stereotypes. However, in spite of the film's shortcomings, this production was important to Robeson, because he believed it was the first

> to give a true picture of many aspects of the life of the coloured man in the west. Hitherto, on the screen, he has been caricatured or presented only as a comedy character. This film shows him as a real man, with problems to be solved, difficulties to be overcome. I am sure you will appreciate the picture as much for this unusual honesty of characterization as for the dramatic intensity of its story.[23]

The first half of *Song of Freedom* is impressive, and lives up to Robeson's expectations. The prologue is extraordinarily moving, with a montage depicting the historical process by which people of African descent came to settle in Britain. Rarely seen in a British film, the horrors of the eighteenth-century slave trade are exposed, as well as its abolition in 1838. Throughout the prologue the King of Casanga's song and medallion are passed down from generation to generation. Zinga acknowledges his African ancestry by wearing the Casanga medallion and singing fragments of the King's song he had been taught as a child. 'It's been at the back of my head since I was a little fella,' he explains. *Song of Freedom* was also the first British film to acknowledge London's multicultural dockland community. Zinga and his wife, Ruth, played by Elisabeth Welch, are part of this community, though some critics have found the portrayal of the couple unrealistic and bourgeois.[24]

Apart from Zinga, the racially integrated workforce includes two of his pals: Monty, an African-Caribbean (Robert Adams), and Bert Puddick, a cockney (George Mozart). The three men enjoy each others' company but Zinga stands out because he is preoccupied with his dream of visiting Africa. In the pub he meets Harry, a sailor who is about to depart to the west coast of Africa. 'What part do you come from?' he asks Zinga, who replies, thoughtfully, 'I don't know. Wish I did.' At home, Ruth departs from the stereotypical depiction of black women in films up to that time. In Hollywood cinema of the 1930s, black women were portrayed as either mammies or whores, but Ruth is neither. She is a well-spoken, warm and loving wife, but is upset about her husband's desire to visit Africa. She doesn't understand why he wants to leave their comfortable home and supportive, friendly community to enter the unknown. Zinga comforts her in a sentimental but emotional musical interlude in which he sings

'Sleepy River'. Says Douglas McVay in *The Musical Film*: 'In Britain, the young Paul Robeson makes another haunting song, "River of Dreams" [*sic*], with the help of tranquil people-at-evening images, a moving flash of film poetry.'[25] At the end of this sequence, Robeson and Welch kiss, probably the first time a black couple were permitted to do so in a film.

In spite of its sentimentality, the 'Sleepy River' sequence acknowledges the racially integrated working-class communities of London's East End. Several families of different nationalities are seen at their windows listening to Robeson, and Monty is shown lodging with Bert Puddick and his wife Nell. This is continued in the following sequence, the singsong in the Crown and Anchor pub. Here, Zinga performs the rousing 'Lonely Road' with the local community. Discovered and coached by an Italian impresario, Gabriel Donozetti (Esmé Percy), he is launched in London's West End in a 'Negro opera' called *The Black Emperor*, and, after a triumphant opening performance, Zinga is persuaded to return to the stage for an encore. The song he chooses, 'Song of Freedom', is recognized by Sir James Pyrie (Bernard Ansell), an explorer and anthropologist, who happens to be in the audience. On meeting Zinga, Pyrie identifies the medallion around his neck, and informs him that he is the descendant of an African kingship called Casanga. Pyrie explains that the 'Song of Freedom' is the King's song: 'I'm probably the only white man who's ever heard it.' Armed with this news, Zinga turns down a lucrative offer to sing at the Metropolitan Opera House in New York so that he can travel to Casanga and meet his people.

At this point in the film the plot has become highly improbable and it gradually descends into nonsense. Monty leaves the docks to become Zinga's dresser and insists on calling him 'boss'. It is embarrassing and Robert Adams's performance doesn't help, acting for all he's worth like Hollywood's shufflin' buffoon Stepin' Fetchit. When Zinga, Ruth and Monty arrive on the island of Casanga, the west coast of Africa looks suspiciously like Richmond-upon-Thames. To their dismay, the trio discover the inhabitants of Casanga living in primitive conditions, and the strangers receive a frosty welcome. Zinga and Ruth look ridiculous in their white pith helmets and matching white safari suits, and it's hardly surprising that the witch doctor, Indobo (Arthur Williams), is unimpressed. 'You think you are a king because you come to us dressed up in white man's clothes,' he sneers. Not only are the islanders suspicious of the visitors, they are also superstitious and ignorant, firmly under the influence of Indobo. The exception is a wise village elder called Mandingo (Tony Wane). He befriends the visitors, and believes Zinga when he reveals that he is the true King of Casanga. However, Mandingo has a warning for Zinga: 'although you are of our colour, you are not of us. A lion who has not lived in the jungle does not know jungle ways.'

The Zingas have difficulty convincing the islanders of their good intentions and when Indobo makes mischief for them, who can blame him? Finally, just as the islanders are about to throw Ruth into a snake pit, Zinga remembers 'Song of Freedom'. After his rendition of the song, they accept him as their true king and Ruth escapes the snake pit. In the final scene, Zinga has returned to London to give a concert. In the audience Donozetti explains to Pyrie: 'every season he returns to sing. Tomorrow, he goes back again.' When Zinga bursts into a chorus of 'Lonely Road', he looks happy and relaxed for the first time in the film, surrounded by African sculptures, with his Casanga medallion on full view. In spite of the film's stereotypical vision of 'Africa', it ends positively by showing Zinga at peace with himself, a man who has found his people and an identity. In *Africa on Film: Beyond Black and White* (1994), Kenneth M. Cameron finds much to recommend in the film's portrayal of a black man:

[*Song of Freedom*] exploited stereotypes as part of a strategy to dramatize Robeson's myth. It acknowledged 'savagery' but did not use it as a stick with which to beat Africans, suggesting rather that problems could be corrected without white presence. It sees a high place for returned blacks in Africa. It asserts that the real triumph is not the fame and wealth to be found in white culture, but the productive life to be found in black culture: 'Tomorrow, he goes back again.' It takes the African stereotypes of commercial motion pictures and stands them on their heads.[26]

One of the most striking features of *Song of Freedom*, and one that has been completely ignored, is the warm, loving relationship between Zinga and Ruth. Off screen, Robeson and his co-star, Elisabeth Welch, admired and respected each other, and this is evident in their acting. Art mirrored life in this film, for it reflected Robeson's growing interest in his African heritage and Welch's apolitical stance. Unlike Robeson, Welch was the child of a mixed marriage, and didn't identify herself as black. She also kept her distance from 'politics'. However, she had nothing but admiration for Robeson's wish to combat racism:

It was during the shooting of the film *Song of Freedom* that I got to know – and love – Paul Robeson. Arriving to play opposite that great man – and it being my first speaking part in a film – I was overwhelmed, and as nervous as a kitten. The nerves were soon calmed, however, when I saw that huge smile light up his face, and felt the warmth of a friendly giant when he pressed my hand in both of his, and welcomed me.

It was a happy time for me, working with Paul and watching him work. I found him a man of great intensity, both in his work and in his beliefs but – thank goodness – not lacking in humour. We'd sometimes sit outdoors with our lunch trays, chatting about life and living. These were times I can never forget. Often he spoke of his desires and his determination for making a better world and, as often, we argued as to how it could be achieved. Once he tried to persuade me to do something for our people. I had an answer. I'm of mixed blood – African, American Indian, Scots and Irish. So I said: 'Paul, I belong to *four* peoples! I can't make a stand for all of them. You must excuse me!' And he laughed really hard at that. Sometimes there was anger in his voice. There was sadness too. The lunch break over, he'd laugh and say 'to be continued tomorrow' and back we'd go to the life and lights of the film studio.[27]

In 1937 Robeson teamed up with Elisabeth Welch and director J. Elder Wills again for a charming, light-hearted musical called *Big Fella*. It was based on the novel *Banjo* by Claude McKay, a popular Jamaican writer

Paul Robeson and Elisabeth Welch in *Big Fella* (1937)

of the Harlem Renaissance. Set in a racially integrated community on the Marseilles waterfront, this uncomplicated tale of a black man who is hired by a wealthy English couple to find their missing son is far removed from *Song of Freedom*. Easygoing and relaxed, Robeson's character, Joe, is quite unlike John Zinga. He's a happy-go-lucky fellow who enjoys taking it easy with his pals at the docks: Chuck (James Hayter) and Corney, played by Lawrence Brown, Robeson's accompanist and arranger from 1925 to 1963. The role of the proprietress of the waterfront café is taken by Robeson's wife, Eslanda. She welcomes black and white patrons, and employs a racially integrated band to accompany her singer, Manda, played by Welch. The scenes between Robeson and Eslanda are memorable. When she reprimands him for starting an argument in her café, she calls him a big bozo.

Manda is Joe's sweetheart. As in *Song of Freedom*, Robeson and Welch are perfectly matched, and it is impossible to think of another film that depicts a light-hearted romance between a black couple. In American films of the 1930s black couples were portrayed as asexual, comic, childlike servants. (Just compare Robeson and Welch to Bill 'Bojangles' Robinson and Hattie McDaniel in *The Little Colonel* [1935], starring Shirley Temple.) Perhaps the film's most memorable scene is the musical interlude in Eslanda's café when Robeson and the racially mixed waterfront community sing 'Roll Up, Sailorman'. Robeson's delivery is a joy.

Big Fella is most interesting for the way it allows its two black women characters to be assertive, humorous and sassy. Welch's Manda doesn't refrain from insulting the flirtatious Lorietta (Marcelle Rogez), a white Frenchwoman who is after Joe's money. 'What's wrong with the Monte Video tonight? They thrown you out already?' Manda snaps when she discovers Lorietta hanging around the bar of the café. No black woman in American cinema would have been permitted to speak to a white woman like that. In the closing shot, Joe and Manda walk away with their arms around each other. A perfect end to an imperfect, but enjoyable, film.

When *Big Fella* was released in America, several black critics expressed their dissatisfaction with Robeson for playing, what they felt, was the stereotypical role of a lazy good-for-nothing. However, other critics exhibited nothing but enthusiasm for Robeson and *Big Fella*. In Britain, *Picturegoer* informed its readers: 'If you like Paul Robeson's voice (and who doesn't?) you will like *Big Fella*', and *Film Weekly* declared: 'Paul Robeson and Elisabeth Welch sing superbly in a comedy about Marseilles kidnappers. Robeson fans will love it.' Interestingly, the title of the film was changed from *Banjo* to *Big Fella* because it was felt that audiences would expect to see Robeson in a story set on a cotton plantation if the original was retained. As biographer Martin Bauml Duberman reveals, the change meant that 'Robeson was thus enabled to make a racial statement about an ordinary but admirable black man, functioning well in a contemporary, European setting.'[28] Unfortunately, *Big Fella* suffered the fate of Josephine Baker's French films, *Zou Zou* (1934) and *Princess Tam-Tam* (1935) – lack of distribution in America and limited availability since the 1930s. For years it was impossible to see *Big Fella*, and for this reason studies of Robeson's films barely mention it and, if they do, it is dismissed as lightweight rubbish, not worthy of the great man. It is a shame, for, in spite of its faults, *Big Fella* remains one of the few films to have black stars in romantic leading roles.

Robeson was expected to sing in all of his films, even if the plots did not necessarily require him to do so. Consequently, he sang – magnificently – in two adventure-dramas: *King Solomon's Mines* (1937) and *Jericho* (1937). However, these films did not stretch him as an actor. *King Solomon's Mines* is based on the novel by H. Rider Haggard. Set in Africa in the 1880s, Robeson plays Umbopa, a dispossessed king who accompanies a group of English adventurers on a perilous journey to find the gold mines of King Solomon. The production values of the film are superior to *Sanders of the River*: Africa looks like Africa, rather than a stretch of the River Thames. However, the depiction of African people as little more than exotic primitives is essentially the same as the earlier film. Though Umbopa is a more interesting and charismatic character than Bosambo, Robeson is given little scope for his acting:

> Robeson was already a major star ... As well, he had to sing, so that at times the film sounds like *Old King Solomon's River*. Nonetheless, Robeson's presence gave the film importance, whereas it easily could have fallen flat, and he made it impossible to cast white actors in blackface in other African roles. (The practice was still common.) Instead, black actors like Robert Adams and the gorgeously screen-named Ecce Homo Toto were given good roles.[29]

In *Jericho* (released in America as *Dark Sands*) Robeson plays Jericho Jackson, an American medical student drafted into the army during the First World War. Court-martialled for the accidental death of a bullying (black) sergeant, he escapes to North Africa where he becomes the chief of an Arab tribe. Meanwhile, Captain Mack (Henry Wilcoxon), a white American officer who had befriended Jackson, is blamed for his escape, thrown out of the army and imprisoned. Years later, Mack seeks Jericho out for revenge, but on meeting him again, his hatred turns to respect. The plot of *Jericho* contains almost as many improbabilities as *Song of*

Freedom, but Robeson agreed to star in the film because he wanted to play a black hero of courage and intelligence. Unfortunately, there were some lapses. For instance, though he is shown to be a strong and sympathetic leader of the black troops, Jericho is just a little bit *too* servile in the company of the white officers. However, once he has escaped from the army, a transformation takes place. He relaxes, takes control of his life and marries the beautiful Gara (Princess Kouka), daughter of a Tuareg chieftain. Made leader of a Arab tribe, he uses his medical knowledge to help the sick. Sheik Agouba (Frank Cochrane) is impressed and describes Jericho as a 'brave and strong leader'.

In 1936 Andre van Gysegham, the left-winger who had directed Robeson in *Stevedore*, co-founded the socialist Unity Theatre in London. Unity aimed to provide a showcase for left-wing dramatists. When it opened at new premises on 25 November 1937, Robeson took part in the opening ceremony, singing spirituals, and 'Ol' Man River'. For the latter he altered Oscar Hammerstein II's lyrics from 'tired o'living and scared o'dying' to 'I must keep struggling until I'm dying'. Says Sean Creighton in *Politics and Culture: Paul Robeson in the UK* (1998), 'Explaining his involvement in Unity, he said that as an artist he needed a working-class audience. Most scripts sent to him went into the wastepaper basket because they did not deal with ideas of social progress.'[30]

One of the scripts that went into the wastepaper basket was *The Sun Never Sets*, a 'melodrama based on the West African stories of Edgar Wallace'. Rejecting a lucrative offer to resurrect Bosambo from *Sanders of the River* in this lavish West End production, Robeson instead agreed to act in a Unity production, Ben Bengal's American strike drama, *Plant in the Sun* (1938). In his autobiography, *Reflected Glory* (1958), Peter Noble remembered going to see the play,

> which had become an enormous success at Unity Theatre due to Paul Robeson playing the leading role. After a long and honourable career as an actor and singer all over the world, Robeson had announced his strong affiliation to socialism, had also visited the Soviet Union and had sent his small son to school there for a time. One of the most revered and most popular figures in the left-wing movement, Paul had given up a great deal of money to work at Unity Theatre ... Robeson's name and personality attracted people who had never been to Unity Theatre before, so that by the time David Newman took us there Unity was well and truly on the theatrical map.[31]

In 1938 Alexander Korda announced that, apart from Sabu, the stars of his next production, *The Thief of Bagdad*, would include Vivien Leigh, Jon

Hall and Robeson as the genie. However, by the time filming commenced, Leigh was in Hollywood making *Gone with the Wind* and Robeson was completing his final British film, *The Proud Valley*, before returning to America. Another impressive African-American actor, Rex Ingram, was imported to play the role intended for Robeson.

The Proud Valley was based on an original idea by Herbert Marshall and his wife, Alfredda Brilliant. They were associated with the Unity Theatre and Marshall had directed Robeson in *Plant in the Sun*. The script for *The Proud Valley* enabled Robeson to express his socialist beliefs and portray the struggles of the working-class people of South Wales. In the film, which is set in the year leading up to the outbreak of the Second World War, Robeson plays David Goliath, a friendly, gentle giant with a giant's name. He once worked down a mine for five years in America and was 'laid up at Cardiff three months ago'. Looking for work ever since, he has travelled into the Welsh countryside, hoping to find a job in the valleys. On his journey David befriends Bert (Edward Rigby), who tells him about a 'a coloured bloke [who] used to work in the Glen Colliery. Blackie Ellis they called him.' This reassures David that, even in the Depression, not all collieries operated a 'colour bar'.

Arriving in the mining village of Blaendy, David and Bert busk in the street for money, where they are overheard by Blaendy's choirmaster, Dick Parry (Edward Chapman). Impressed with David's singing, Dick takes him home to meet his wife (Rachel Thomas). 'He's got a bottom base like an organ,' he tells her. 'The finest I ever heard in these valleys. It floated in that hall like thunder from a distance.' David becomes their lodger, and Dick finds him a job in the local colliery and a place in their choir, but not everyone is impressed with the newcomer. Seth Jones (Clifford Evans) resents David's employment. 'This fellow is a black man to work down the pit,' he complains. 'Well, what about it?' demands David angrily. Dick's response is to support his new friend: 'Damn and blast it, man, aren't we all black down that pit?' David Berry, in *Wales and Cinema* (1994), praises the film's attempts to portray racism:

> It may seem coy in its treatment of racism but it broaches the subject openly and courageously enough for the 1940s, even though the film is careful to avoid presenting racial conflict in the wider community outside the mine, or in the Parry home.[32]

However, Seth is on his own, for the rest of the Blaendy community welcome David. Settling in with the Parry family, he looks forward to performing with the Blaendy Male-Voice Choir at the forthcoming eisteddfod. But tragedy lies ahead. On the day of the eisteddfod, Dick is killed in a pit disaster. To its credit, *The Proud Valley* does not skirt around the grim horror of life – and death – underground. At the eisteddfod, which has been postponed for one month, David pays tribute to his pal with a moving rendition of 'Deep River', one of the most emotional sequences ever seen in a British film. After the eisteddfod, David joins the community in their fight against the closure of their colliery, but more tragedy follows when he sacrifices himself to save Dick's son, Emlyn (Simon Lack), in another pit disaster. Some critics have complained that David is used as nothing more than the stereotypical noble black man sacrificing himself for the white man. But this is unfair. It is the first British film in which Robeson dies at the end, and his reasons for saving Emlyn are clear. 'Your father was my friend,' he explains. 'He took me in, gave me food and shelter, found me work. What kind of a man would I be if I left now when things are bad?'

The Proud Valley stands out from most British films of its time because it contains believable working-class characters, not caricatures. Unlike the cockneys, Bert and Nell Puddick, in *Song of Freedom*, Dick Parry and his wife are not one-dimensional comic stereotypes; they're resourceful human beings, and the film treats them with respect. The story affords David a similar respect and, like the Parrys, he is a convincing working-class character, kind, generous and good-natured. But it was extremely rare for a black character to be presented in this way in the 1930s and 1940s when cinema audiences were used to seeing Stepin' Fetchit playing the fool. However, not everyone was impressed with Paul Robeson's performance. Graham Greene was particularly scathing in his review in the *Spectator*, describing him as a 'big black Pollyanna' who kept 'everybody cheerful and dying nobly at the end'.[33]

The Proud Valley was directed with great passion and sincerity by a promising young director, and ex-Etonian, Pen Tennyson, who tragically died shortly after the film's completion while serving in the Fleet Air Arm. The Welsh actors in the supporting cast, notably Rachel Thomas, Charles Williams, Jack Jones (who also contributed to the script) and Clifford Evans, give the film its authenticity. The setting of the film is realistic, too. Some location work actually took place in the Rhondda Valley and the film refuses to glamorize working-class life. The pit disaster at the end is horrifying, and Robeson's 'death' at the conclusion of the film symbolically marks the end of his British film career. But just before the final credits appear, Robeson's rich, glorious voice can be heard singing 'Land of My Fathers' over a tracking shot of the Welsh mountains.

For Robeson, making *The Proud Valley* was a rewarding experience, both on and off camera. His biographer Marie Seton describes how the Welsh people took Robeson to their hearts:

The Welsh looked at Robeson. They knew he was a great singer. That meant a lot to them for music was as deep a part of their heritage as it was of his: but it seemed they found something else in him; the decency and simplicity of their own folk. They took him into their homes, fed him and wrapped him around tight and close in the intimacy of warmth and humour, and in the aspirations of a people in whom a national spirit had never died ... Paul felt he was at home, back where he had been as the 'preacher's son' in Westfield and Somerville, New Jersey, among the people to whom he belonged. Never had he felt so much at home since he grew up ... 'It was the one film I could be proud of having played in,' said Robeson. 'That, and the early part of *Song of Freedom*.'[34]

On 25 February 1940 *The Proud Valley* became the first film to be premiered on radio. That evening the BBC broadcast a sixty-minute version of the film, reproduced from its soundtrack, on their Home Service. After its release on 8 March 1940 at the Leicester Square Theatre in London's West End, its success in Britain was harmed by newspaper magnate Lord Beaverbrook, who banned any mention of Robeson and the film in his newspapers. Apparently, he objected to certain pro-Russian remarks Robeson had made after his return to America in September 1939. The film's producer, Michael Balcon, later recalled the affair:

> while a number of people in films, both British and American, had found it convenient to leave for America either immediately before or after the war began, Paul Robeson had remained to fulfil his contract with us. A few days later my telephone rang and it was Lord Beaverbrook. He gave me a very uncomfortable time, telling me in his forthright manner what he thought of Robeson. At the end of the conversation he said that there would be no attack on Robeson or the film but he thought it was appropriate for his papers to ignore it entirely. Thus *The Proud Valley*, one of the first British films to be shown after the outbreak of war, went without a single reference in three important papers – two of them with national circulations.[35]

After appearing in *The Proud Valley*, Robeson was never forgotten in South Wales. In the years that the American government denied him a passport (1950–58), the Welsh people were one of the most vocal and active groups who came to his support.

After returning to America, nothing had changed as far as Hollywood was concerned. In the *Los Angeles Examiner* (19 February 1940), gossip columnist Louella O. Parsons announced that Universal were planning to remake *Uncle Tom's Cabin* with Robeson as Uncle Tom: 'Since *Gone with the Wind* broke box-office records right and left and every studio has been hunting for a road show idea', she explained. Robeson had no intention of playing Uncle Tom, but in 1942 he did accept an offer to play a sharecropper in a segment of a film called *Tales of Manhattan*. Ethel Waters co-starred, but it was a decision he deeply regretted making, as he was subsequently condemned for perpetuating a racist stereotype. It was *Sanders of the River* all over again. David Shipman has described the segment as 'folksy and patronizing . . . a negation of everything both artists stood for'.[36] Robeson agreed with his critics, and publicly stated that he 'wouldn't blame any Negro for picketing the film'. He even volunteered to join protestors outside cinemas where the film was being shown. He never made another film appearance as an actor. Thomas Cripps has described the dilemma that Robeson faced:

> Robeson, despondent and bitter, told an interviewer that his film career was at an end . . . Forced to choose between long-standing loyalty to cinema and his faith in the politics of the left, he chose the latter and blasted the picture he had liked enough to appear in and fight to change.[37]

Paul Robeson died in 1976 at the age of seventy-seven. Two years later controversy arose in Hollywood when the Chamber of Commerce turned down requests from Actors' Equity, and the Screen Actors' Guild to place a posthumous star in his name on Hollywood's Walk of Fame. The Chamber's selection committee claimed Robeson had been rejected because he 'lacked sufficient professional achievements' *not*, they stressed, because of his political beliefs. However, following protests from groups such as Equity, as well as individuals like Lena Horne and Paul Robeson Jr, they relented and on 10 April 1979 Paul Robeson had a star bearing his name placed on the Walk of Fame. In 1981 Robeson's granddaughter, Susan Robeson, provided this fitting testimony to her grandfather:

> My grandfather challenged the inherent racism of the film industry to its foundations, for which he paid a price perhaps greater than that of any artist in American history. He did so proudly, as a matter of principle and with no regrets.[38]

NOTES

1 John Kobal, letter to Stephen Bourne, 24 March 1986.
2 Robin Gibson, letter to Stephen Bourne, 13 March 1986.
3 Paul Robeson, *Film Weekly*, 1 September 1933.
4 David Shipman, *The Great Movie Stars: The Golden Years* (London: Hamlyn, 1970), p. 463.

5 Paul Robeson, BBC radio interview, 6 September 1959.

6 Eslanda Goode Robeson, *Paul Robeson: Negro* (London, Victor Gollancz, 1930), pp. 96–7.

7 Eric Johns, 'When Edith Day flipped a coin', *Theatre World*, October 1960. Courtesy of Ken Sephton.

8 Stephen Bourne, 'Heydays: Amanda Ira Aldridge', *The Stage*, 13 July 2000.

9 Pauline Henriques, interview with Stephen Bourne, in Jim Pines (ed.), *Black and White in Colour: Black People in British Television Since 1936* (London: British Film Institute, 1992), pp. 25–6.

10 Kenneth Barrow, *Flora: An Appreciation of the Life and Work of Dame Flora Robson* (London: Heinemann, 1981), pp. 80–1.

11 Marie Seton, *Paul Robeson* (London: Dennis Dobson, 1958), p. 78.

12 Paul Robeson, *Sunday Worker*, 10 May 1936.

13 Eslanda Goode Robeson, *African Journey* (London: Victor Gollancz, 1946), p. 9.

14 *Ibid.*, p. 49.

15 Flora Robson, interviewed in *Paul Robeson* (BBC television, tx 26 November 1978).

16 Paul Robeson Jr, interviewed in *Songs of Freedom: Paul Robeson and the Black American Struggle* (Channel 4 television, tx 30 June 1986).

17 Dr Nnamdi Azikiwe, *Renascent Africa* (Lagos, 1968), pp. 153–5.

18 *The Keys*, Vol. 2, No. 4, April–June 1935.

19 Marcus Garvey, *Black Man*, Vol. 1, No. 7, June 1935.

20 Rupert Lewis, *Marcus Garvey: Anti-Colonial Champion* (Karia Press, 1987), p. 250.

21 Paul Robeson, 'Why Robeson rebelled', *Film Weekly*, 8 October 1938.

22 Paul Robeson, *The Cine-Technician*, September–October 1938, pp. 74–5.

23 Paul Robeson, *Film Weekly*, 23 May 1936.

24 See Donald Bogle, *Toms, Coons, Mulattoes, Mammies and Bucks: An Interpretive History of Blacks in Americans Films* (New York: The Viking Press, 1973), p. 137; and Lola Young, *Fear of the Dark: Race, Gender and Sexuality in the Cinema* (London and New York: Routledge, 1996), pp. 71–9.

25 Douglas McVay, *The Musical Film* (London: Zwemmer, 1967), p. 22.

26 Kenneth M. Cameron, *Africa on Film: Beyond Black and White* (New York: Continuum, 1994), p. 102.

27 Elisabeth Welch, letter to Stephen Bourne, 19 January 1984.

28 Martin Bauml Duberman, *Paul Robeson* (London: Bodley Head, 1989), p. 208.

29 Cameron, *Africa on Film*, p. 26.

30 Sean Creighton, *Politics and Culture: Paul Robeson in the UK* (London: Agenda Services, 1998), p. 4.

31 Peter Noble, *Reflected Glory* (London: Jarrolds, 1958), p. 37.

32 David Berry, *Wales and Cinema* (Cardiff: University of Wales Press, 1994), p. 168.

33 Graham Greene, *Spectator*, 15 March 1940.

34 Seton, *Paul Robeson*, p. 121.

35 Michael Balcon, *Michael Balcon Presents . . . A Lifetime of Films* (London: Hutchinson, 1969), p. 127.

36 Shipman, *Great Movie Stars*, p. 465.

37 Thomas Cripps, *Slow Fade to Black: The Negro in American Film, 1900–1942* (Oxford: Oxford University Press, 1977), p. 384.

38 Susan Robeson, *The Whole World in His Hands: A Pictorial Biography of Paul Robeson* (Secaucus, NJ: Citadel Press, 1981), p. 64.

FURTHER READING

Anthony Aldgate, and Jeffrey Richards, 'The sun never sets: *Sanders of the River*', in *Best of British Cinema and Society 1930–1970* (Oxford: Blackwell, 1983).

Lloyd L. Brown, *The Young Paul Robeson: 'On My Journey Now'* (Westview Press, 1997).

Colin Chambers, *The Story of Unity Theatre* (London: Lawrence and Wishart, 1989).

Richard Dyer, 'Paul Robeson: crossing over', in *Heavenly Bodies: Film Stars and Society* (London: British Film Institute/Macmillan, 1987).

Philip S. Foner (ed.), *Paul Robeson Speaks: Writings, Speeches, Interviews 1918–1974.* (London: Quartet Books, 1978).

G. D. Hamann, *Paul Robeson in the 30s and 40s* (Hollywood, Ca: Filming Today Press, 2000).

C. L. R. James, 'Paul Robeson: black star', *Black World*, November 1970.

Virginia Mason Vaughan, ' "The Ethiopian Moor": Paul Robeson's Othello', in *Othello: A Contextual History* (Cambridge: Cambridge University Press, 1994).

Jeffrey Richards, 'The black man as hero', in *Films and British National Identity: From Dickens to Dad's Army* (Manchester and New York: Manchester University Press, 1997).

Paul Robeson, *Here I Stand* (1958). Reprinted by Beacon Press, Boston (1971) and Cassell, London (1998).

Paul Robeson, Jr, *The Undiscovered Paul Robeson: an Artist's Journey, 1898–1939* (New York: John Wiley, 2001).

Anatol I. Schlosser, 'Paul Robeson in film: an iconoclast's quest for a role', in *Paul Robeson: The Great Forerunner* (New York: Dodd, Mead and Company, 1985).

Jeffrey C. Stewart (ed.), *Paul Robeson: Artist and Citizen* (New Brunswick, NJ, Rutgers University Press: Solidus London, The Paul Robeson Cultural Center, 1998).

Allan Lord Thompson, *Paul Robeson: Artist and Activist on Records, Radio and Television* (Allan Lord Thompson, 2000).

4

A Guinea a Day
Film Extras and Bit Players

It is a little-known fact that, in the 1930s, the British film industry became a major source of income for Britain's black population. Hired as extras and bit players, both adults and children made their way from all over the country to film studios in places like Beaconsfield and Shepperton. Mostly they were hired to play Africans in films that glorified the Empire. However, though this work was demeaning, the extras and bit players mostly came from working-class communities striving to overcome hardship. For them, film work became an invaluable source of income. Some were aware of the struggles of Paul Robeson, the star of most of these films. With the exception of *The Proud Valley*, all of them employed black actors in supporting roles, as well as many extras and bit players.

In the early part of the twentieth century, most working-class black people lived in communities in the dockland areas of Cardiff, Liverpool, Glasgow, Bristol and Canning Town in the East End of London. However, when Joseph Bruce came to Britain from Guyana, he differed from most of his contemporaries by making his home in a predominantly white community in Fulham, west London. When his daughter Esther was born in 1912, people of African birth or descent who lived in Britain at that time could be found in every social group. Jeffrey Green explains:

Edwardian Britain's widespread population of African birth or descent was resident at the centre of the world's largest empire, participating in the affairs of the leading industrial nation. Some knew no other land and others were self-motivated migrants. There were ambitious professionals, youths anxious for an education, parents concerned about the future, adults seeking tranquillity and workers seeking money, as well as descendants of earlier generations.[1]

Now and again, Joseph Bruce supplemented his main income as a builder's labourer by portraying an exotically dressed slave in an Arabian Nights fantasy like *Chu Chin Chow* (1934), or an African spear carrier in a Paul Robeson adventure like *Sanders of the River* (1935). Black film extras could earn up to a guinea a day, which put food on the table and helped clothe their children. In *Aunt Esther's Story*, a lively and entertaining account of her experiences of working-class black life in Britain in the twentieth century, Esther remembered how her father became a film extra:

> There weren't many black people living in Fulham before the war. Apart from Marcus Garvey there was Old Mr Fahmey. He was African. A tall, distinguished-looking bloke who was over six foot tall and very thin. He dressed very smart and was a friendly, outgoing chap. All the kids talked to him. He must have been about one hundred years old but nobody knew exactly how old he was. He earned a living working as a film extra. Now and again Mr Fahmey asked Dad if he would like to earn a bit of pocket money working as a film extra. They were in *Chu Chin Chow* with Anna May Wong and *The Thief of Bagdad* with Sabu. They also appeared as spear carriers in some of Paul Robeson's films including *Sanders of the River*, *Song of Freedom* and *King Solomon's Mines*. Sometimes whole families appeared in the same films. Dad said they came from all over the place. Cardiff. Liverpool. The East End. When Dad appeared in *Sanders of the River* he told me that the little children cried when they saw their Mums and Dads take their clothes off and pretend to be African natives. Today people would think it was offensive, and they'd be right, but in those days black people earned good money working as film extras.[2]

Joseph Bruce did not regard himself as a professional actor, and film-extra work was not his main source of income. However, some black men of his generation, like Napoleon Florent, did pursue full-time careers as professional actors. His daughter, Josephine, describes how Napoleon arrived in this country in the early part of the century:

> My father was born in St Lucia in the 1870s. He was about seventeen or eighteen years old when he left. His mother was friendly with a captain of a ship who exported sugar and bananas from St Lucia. My father was chosen to travel with the captain and he travelled to places like Germany and France. He did not come to England until 1907. I remember being taken to see my father on the West End stage in *Kismet* at the Garrick Theatre [1914]. Another show he appeared in was *Chu Chin Chow* at His Majesty's Theatre [1916]. That ran for five years and kept father in work for a very long time. I was a very small child at the time, but I do vividly remember seeing my father on stage in those productions wearing the most wonderful,

exotic costumes. He didn't have speaking roles. He was an exotic extra, usually a eunuch. Father also worked as an extra and bit player in silent films, and he was a very good actor, as well as a fine raconteur on and off the stage. To put it simply, if father got work in a film or on the stage, we ate.

Father worked a lot in the early days, but by the time I was twelve, around 1922, the work dried up. The slump lasted until 1930. To help out financially, my mother went to work, even though she had a home and eight children to take care of. She worked all her life and could turn her hand to anything. They were not very glamorous jobs, either! After I left school, I tried to get into show business to earn some money for the family. In 1926, when I was just sixteen years old, I auditioned for a famous West End stage revue called *Blackbirds* which starred that marvellous American entertainer, Florence Mills. This was going to be a big musical production, with a huge cast of black singers and dancers. But I couldn't sing or dance, so for the audition I recited a poem! Can you imagine that? They must have thought I was mad. Needless to say, I didn't get a job in the show![3]

After 1930, Napoleon Florent began to find occasional stage roles. However, the range of parts open to him was extremely limited. Though he had ceased to play exotic eunuchs, Florent can be found listed in the casts of several West End plays as 'pullman porter' or 'witch doctor'. Away from the stage, he continued to work in films as a bit player and extra, but the roles were mostly comical stereotypes.

Paul Robeson's films provided Florent with a fairly regular source of income. For instance, he's visible as one of King Mofolaba's henchmen in *Sanders of the River*, and is recognizable in at least three different scenes in *Song of Freedom* (1936). In the prologue he appears as a spear carrier on the island of Casanga and also as one of the slaves on board the slave ship. Later, when Robeson arrives on the island of Casanga, Napoleon is visible again as one of the villagers. In *King Solomon's Mines* (1937) he took the part of one of the village elders. Florent also appeared in three comedies starring Will Hay, who, during that period, was one of the most popular stars in British films. In *Windbag the Sailor* (1936) Hay is cast away on a cannibal island, and Florent played the cannibal king's right-hand man. In *Hey! Hey! USA* (1938) Florent appears as an extra in the large crowd scene at the end of the film, and in *Old Bones of the River* (1938) he makes a brief appearance as Chief Tahiti, from whom Hay tries to collect taxes. Of the guinea a day Napoleon was paid for film-extra work, 10 per cent went to his agent. In 1935 his participation as an extra in *Sanders of the River* upset Josephine:

We had an argument about that film because, after it was shown, Paul Robeson complained that it showed black people as ignorant savages. He

Song of Freedom (1936)

said he wasn't going to appear in any more 'jungle' or 'Uncle Tom' films. This upset my father. He said Robeson would put him, and many other black people, out of work. But I said 'Good for Paul Robeson! Why should British films always show us as being subservient?' Father said: 'I've been out of work for six years. Paul Robeson comes along and I'm working again. *Sanders of the River* pays the rent and puts food on the table. You're only a child. What do you know?' A few years later Robeson made *The Proud Valley* and he was wonderful in that. So he did break away from the jungle films.[4]

In 1946 Florent played his most important screen role as the father of Robert Adams in *Men of Two Worlds*:

Father had a good speaking role as an elderly African villager in *Men of Two Worlds*. My sister Elvira and I went to see it and we were horrible girls. First, we arrived late at the cinema in Marble Arch where it was being shown. After we found our seats, Elvira turned to me and said: 'Oh, my God, there's father dying.' We had walked in during his death scene! Father was dying very convincingly but, instead of crying, Elvira and I shrieked with laughter. We didn't tell father about that. At home, father could be very stern. He definitely had a Victorian attitude to raising his children. That generation of West Indians could be very strict. But now and again we were allowed to laugh.[5]

In 1948 Florent made his last film appearance in David Lean's screen version of Charles Dickens's *Oliver Twist*. He is clearly visible as the elderly white-haired gentleman in the sequence set in the Three Cripples pub. He died at the age of eighty-four on 6 March 1959 and on his death certificate his occupation is entered as 'Theatrical Artist (Retired)'.

Joseph Bruce and Napoleon Florent joined about three hundred black men recruited to appear as 'spear carriers' in *Sanders of the River*. In 1934 Alexander Korda's casting director, Dorothy Holloway, visited the Cardiff, Glasgow, Liverpool and London docks to find African seaman to appear in the crowd scenes. These were filmed in the African village constructed at Korda's studios in Shepperton in Middlesex. African students also found their way onto the set, eager to earn some extra money. Between 1934 and 1937 Jomo Kenyatta studied at two London universities, and appeared in a minor role as a chieftain in *Sanders*. In 1964 Kenyatta became President of the Republic of Kenya. Martin Bauml Duberman draws attention to the apparent contradiction between his appearance in such a film and his political activities:

> It's worth noting that Jomo Kenyatta seems to have felt no qualms about the direction the film was taking, expressing 'delight' in 'the music and the spirit of the African scenes'. Even after its completion, Kenyatta joined in the presentation of a cigarette case to Korda, adding his name to the inscription inside ('With deep admiration and gratitude'), and no one has ever accused Kenyatta of insufficient dedication to the cause of African independence and the integrity of African culture. Kenyatta never again spoke of the film.[6]

Another extra who appeared in *Sanders of the River* was Ernest Marke, who was born in Freetown, Sierra Leone. Marke's mother was a member of a Nigerian royal tribe and one of the first African women to complete her education in Britain. Marke first came to Britain in 1917 after stowing away on a merchant ship. Demobbed in Liverpool, Marke was attacked in the anti-black riots of 1919. He recalled his eventful life in his autobiography, first published as *Old Man Trouble* in 1975 and reissued in 1986 as *In Troubled Waters: Memoirs of Seventy Years in England*. Like other black people of his generation, he lived by his wits and earned a living the best way he could: as a seller of quack (but harmless) 'medicine', as a showman, a boxer, a racing tipster and a gambler. Heading for London in the 1930s, he opened a nightclub in Soho and, later, the Coloured Colonial Social Club. He also formed the Coloured Workers' Association, and in 1945 represented them in the historic fifth Pan-African Conference in Manchester, chaired by W. E. B. DuBois. From 1956

Marke worked as a boilerman in Chelsea until his retirement in 1968. He died in 1995. In his autobiography he remembered Kenyatta:

> I think Nkrumah was the greatest African I ever had the pleasure of knowing – if for no other reason than that he started the wind of change in Africa. I am also proud to have known Jomo Kenyatta, now President of Kenya. We first met in the early thirties when filming *Sanders of the River* with Paul Robeson. I was an extra, and Jomo took the part of one of the tribal chiefs. No one then, including himself, would have dreamt that he was destined to become the liberator and president of his country.[7]

Some of the extras in Paul Robeson's films were found as far away as Bute Town, also known as Tiger Bay, in Cardiff. Robeson enjoyed enormous popularity in Wales, and occasionally visited the black community in Tiger Bay, as local historian Neil M. C. Sinclair describes in *The Tiger Bay Story*:

> With his marvellous voice Robeson found a great 'welcome in the hillside' and sang with many a Welsh male-voice choir. . . . Paul Robeson also found a welcome in Tiger Bay where he made several visits to the Jason home on the west side of Loudoun Square. There he used to visit the African-American, Aaron Mossell, who lodged with the Jason family at that time in 9 Loudoun Square. In actuality Mr Mossell was uncle by marriage to Paul Robeson. No doubt that relationship was one of the reasons he came to visit . . . this American film actor thrilled us immensely because he had a wonderful voice and had the essential quality of being black. He was someone like us – at least those of us of African descent! It must be recalled that in the media of those days one rarely saw a black face that wasn't a white face painted black with white eyes and mouth . . . many of the extras in the film *Sanders of the River* came from Tiger Bay. We all knew that the witch doctor dancing wildly in the centre of the film's version of an African village was Mr Graham, the 'Bengal Tiger', from Sophia Street. And that was Uncle Willy Needham leaping around in the loin cloth which he kept for years after the film was made![8]

The Cozier family from Canning Town in London's East End nearly all worked as film extras. Joseph Cozier was born in British Guiana in 1896 and, to escape a strict father, he ran away to sea. His eldest daughter, Anita, takes up the story:

> Dad was just fourteen when he stowed away on a ship and came all that way from British Guiana. He was on the ship for a little while before he got discovered, and he was frightened. He told us the captain was a nice man

and said 'How would you like to help out in the galleys?' Dad said: 'Well, I'll do anything because I want to come to England.' The captain said: 'Well, I don't know what will happen when you get there.' Dad met a fella in the galley and they became friends. His name was Mr Gerald. He was my Dad's friend for years and years. He became a friend of the family. During World War One, Dad was a chief cook in the navy. After the war, Dad came to the East End, and stayed in a lodging house in Victoria Dock Road. Mrs MacKenzie took in all the coloured seamen as lodgers. Her lodging house was near Custom House Station where the park is now.[9]

A number of black families lived in the area around the Royal Group of Docks in the East End of London, even before the First World War. These docks were the largest in the world, and the Port of London was the most famous in the British Empire. Historian Howard Bloch has researched the lives of the local black community between the wars. He says:

Some black seaman chose to make new homes in London while others, because of a downturn in world trade, and the colour bar, found it difficult to obtain a passage home. Many of them settled in the streets around the 'sailor town' area of Victoria Dock Road which ran from west to east from Canning Town to Custom House.

The number of black seamen who settled in the district increased during the First World War. Some black men stowed away on ships from the Caribbean in order to volunteer to fight with the British armed forces. They were not allowed to serve in the white army regiments, although some were informed that they might be able to enlist in a black regiment which had been formed. Many of them served in the Merchant Navy. Their presence in the area was not always welcomed by the white population. Some considered that the white women were infatuated with the black men and the houses of black men from Jamaica in Crown Street were attacked by gangs of men and boys in July 1917.

At the end of the First World War, demobilisation and the lack of employment led to resentment by white people against the black people who had settled in what they considered to be their neighbourhood. Further attacks occurred on black people in Crown Street in August 1919. These were not on anything like the scale of those in Cardiff, Liverpool and other port towns. Crown Street off Victoria Dock Road was the main street where black people lived. It was known locally as 'Draughtboard Alley' – because black and white people lived together there. They also lived in other nearby streets.[10]

In 1920 Joseph Cozier married an Englishwoman, Florence Tindling, and they had eight children including Christopher, who remembers the respect shown towards their father who died in 1967:

> Dad was very educated. He could speak three languages. After a series of strokes, he had to give up his job in the navy but he always found work. He took menial jobs on the railways – engine cleaning, that sort of thing. Dad was respected in our community. Everyone called him 'Mr Cozier'. All the old coloured men were respected and addressed as 'Mr'. When I grew up in the 1930s, black and white people respected each other. Racial prejudice did not exist in our community.[11]

Anita remembers that at the time she was growing up, there were very few black women in the community:

> So black seamen married white women and quite a lot of mixed marriages turned out all right because they were good to each other. Where we lived there was no feeling that mixed marriages were wrong. The white people we lived with accepted it. I feel there is more racism here now than we ever had before the war. We never had any racism when I was young. I remember when I played in the street with my brothers and sisters the policemen would come along on their horses. They knew us all by name, and gave us rides on their horses. Afterwards they took us to the police station for a treat – a piece of cake baked by the station cook. The only drawback was that if any of us got into trouble, the local policemen would scream out our names and threaten to go and see our Mum. Now and again a white kid at school called us names like 'darkie walla', but we always got our own back. I remember pulling a girl's hair because she called my sister Joan 'darkie'. I remember that. So we called the white kids names like 'whitewash' and, after that, we became friends. It isn't like that today. When we were kids, we was all one.[12]

Anita didn't work as a film extra herself, and she doesn't remember how her family started working in films, but she believes it had something to do with the Coloured Men's Institute in Tidal Basin Road. This was known in the local community as 'the Mission', and provided a meeting place for black seamen who were waiting for a ship. They occupied themselves by playing darts or draughts, and there was a fountain outside where they could be seen standing and chatting. Anita remembers how the film companies would come to the Mission to recruit extras:

> Now and again, when there was an African film being made like *Sanders of the River*, someone would call at the Mission and ask if we wanted to be in it. An arrangement would be made to take a number of children from the

neighbourhood to the film studio. Mum and another lady arranged to take the children to the studio. Everything would be layed on – their fare and that. But Mum and this lady had to chaperone the children. My brothers and sisters were only little. They'd arrive at Shepperton, or wherever, and be taken to the wardrobe department for their costumes, and to see if their hair was all right. Most of the children got a job. If it was an African film, they'd have to be dark, but some of the children were not dark enough to play Africans. So they used something called cocoa stick on them. At the studio they'd say, 'You can darken up a bit there'. The make-up people put it on for them. Then they'd have to have tight, curly hair. My brother Joe was all right because he had tight hair anyway. My other brothers and sisters had loose hair, but the film people knew how to tighten it for them. I remember they even blacked Mum up once to play the wife of somebody. When I saw her she had a scarf wrapped around her head as African women do, and she looked lovely. But they only had fleeting little bits in these films.

Dad was in *Sanders of the River* and *King Solomon's Mines* with a lot of the coloured seamen. They played warriors and they were done up in feathers, carrying spears, and all that sort of thing. I remember Dad's old mate, Mr Boucher, who was a bit of a character. He used to get his face in lots of films, and if we recognized him we said, 'Oh, where's Dad?' because they always stuck together. They didn't think it was degrading. They were only too pleased to get the work and earn the money. Today people would feel it was degrading and refuse to play a savage or whatever. But there wasn't that sort of feeling in those days. The coloured men who appeared in these films were proud of their colour, and wouldn't have anything said against themselves or their families. Playing African natives in films like *Sanders of the River* didn't bother them. They had a good time.

We recognized Dad in *The Thief of Bagdad* because he was one of the fishermen waving angrily at Sabu, the little thief who's nicked his fish. When we saw the film we said, 'Oh, look, there's Dad!' *The Thief of Bagdad* is a lovely film.[13]

Christopher was very young when he worked as a film extra, but he does remember Mrs Campbell, a 'coloured woman', who acted as an agent for the film studios. Christopher believes she might have had an office in the West End. When film extras were needed, Mrs Campbell came to Canning Town and contacted Mrs Cozier, who rounded up the number of children required by the film studio. He has nothing but happy memories of his experiences of working as a film extra:

When we went to the film studios from the streets of the East End it was always a very exciting experience for us. It was a big adventure, and we were spoilt with ice creams and sweets. When we worked as film extras we lived like little princes and princesses! All our mates at school asked us if we were film stars! It was a game to us, a chance to bunk off school and make a bit of money for the family. The money we earned was needed because Dad had suffered a stroke and work was scarce in the 1930s. Mum and Dad had eight kids to support. We were well paid. Each child could earn up to three pounds a day. Mum was always responsible for us. She was our chaperone. When we arrived at the studio we'd have our make-up done, and once we were on the film set, we behaved ourselves. Mum watched over us to make sure we didn't play up. We couldn't afford to get sacked and lose money. We enjoyed ourselves but sometimes, if the hours were long, we fell asleep. It could be a bit boring for young children.

Film extra work usually took place after school hours. Mum would rush us home, scrub us clean, and take us to the film studio. We worked at Denham, Beaconsfield, Shepperton, Pinewood and Elstree. She worked in a couple of films herself, including *Sanders of the River*. I remember she spoke to the producer Alexander Korda. *Sanders of the River* was the first film we worked in. We were surprised to see so many black people on the set. Most of them were Africans. I remember being astonished by one who laughed at us, showing his gold teeth! I remember meeting Jomo Kenyatta, a friendly man. But I didn't know anything about him until much, much later. Paul Robeson was a very nice man. We knew he was famous. I remember him as a massive, gentle giant with a big, smiling face. To us children he was the King. I also remember appearing in *East Meets West* [1936] with George Arliss, a funny-looking old chap. Then Dad, Joe and I worked together in *The Four Feathers* [1939].

I worked with Will Hay in two films, *Hey! Hey! USA* and *Old Bones of the River*. Will Hay didn't have much to do with us, but we liked him because he behaved like a favourite schoolteacher. He was a comical, funny old man. We were sitting on old wooden benches, and he's trying to tell us about the shape of the world on this blackboard. Then there's this native who resents the kids being educated by this white man. He throws a spear at the blackboard, but the man playing the native didn't throw it. The spear was supposed to be fired by air. I remember the first time they tried it the spear split the blackboard into little pieces! When Joan, Joe and I worked in *Old Bones of the River* it was like winning the pools. I mean, three of us in one film – that came to about £12 a day! It was a fortune!

When we worked as film extras we had to keep it a secret because our family was means-tested by the dole people. If we needed financial assistance, Mum used to hide all her prized possessions when the dole people visited us. So when we took time off school to go to the film studios, Mum told us to pretend to our teachers we had colds, chicken pox or measles. I remember when I went too far and told a teacher that my brother Eugene couldn't come to school because he had swallowed a needle and died! In fact, he had a contract to appear in a Paul Robeson film called *Jericho*. Imagine my Mum's embarrassment when the teacher told her how sorry she was to hear about young Eugene! We loved going to the pictures, too. We went to three cinemas in Canning Town. There was a 'tuppeny rush' on a Saturday morning to the 'Addo' in Addison Road. Other times we went to the 'Pollo' [Apollo] or The Old Grand by the Abbey Arms. My favourites were Tarzan, Flash Gordon, Charlie Chan and comedy films with Old Mother Riley and Will Hay. There was always a lot of noise from the kids in the audience, and we were always throwing orange peel at each other. I also remember a bloke who came round and said, 'legs up'. Then he'd spray everything with disinfectant.[14]

Eugene was the only Cozier child to sign a film contract, when he played Paul Robeson's son in *Jericho* (1937). Aged about three, the smiling, happy toddler appears towards the end of the film, sitting on Robeson's lap, while Robeson sings 'Shortnin' Bread' to him. Anita recalls her brother's all-too-brief film career:

Eugene was the worker and he was only a few years old when he appeared in *Jericho*. He worked for about a month in that film. He earned one guinea a day. I remember Mum was able to put something by for little suits for Eugene, and clothes for my brothers and sisters. It was quite good, really. Eugene was only fourteen years old when he died from peritonitis.[15]

When the war broke out, most of the film studios in Britain closed down. The vogue for films about the British Empire was over, at least for the time being, and the services of the Cozier family were no longer required. Anita left school at the age of fourteen in 1939 and went to work for the Co-Operative Wholesale Society, in a sweet factory in Silvertown. Joan (aged twelve), Joseph (aged ten) and Christopher (aged eight) were evacuated, as Joseph explains:

In 1939 I was evacuated with Joan and Chris with our school, St Joachim's, a Catholic school in Custom House. We were taken to Great Bedwin near Malborough in Wiltshire. There was a crowd of us from the East End, but we were the only coloured children. It was quite an adventure, because we'd never left home before. We were taken to the village hall where the vicar and some women from the village offered different children to villagers for fostering. Each child had its name called out and was told to stand on the stage, and the villagers came and picked the children they wanted, but we were left out. They only picked the white children, except a little boy who had impetigo. Afterwards there was just Joan, Chris, myself and this boy with impetigo left in the village hall. I thought to myself, 'I won't let this bother me'. I was with my brother and sister anyway. At the end of the day the vicar took us to his vicarage, but he wasn't married, and didn't have a clue how to look after us. So he asked one of our teachers to feed us. But she was a spinster and couldn't cook either. Instead she fed us Garibaldi biscuits with milk and raisins for breakfast, dinner and tea! When the health visitor came she told the vicar we must be given proper meals. Luckily for us, Mrs MacDonald, an Irish woman who had been evacuated to the same village with her two daughters, knew our family and took us under her wing. She was a lovely woman. She mended our clothes, and took us for walks in the countryside. We were together for about two years. I don't know what would have happened to us if she hadn't been there. We had the run of the vicarage, and access to orchards and forests. We even had a canal, something we'd never seen before. It was a very happy experience. We roamed all over the countryside. It was an adventure. Mum and Dad visited us when they could, and Dad wrote us letters. Mum couldn't read or write. When we returned to London, we had great difficulties adjusting. We lived right on the docks. We could see the funnels of the ships at the top of our street.[16]

Cleo Laine was another mixed-race child who experienced the fun and excitement of working as a pre-war film extra. Born in Southall, Middlesex, she was the daughter of Alexander Sylvan Campbell, a Jamaican, and Minnie Hitchen, who was born and brought up in Swindon in Wiltshire. Minnie was disowned by her family for marrying a black man. In the summer of 1939, when she was eleven years old, Cleo, her older sister Sylvia and younger brother Alexander took part in the filming of Alexander Korda's spectacular Arabian Nights fantasy *The Thief of Bagdad*, starring the Indian child actor, Sabu. The Campbell children appeared as urchins in the Bagdad market sequence. In her autobiography she describes how a family friend called Bill Betts, a 'blue black' Londoner who wore 'African robes' and spoke with an 'affected African accent', helped launch the little girl into the world of entertainment:

he suggested something that turned out to be the start of my professional career in show business As a member of the 'Actor's Extra Union', Bill had heard that they needed children for the crowd scenes in the film *The Thief of Baghdad* [*sic*]. Would Mother agree to us going along to try for it? And did we want to do it? If we didn't he wouldn't bother to put in a good word for us. Did we want to! Do cats refuse milk? The room became a circus of joy in which we jumped, cart-wheeled and hollered. ... It was the summer holidays so school wasn't a problem.

We saw very little of Sabu, except for one scene, when he had to tip a basket of oranges over to escape from Conrad Veidt's evil threats. The urchins (the extras – me) had to dive after the fruit with glee, helping him to get away in the confusion. I did my whooping and hollering wholeheartedly, flinging myself on the oranges and keeping a couple to eat later. Rex Ingram, the impressive black actor who played the Genie in the film, was very visible though throughout my period of filming, calling out 'Hi!' to us all every morning as he passed on his way to makeup or wardrobe. He had a very friendly manner towards us lowlier participants in the film. Most of the other stars, if they passed by, passed with nothing to say – Rex Ingram was really most unusual. But for me it was enough to be on the same studio lot as all of them, picking up the vibes ...

The journeys home were extremely embarrassing for sister Sylvia ... I was now a movie actress, who had to polish up her act continually. We would both get on the Greenline bus to Hayes End and home, sixpenny fare in hand, and wait for the conductor to confront us with 'fares please'. Sylvia, in her best English, would ask for her sixpenny fare. When it was my turn, ignoring the fact that we were together and obviously related, I would plunge into the most idiotic accent that had nothing to do with Sylvia's ... 'Seexerpineez' didn't fox the conductor who probably came into contact with a lot of nutters on his daily route.[17]

One of the most best-known – and flamboyant – showmen in Britain in the twentieth century was a racing tipster called Ras Prince Monolulu. From the 1930s to the 1960s there were few people in this country who had not heard of him. Many had seen him, at Ascot and Epsom, in Oxford Street or the East End. Indeed, you couldn't mistake him, with his head-dress of ostrich feathers, multicoloured cloak and gaiters, tartan shawl wrapped around his waist, a huge shooting stick-cum-umbrella in his hand and a lion-claw necklace round his neck. Then there was his famous catchphrase, 'I gotta horse!', which he shouted at the top of his voice.

Though he claimed to have been born in Addis Ababa, the capital of Ethiopia, the son of a chieftain of the wandering Jewish tribe, he was actually born Peter Carl McKay in British Guiana in 1881. When he arrived in Britain in 1902, he earned a living the best way he could, singing in the streets and taking menial jobs until joining the chorus of the all-black show *In Dahomey* in 1903. Before he became a racing tipster in the 1920s, Monolulu travelled around the world, working in a variety of jobs including fortune-teller, violinist, singer, lion tamer, horseback rider in a circus and 'cannibal' in a roadshow. His association with the world of racing began when he worked as a stablehand. Within a few years he had become an accomplished tipster. In 1920 he reputedly won more than £3,000 on the Derby when he put all his money on Spion Kop. His fate as a tipster was sealed, and from that point on he was feted by racing's rich and famous all over the world. In the 1930s Monolulu, pianist Leslie 'Hutch' Hutchinson and Paul Robeson were the three most famous black men in Britain.

It was inevitable that Ras Prince Monolulu would appear in British films. Virtually every film with a racecourse setting includes an appearance by this legendary character. In his autobiography *I Gotta Horse* (1950) he declares, 'it is only natural that where there have been racing films producers have made use of my services to give colour to crowd scenes'.[18] As himself, Monolulu made fleeting appearances in *The Sport of Kings* (1931), *Educated Evans* (1936), *Wings of the Morning* (1937), *Derby Day* (1952), *The Gambler and the Lady* (1952), *Make Mine a Million* (1959) and *The Criminal* (1960). However, he never took an acting role in a film, though he came close in 1945 when he joined the cast of an epic screen version of a play by George Bernard Shaw:

> Believe it or not, I played a small part in *Caesar and Cleopatra*. It would have been a larger part, but someone who saw the 'rushes' – the first pictures of the previous day's work – recognized me as a tipster and the film company thought it wasn't at all funny to have someone whose face was too well known on the racecourses to play the part of an Ethiopian in the Council Chamber![19]

In 1993 he was remembered with affection by Ernest Marke in the BBC series *The Nineties* and, in the collection of interviews published to coincide with the series, he said:

> When he went to Doncaster for the St Leger race, everybody know him, so he can get digs. It was very hard for the black people to get digs. He accepted me like a son or a little brother. He used to book digs and write to me. 'I've booked a room for you, son, come along.' So we sleep in the same bed, one big bed, so I know all about him. I know more about Monolulu than even his wife know. But the only thing he did was tell me off when he found out I was selling tips. I don't blame him. 'No messing about tipping, I'm the one who sell the tips around.' But I said, 'Who are we against you? You are the tops. So what are you worried about?' 'Oh, well maybe you're right, dear boy.'
>
> We called him Lulu. Tall fellow, dressed like an Abyssinian. He said he was an Abyssinian prince. He was a character, everybody knew him. He showed me the tricks of the trade. He was from the British West Indies, but he told me, 'You better keep that to yourself. I told them I'm from Abyssinia because they respect people who've never been conquered. Abyssinia has never been conquered, so they respect me.' Lulu wore about five, six or seven feathers on his head, all different colours. He used to shout, 'I gotta horse, I gotta horse.' He was the first black man on the course and people used to say, 'My God!' They used to buy – 'black is luck!'[20]

Ras Prince Monolulu died in London in 1965 at the age of eighty-four. On his death certificate his occupation is entered as 'Racehorse Betting Adviser'. In 1992 a pub was named after him in Maple Street, Camden, in North London. Interviewed in a local newspaper, his son Peter maintained:

> There should have been more done for my father. He was a legend and an institution. There should have been a monument of him at Epsom or Ireland. You mention Prince Monolulu to anybody and their face lights up with a smile. My father brought happiness on this earth.[21]

NOTES

1 Jeffrey Green, *Black Edwardians: Black People in Britain 1901–1914* (London: Frank Cass, 1998), p. xiii.

2 Stephen Bourne and Esther Bruce, *Aunt Esther's Story* (London: Hammersmith and Fulham Ethnic Communities Oral History Project, 1996), pp. 2–3.

3 Josephine Florent, interview with Stephen Bourne, London, 21 August 1995.

4 *Ibid.*

5 *Ibid.*

6 Martin Bauml Duberman, *Paul Robeson* (London: Bodley Head, 1989), p. 180.

7 Ernest Marke, *In Troubled Waters: Memoirs of Seventy Years in England* (London: Karia Press, 1986), p. 136.

8 Neil M. C. Sinclair, *The Tiger Bay Story* (Bute Town History and Arts Project, 1993), pp. 41–4.

9 Anita Bowes, interview with Stephen Bourne, London, 27 January 1996.

10 Howard Bloch, 'Black people in Canning Town and Custom House between the wars', Black and Asian Studies Association, Newsletter No. 14, January 1996, p. 5.

11 Christopher Cozier, interview with Stephen Bourne, London, 1 March 1996.

12 Bowes, interview with Stephen Bourne.

13 *Ibid.*

14 Cozier, interview with Stephen Bourne.

15 Bowes, interview with Stephen Bourne.

16 Joseph Cozier, interview with Stephen Bourne, London, 9 March 1996.

17 Cleo Laine, *Cleo* (London: Simon and Schuster, 1994), pp. 49–52.

18 Ras Prince Monolulu, *I Gotta Horse* (London: Hurst and Blackett, 1950), p. 161.

19 *Ibid.*, p. 162.

20 Ernest Marke, *The Nineties: Personal Recollections of the 20th Century* (London: BBC Books, 1993), pp. 124–5.

21 Peter McKay, *Camden New Journal*, 5 November 1992.

5

Buddy Bradley and Elisabeth Welch
Harlem Comes to London

In the 1920s America witnessed the Harlem Renaissance – a large-scale explosion of creative energy and artistic expression from African-American artists and intellectuals. The event most frequently cited as marking the beginning of this period was the Broadway musical revue *Shuffle Along*, which opened in 1921, as writer Langston Hughes explains:

> The 1920s were the years of Manhattan's black Renaissance ... it was the musical revue, *Shuffle Along*, that gave a scintillating send-off to that Negro vogue in Manhattan, which reached its peak just before the crash of 1929 ... It gave just the proper push – a pre-Charleston kick – to that Negro vogue of the 20s, that spread to books, African sculpture, music and dancing.[1]

Stage musicals and revues, as well as nightclubs like the Cotton Club, showcased black talent, and African-American performers enjoyed unprecedented success and popularity in white and urban black America. But there were other, unpleasant, sides to this. Singer Lena Horne, whose career was launched at the Cotton Club in 1933, later explained:

> Nostalgia has not played anyone false about the Cotton Club shows. They were wonderful. But for the employees, it was an exploitative system ... The club got great talent very cheap, because there were so few places for great Negro performers to work. ... As for the 'exotic', wonderful, rhythmic, happy-go-lucky quality of our lives, that was a real joke. Especially for my family. We lived in a typical, roach-infested tenement.[2]

At one time or another the majority of performers who appeared in these shows and nightclubs found popularity and acclaim in Britain. They were featured in recordings, music halls, cabaret, West End revues, radio and, almost without exception, British films and/or television. Recalled blues singer Alberta Hunter: 'The Negro artists went to Europe because we were recognized and given a chance. In Europe they had your name up in lights. People in the United States would not give us that chance.'[3] It is hardly surprising, then, that historian Jeffrey Green suggests that, in Britain, another 'Harlem Renaissance' took place, in particular after the economic crash of 1929: 'The occurrence of a Harlem Renaissance in England seems unlikely, if not absurd, but New York did not have sole possession of the ideals that led to the black artistic outflow of the Renaissance.'[4]

It is important to acknowledge that some black entertainers who worked here between the two world wars received not only acclaim and popularity but also positions in high society. In fact, the association of black entertainers with Britain's upper classes and royalty can be traced back to the Victorian era when African-Americans performed for Queen Victoria. These included concert singer Elizabeth Taylor Greenfield in 1854, and the Fisk Jubilee Singers in the 1870s. The cast of *In Dahomey*, led by Bert Williams and George Walker, were invited to perform for King Edward VII at Buckingham Palace in 1903 but, though such contacts suggest a level of social acceptance, Jeffrey Green reveals that

> further investigation shows that to be a superficial view, for black entertainers were seldom truly accepted as individuals, but in general only as symbols. This led to a paradox, since the association of black people with the aristocratic and ruling elite of Britain was seen in America as a social triumph, and was reported as such in the press, biographies, and autobiographies ... If the Americans saw the association of black entertainers and Britain's high society as a black success, it would seem likely that a number of Britons, black and white, would conclude the same. British liberals, aghast at lynching, Jim Crow, and other manifestations of racialism in America, could show that the mingling of black people in British high society proved how different life was in Britain. The reality was that black access to high society was as volatile as show business, and friends were as fickle as audiences.[5]

Black entertainers and musicians were employed in British films from the introduction of sound at the end of the 1920s. The likeliest candidate for the first black performer to appear in a British sound film is Frisco (Jocelyn Bingham), an entertainer and nightclub owner who, in 1928, performed two spirituals in a series called *Phototone Reels*, produced by British Phototone. However, two of the most famous African-Americans working in British films and theatre in the 1930s and 1940s were choreographer Buddy Bradley and singer Elisabeth Welch. Bradley's collaborations with Britain's top musical star Jessie Matthews earned him the title 'Britain's Busby Berkeley'. Welch projected a glamorous and sophisticated image far removed from the bandanna-wearing mammies of Hollywood cinema.

Buddy Bradley was a major influence in jazz and tap dancing, but he has yet to be fully recognized and appreciated. He taught dance techniques to many Broadway and West End stars of the 1920s and 1930s, but he was known only within show-business circles. The name Buddy Bradley meant little to the general public. His dance ideas were well ahead of their time but, for too long, Bradley's major contribution to the art of dance in 1930s British film musicals has been ignored. His work is comparable to Busby Berkeley in Hollywood, and for years he collaborated with Jessie Matthews, Britain's top musical star in films. Together they created some of the most outstanding dance routines in the history of film musicals, as Matthews acknowledges: 'No praise is too great for Buddy, he's a genius of the dance.'[6]

Bradley was born in Harrisburg, Pennsylvania, and made his first appearance on the stage in 1926 in a New York revue with Florence Mills. He subsequently became the dance teacher and arranger for a number of Broadway musicals in the late 1920s and early 1930s, coaching many stars, including Mae West, Ruby Keeler, Lucille Ball, Eleanor Powell, as well as Fred Astaire and his sister Adele. However, Bradley never choreographed a show with a white cast in America. For instance, in 1928 he re-choreographed *Greenwich Village Follies*, even though Busby Berkeley's name appeared in the programme: 'They called me in to patch them up when they realised how bad the dancing was. I never saw half the shows my stuff appeared in ... I wasn't invited, and besides I was too busy teaching.'[7]

Jessie Matthews's biographer, Michael Thornton, reveals that it was at Fred Astaire's suggestion that she persuaded Charles B. Cochran to bring Buddy and another black dancer, Billy Pierce, over to London to stage the dances for her show *Ever Green* (the title had two words originally) at the Adelphi Theatre in December 1930, which became Jessie's greatest hit:

After *Ever Green*, Bradley worked with Jessie on her dances for *Hold My Hand*, at the Gaiety Theatre, London, 1931–32, by which time he had also made his first appearance on the British stage at the London Pavilion on 19 March 1931 in *Cochran's 1931 Revue*. In 1932 he staged the dances for Jerome Kern's *The Cat and the Fiddle*, at the Palace Theatre, and was then signed by Gaumont British, at Jessie's express request, to choreograph her dances for the film version of *Evergreen* (the title became one word), which began filming at the Gainsborough Studios in December 1933.[8]

Bradley made his one and only screen appearance in *Evergreen* (1934). In the spectacular production number, 'Springtime in Your Heart', he can be glimpsed dancing with some children on the pavement of a London street. Bradley and Matthews also collaborated on *It's Love Again* (1936), *Head Over Heels* (1937), *Gangway* (1937) and *Sailing Along* (1938). Ralph Reader is credited as the dance arranger for *First a Girl* (1935), though Bradley helped out.

The Bradley–Matthews partnership is one of the most important in the history of dance, especially in film, and yet it is barely acknowledged. For example, Jeffrey Richards only mentions him once in his chapter 'Jessie Matthews: The Dancing Divinity' in *The Age of the Dream Palace: Cinema and Society in Britain 1930–1939* (1984). David Shipman fails to mention him at all in his otherwise excellent study of Matthews in *The Great Movie Stars: The Golden Years* (1970), and there is no entry for Bradley in Colin Larkin's *The Guinness Who's Who of Film Musicals and Musical Films* (1994). John Kobal makes a brief reference to Bradley's collaboration with Matthews in *Gotta Sing Gotta Dance: A Pictorial History of Film Musicals* (1971):

> Her usual choreographic collaborator, and American resident in England, Buddy Bradley, must have understood Jessie Matthews and her abilities as a dancer almost as well as she did herself. There is hardly ever a moment in her dances that is not lyrical and harmonious or which looks awkward for

Buddey Bradley in *Evergreen* (1934)

her to do. She feels the music. At times she almost seems to *be* the music, always anticipating the next movement – not just clever choreography, but her body's intuitive expression of the pleasure she gets from dancing.[9]

One of the most memorable sequences in a Jessie Matthews musical is the 'Dancing on the Ceiling' number in *Evergreen*. Matthews is seen at her best, enchanting and graceful, dancing sensuously through a house. But her versions of the facts could never be wholly relied upon, and she was fond of saying that this long dance sequence was created by her alone at the very last moment before shooting. Bradley refuted this, saying that they worked out every single move and step together. Of Bradley, she said:

> We worked on most of my films together marvellously well! We created together. Had he tied me down to his one type of dancing, I would have rebelled. I was a classical dancer, and I added to the classical arabesques, the high kicks of musical comedy. Buddy then added the coloured rhythm. That's why I think my dances have held up so well, because underlying every movement is the classical ballet, which never dates.[10]

Bradley choreographed a number of other important British film musicals of the 1930s, including *Radio Parade of 1935* (1934), *Oh, Daddy* (1935), *A Fire Has Been Arranged* (1935), starring Flanagan and Allen, and *This'll Make You Whistle* (1936), starring Jack Buchanan and Elsie Randolph. *Brewster's Millions* (1935), starring Jack Buchanan, features some of Bradley's best work, including 'The Caranga'. Said an enthusiastic reviewer in *Film Weekly*:

> the spectacular highlight is the performance of The Caranga, a near-relative of The Carioca [danced by Fred Astaire and Ginger Rogers in the Hollywood musical *Flying Down to Rio*], by hundreds of 'native' dancers. . . . This is the best photographed and best edited, as well as the biggest dance sequence yet seen in a British picture. It lifts the whole film into a class by itself.[11]

Though Bradley preferred to remain out of the limelight, he agreed to be interviewed in two popular British film magazines of the period. *Picturegoer Weekly* (7 March 1936) called him the man who 'gives the stars their legs'. *Film Weekly* described him as 'Our Busby Berkeley' and interviewed him on the set of *Brewster's Millions* about the origins of 'The Caranga':

> 'Well,' replied Buddy, 'let's begin at the beginning. All modern dance creations, like the Caranga, have African rhythm and movement as their

rudimentary bases. People lose sight of the fact that all these modern dance creations, stretching over the past fifteen years, beginning with the Charleston and carrying on through the Black Bottom, Pickin' Cotton, Beguine, Rhumba, and Carioca, all have African origin. The idea is to "localise" that African base ... When I set out to conceive such a dance as the Caranga I first ask, "What is the background?" In *Brewster's Millions* it is "Alvarese," which is meant to portray Ajaccio, Corsica. Very well then, we must introduce Italian touches. We must study the National Dance, and add to it newer movements, mostly African in origin, but now universal in practice. Then I ask "What is the situation?" In this case it is a Feast Day, but also in honour of a Saint. So it must be both vigorous – for the festive atmosphere, and graceful – for the religious atmosphere. Here we have light and shade of tempo and variation of movement.'[12]

In 1932 Bradley collaborated with Frederick Ashton in creating Britain's first jazz ballet, *High Yellow*, in which Alicia Markova starred for Sadler's Wells. He also created a cabaret act for the ballet dancers Vera Zorina and Anton Dolin. In 1935 he choreographed the London production of Cole Porter's *Anything Goes* followed by many other big musicals, including *Blackbirds of 1936*, with a cast that included the Nicholas Brothers, *I Can Take It* (1939) with Jessie Matthews, *Full Swing* (1942), *Big Top* (1942), *Something in the Air* (1943) and *It's Time to Dance* (1943) with Jack Buchanan and Elsie Randolph, in which he also appeared in the role of 'Buddy'. Says Michael Thornton:

> After the war he ran his own dance school in London and in 1949 it was he, as choreographer, who was responsible for Jessie Matthews taking over from Zoe Gail in Cecil Landeau's revue *Sauce Tartare*, at the Cambridge Theatre, which was the last time that they worked together, and Jessie's last West End bow as a dancer. The young Audrey Hepburn was also in the cast of that production. Buddy also choreographed the sequel to this revue, *Sauce Piquante*, again at the Cambridge, in 1950.[13]

By 1950 the Buddy Bradley Dance School in London had over 500 students and it remained in operation until 1968 when he decided to return to New York. In 1961 Bradley made a surprise guest appearance in BBC television's *This Is Your Life* tribute to Jessie Matthews. He died in New York in 1972 at the age of sixty-three.

It took almost thirty years after his death for Bradley's name to be mentioned on British television. When Sir John Mills was interviewed by Michael Parkinson in BBC1's *Parkinson* on 24 March 2001, an extract was shown from the 1937 film *The Green Cockatoo*. After watching Mills tap-dance across the screen, an impressed Parkinson enquired who taught him. Without hesitation, Mills replied, 'Buddy Bradley.' Only a gentleman as kind, considerate and generous as Mills could have acknowledged the importance of Bradley.

Before making London her home in 1933, Elisabeth Welch was featured in several Broadway musicals of the 1920s, including *Runnin' Wild* (1923) – in which she introduced the song 'Charleston' – and *Blackbirds of 1928*, starring the legendary dancer Bill 'Bojangles' Robinson. Since the 1930s Elisabeth has been a permanent fixture on London's West End musical stage, and among the many highlights of her illustrious stage career are Cole Porter's *Nymph Errant* (1933), Ivor Novello's *Glamorous Night* (1935) and *Jerome Kern Goes to Hollywood* (1985). In 1992 the cream of British show business gathered at London's Lyric Theatre to pay tribute to Elisabeth in the Crusaid concert 'A Time to Start Living'. Petula Clark, Sally Ann Howes, Cleo Laine, Julia McKenzie and Millicent Martin were among those who gave her an unprecedented (as far as anyone there could remember) five standing ovations. However, after performing 'Love for Sale' in Cole Porter's *The New Yorkers* in 1931, American audiences had to wait almost fifty years to see her on stage again. Following a brief return to New York for the 1980 revue *Black Broadway*, Elisabeth received critical acclaim and a Tony nomination for the Broadway version of her London hit *Jerome Kern Goes to Hollywood* (1986). Said the theatre critic Frank Rich in the *New York Times*: 'We must write letters to our Congressmen demanding that Miss Welch be detained in the United States forthwith, as a national resource too rare and precious for export.'[14]

The impact Elisabeth has had on other singers is, perhaps, best summed up by Cleo Laine, who, as a child in the 1930s, first heard her singing on the radio:

> I've always admired Elisabeth. Before I came into the business I used to imitate the way she sang. I loved her voice. When I had the opportunity to work with her, that was a dream come true. She's great fun to be with. Elisabeth has been a mentor to a lot of singers. People in the business adore her.[15]

In 1996, at the age of ninety-two, after a career spanning seven decades, Elisabeth decided to call it a day and live quietly in a retirement home in west London. Seven years earlier, in 1989, she was given an Oscar Micheaux Award at the 16th Annual Black Film-makers Hall of Fame Awards ceremony in Oakland, California. She thus became the first artist to be honoured for appearances in British films. Though seldom mentioned in histories of cinema, Elisabeth's contribution should not be overlooked.

Elisabeth was born in New York City to a Scottish mother with Irish ancestry and a father who was of African and American Indian descent. In 1929 Elisabeth left America with the *Blackbirds* revue for an engagement at the Moulin Rouge in Paris. The following year she returned to Paris to launch her career as a cabaret singer. In 1933 Elisabeth arrived in London with a contract from Charles B. Cochran to appear in *Nymph Errant* but, while waiting for rehearsals to begin, he gave her permission to make her London debut in another show. In *Dark Doings* at the Leicester Square Theatre she introduced Harold Arlen and Ted Koehler's Cotton Club hit 'Stormy Weather' to Britain. By the mid-1930s, Elisabeth's name had become well known to the British public following her appearances in a popular BBC radio series called *Soft Lights and Sweet Music*. The BBC also provided the setting for Elisabeth's first film appearance. In the crime thriller *Death at Broadcasting House* (1934) she sings 'Lazy Lady' but, apart from her two starring roles opposite Paul Robeson in *Song of Freedom* (1936) and *Big Fella* (1937) (see Chapter 3), Elisabeth was given little to do in British films other than sing songs in cabaret or nightclub sequences:

> When I made a 'one-song' film appearance I had my gowns fitted in the West End, then a car would arrive to take me to the studio. I never chose the song I would perform. That was done for me. So I was in films, but I wasn't a 'star'. I only appeared as myself.[16]

Elisabeth's other 'one-song' film appearances include *Soft Lights and Sweet Music* (1936), *Around the Town* (1938), *Alibi* (1942) and *This Was Paris* (1942). In the 'Harlem Holiday' segment of *Calling All Stars* (1937), set in the Cotton Club (courtesy of a film studio in Beaconsfield, *not* the real thing in New York!), she performs a haunting blues called 'Nightfall' with music by the African-American jazz legend Benny Carter. 'Harlem Holiday' also features the dance innovators Buck and Bubbles with 'The Rhythm's OK in Harlem', the sophisticated singer-pianist Turner Layton with 'These Foolish Things' and the Nicholas Brothers with 'Za Zu Za Zu' and a dazzling tap dance. This segment showcased some of the best African-American talent then working in Britain, and none of the artists were demeaned. For instance, Turner Layton and the Nicholas Brothers wear tuxedos, and Elisabeth is beautifully gowned.

In the sparkling Technicolor comedy *Over the Moon* (1937), Elisabeth made a lively appearance in a Monte Carlo nightclub singing 'Red Hot Annabelle'. However, she was not impressed with the on-set behaviour of the star of the film, Merle Oberon:

> She was temperamental, and difficult. I remember the time she asked a

young assistant to bring her some gloves. When he returned with the wrong pair, she blew her top, and had him fired on the spot. Being married to the producer of the film [Alexander Korda] she could get away with that sort of behaviour. Maybe this had something to do with the pressure she was under, being mixed-race and passing for white. Of course we all knew that the little Indian lady who lived with her was really her mother even though Merle told everyone she was her *ayah* [maidservant]. But if the press had found out the truth, her career would have been ruined.[17]

It is important to acknowledge that, in American films of the 1930s and 1940s, black women were invariably stereotyped as maids and mammies. Black musicians and singers were never allowed to appear on screen with white performers. For example, when the jazz legends Louis Armstrong and Billie Holiday were featured in *New Orleans* (1947), they had to play servants in between the music sequences. Hollywood studios backed away from challenging distributors in the Southern states who threatened to ban any film featuring a black person in a non-servile role. However, though the British film industry failed to use Elisabeth in acting parts, other than her films with Robeson and two shot at Ealing during the war (*Fiddlers Three*, 1944, and *Dead of Night*, 1945), it did not seem worried about showing her with a white band. As such, Elisabeth appeared on screen accompanied by white musicians in films like *Death at Broadcasting House*, *Over the Moon*, *Alibi* and *Dead of Night*. She was also given 'star status' in the two films she made with Paul Robeson, something Hollywood denied black women for many years.

One of Elisabeth's most interesting film roles was in *Dead of Night*. In the classic 'Ventriloquist's Dummy' segment she played Beulah, a glamorous Parisian nightclub owner, who employs an unhappy, tortured ventriloquist, Maxwell Frere (Michael Redgrave). For the first time in a film, a black woman is portrayed as successful, independent and resourceful. In spite of her name – which conjures up an image of a Hollywood mammy – Beulah serves customers, not a white mistress. Though not a very big part, nevertheless it is significant, as Peter Noble points out in *The Negro in Films* (1948):

> Here she acted as the popular Parisian nightclub owner who sang the blues, joked with the customers, was a good friend to everyone and was altogether an attractive personality. She played an important part in the development of the plot, and was featured in the film's billing with such eminent players as Michael Redgrave, Googie Withers, Mervyn Johns and Frederick Valk.[18]

Elisabeth's role in *Dead of Night* marked a breakthrough in the portrayal of black women in films. In Hollywood at that time, Elisabeth's contemporary, Lena Horne, then under contract to MGM, was never allowed to appear with white performers or musicians. MGM were even forced to cut Horne out of their musicals before they were released in the Southern states.

In spite of her excellent work in the two Robeson films and *Dead of Night*, Elisabeth was not offered another important screen role for more than thirty years. In 1979 the gay film-maker Derek Jarman cast her as a 'Goddess' in his stylish film version of William Shakespeare's *The Tempest* (1979). Elisabeth later recalled:

> I was singing 'Stormy Weather' in a concert at Covent Garden and Derek Jarman was in the audience. Afterwards he rang me and asked me if I wanted to sing in *The Tempest*. I said: 'What tempest?' He said: 'Shakespeare's *Tempest*.' I said: 'You must be mad! What do you want me to do?' He said: 'I want you to sing "Stormy Weather".' I said: 'You're joking.' But I went ahead with it and we had a lot of fun. Derek Jarman is a good director and anyone with any sense wants that.[19]

Dressed in gold from head to foot, and surrounded by handsome young sailors, she interrupts Miranda and Ferdinand's wedding feast. Walking

Elisabeth Welch in *The Tempest* (1979)

through a rain of confetti in a room garlanded with flowers, Elisabeth sings 'Stormy Weather'. It is a sequence which writer and jazz singer George Melly has described as 'arguably the campest, most sparkling moment in the history of cinema'.[20] In 1984 Jarman recalled the filming of Elisabeth's sequence in his autobiography:

> She entranced all the young sailor boys. Her singing was an enchantment. In the cold ballroom she worked non-stop through the day, never missing a cue, and still had the energy to entertain everyone at the dinner-table in the refectory. 'One song Welch', as she called herself, had one song in *The Tempest* and true to form she stopped the show.[21]

In 1987 Steven Spielberg used Elisabeth's wartime recording of 'These Foolish Things/A Nightingale Sang in Berkeley Square' on the soundtrack of *Empire of the Sun*, and she was the subject of a documentary film called *Keeping Love Alive*, described as 'a self-portrait in words and songs'.

In a career that began on Broadway in a show called *Liza* in 1922 to her most recent professional appearance in 1996 in a British television documentary called *Black Divas*, there was only one occasion when Elisabeth was asked to audition. The hit Broadway musical *Pippin* was due to open in London in 1973, and a friend urged her to try out for the show: 'But what do I sing?' she asked. 'I've never auditioned before.' So Elisabeth chose 'Solomon', the song Cole Porter wrote for her to perform in *Nymph Errant* forty years earlier:

> But I made a terrible *faux pas* at the audition. When the director, Bob Fosse, asked me what I was going to sing, I said, 'You're too young to know it, but I think perhaps just the first of the songs that Cole Porter wrote for me.'

Every time Elisabeth recollects this encounter, she bursts into fits of laughter. Bob Fosse gave her the part.

NOTES

1 Langston Hughes, 'When the Negro was in vogue', in *The Big Sea* (New York: Knopf, 1940), pp. 223–4.
2 Lena Horne and Richard Schickel, *Lena* (London: Andre Deutsch, 1966), pp. 53–5.
3 Frank C. Taylor with Gerald Cook, *Alberta: A Celebration in Blues* (New York: McGraw-Hill, 1987), p. 88.
4 Jeffrey Green, 'The Negro Renaissance in England', in Samuel A. Floyd Jr (ed.), *Black Music in the Harlem Renaissance: A Collection of Essays* (Knoxville Greenwood Press, 1990), p. 151.

5 Jeffrey Green, 'High society and black entertainers in the 1920s and 1930s', *New Community*, Vol. 13, No. 3, Spring 1987.

6 Jessie Matthews, *Over My Shoulder* (London: W. H. Allen, 1974), p. 118.

7 Marshall Stearns and Jean Stearns, 'Choreography: Buddy Bradley', in *Jazz Dance: The Story of American Vernacular Dance* (New York: Macmillan, 1968), p. 162.

8 Michael Thornton, letter to Stephen Bourne, 13 November 1990. See also Michael Thornton, *Jessie Matthews* (London: Hart-Davis, MacGibbon, 1974).

9 John Kobal, *Gotta Sing Gotta Dance: A Pictorial History of Film Musicals* (London: Hamlyn, 1971), p. 95.

10 *Ibid.*, p. 100.

11 *Film Weekly*, 1 March 1935.

12 *Ibid.*, 25 January 1935.

13 Thornton, letter to Bourne.

14 Frank Rich, *New York Times*, 24 January 1986.

15 Cleo Laine, interview with Stephen Bourne, London, 2 June 1994.

16 Anthony Slide, 'Elisabeth Welch', *Films in Review*, Vol. 38, No. 10, October 1987, pp. 480–3.

17 Stephen Bourne, 'Elisabeth Welch: a touch of class', *Classic Images*, No. 295, January 2000, pp. 73–7.

18 Peter Noble, *The Negro in Films* (London: Skelton Robinson, 1948), p. 128.

19 Bourne, 'A touch of class'.

20 George Melly, 'Cole's nymph errant', *Independent Magazine*, 13 May 1989.

21 Derek Jarman, *Dancing Ledge* (London: Quartet Books, 1984), p. 191.

6

A Sort of Magic

Television – The First Thirty Years 1932–61

In 1988 the British Film Institute and the BBC launched a ground-breaking research project which pieced together the history of black people in British television from the 1930s to the early 1990s. This resulted in a two-part television documentary called *Black and White in Colour*, first shown on BBC2 in 1992. There were, it turned out, many more programmes featuring black people in the early years than had been anticipated. Themes explored included decolonization, the settlement of African-Caribbeans in post-war Britain (*A Man from the Sun*, BBC, 1956) and mixed marriages (*Hot Summer Night*, ABC, 1959). Racism was hardly absent, the BBC's *Black and White Minstrel Show* ran from 1958 to 1978, but it coexisted with the assignation of major roles to black actors in television drama, such as Gordon Heath in *Othello* and *Cry, the Beloved Country*, and prominence was given not only to them but also to black singers and entertainers. For example, from the mid-1950s artistes like Gordon Heath, Eartha Kitt, Cy Grant and Paul Robeson could be found on the covers of the *Radio Times* and *TV Times*. Indeed, as the project discovered, the story began at the birth of television itself, in experimental programmes of the early 1930s. There was also a black presence in the BBC's pre-war service, which was broadcast live from the Alexandra Palace studios from 1936–1939. And yet, almost without exception, this 'secret history' has been ignored in books about British television.

The first black person to appear before a television camera was the African-American film star and cabaret entertainer Nina Mae McKinney. She made this historic appearance from the BBC's John Logie Baird experimental television studio at 16 Portland Place, London, on

Nina Mae McKinney in *Television Demonstration Film* (1937). Pianist Yorke de Souza on left, director Dallas Bower sitting under the camera

17 February 1933. The legendary entertainer Josephine Baker made a similar appear-ance on 4 October 1933. A photograph of Baker at the studio, wearing a striped blazer and black skirt, has survived and can be seen in Bryan Hammond and Patrick O'Connor's acclaimed biography *Josephine Baker* (1988).

The British Broadcasting Corporation officially opened its regular, high-definition television service at Alexandra Palace on 2 November 1936. Following opening speeches, a variety programme commenced at 3.23 p.m. with musical-comedy star Adele Dixon singing 'Television', followed by an appearance by the African-American double-act Buck and Bubbles. The *Radio Times* described Buck and Bubbles as 'a coloured pair who are versatile comedians who dance, play the piano, sing and cross-chat'. At the time Buck and Bubbles made their historic television appearance, they were starring in the West End revue *Transatlantic Rhythm*.

Buck and Bubbles belonged to a generation of African-American entertainers who came to Europe in the 1920s and 1930s, leaving America because they encountered less virulent racism (and more work) abroad. In the pre-war years of the BBC television service, before the Second World War interrupted the service, black entertainers made an important contribution to British entertainment programmes. Says Bruce Norman:

In the first years at Alexandra Palace ... the programme emphasis, if there was an emphasis, was on entertainment ... The first programme on the opening afternoon was called, simply, *Variety*. Saturday nights on television became a variety ghetto. Cecil Madden producer:

'We had such frightfully good entertainment available to us. There were shows going on in all the London nightclubs and a great deal of money was being spent ... There was a cabaret, an artist or two in every place – Quaglinos, the Windmill, the Ritz – everywhere. Of very high class. The sort of people we really wanted and so we were able to draw on a great deal of ready-made entertainment without having to do an awful lot of rehearsing ourselves.'[1]

Some of the pre-war shows were influenced by the black Broadway musicals and revues of the Harlem Renaissance, and some of the black entertainers featured included Leslie 'Hutch' Hutchinson, Eunice Wilson, Alberta Hunter, Fats Waller, Nina Mae McKinney, Valaida Snow, Art Tatum and the Mills Brothers. In 1939 singer Adelaide Hall performed with her accompanist, the Nigerian pianist Fela Sowande, in live broadcasts from her popular West End nightspot, the Florida Club. Also in 1939, the Jamaican tenor Basil Rodgers appeared in *Music Makers*, Buddy Bradley choreographed *Night Lights* and Paul Robeson made his television debut on 23 August. Accompanied by Lawrence Brown at the piano, Robeson gave a ten-minute recital that included 'Water Boy' and 'Ol' Man River' from *Show Boat*. Elisabeth Welch began her television career at Alexandra Palace in 'light musical items'. At that time, television, which was still in its infancy, 'amused' the young singer:

At Alexandra Palace ... You had to climb over a whole sea of cables just to get to the camera ... which never moved, you just stood there in front of it. The cameras were like old-fashioned still cameras used to take pictures – the cameraman wore a black hood over his head ... and you just stood there and sang your song ... It was static, nerve-racking, but amusing. And, when you had a studio with four or five artistes doing a programme, it was chaotic. I mean, we were falling over each other and trying to be quiet at the same time! But we had fun. It was wonderful. Of course, you must also remember that everything was live. If you made a mistake, you couldn't just re-do it from scratch. And the cameras weren't that reliable ... The BBC was called 'Auntie' because it had a reputation for being prim and prissy. The ladies, for example, never had plunges in their dresses – the BBC were very strict about that – and the men ... had to wear evening jackets and a black tie ... But we all kept our sense of humour.[2]

In those early days all television programmes were live, and broadcast for just a few hours a day to a limited audience, which was exclusively white and middle class. Also, between 1936 and 1949, the BBC could only broadcast in the London area. At that time, television was an expensive commodity, costing the same as a new car.

The BBC reopened its television service about a year after the end of the Second World War, on 7 June 1946. Shortly afterwards the Trinidadian folk singer Edric Connor made his television debut. He also appeared in a landmark programme in British television, introducing the work of the black ballet company, Ballets Nègres, in excerpts from their repertoire. Says music historian John Cowley:

> a number of African musicians were performing in London, especially the group [West African Rhythm Brothers] led by Ambrose Campbell, a Nigerian, which provided the accompaniment for *Ballets Nègres*, organized by Jamaican dancer Berto Pasuka, with dancers from Britain, Africa and the Caribbean. Edric Connor performed a selection of his West Indian folk songs and calypsos during their appearance on BBC television on 24 June 1946.[3]

At that time, Edric's popularity on BBC radio in the music series *Serenade in Sepia* was so great that it was transferred to television on 18 July 1946. It proved to be one of the BBC's earliest post-war successes. The *Radio Times* heralded its arrival:

> *Serenade in Sepia* is to be televised in the afternoon and evening of July 18. This sincerely beautiful presentation won a big following of listeners during a series of forty broadcasts. The singers are Edric Connor, from the West Indies, and Evelyn Dove, who is of West African descent. Eugene Pini's Orchestra accompanies. Both artists made a highly photogenic picture in television tests at Alexandra Palace earlier this year. Eric Fawcett, the producer, will aim at presenting them in vision very much as they appeared in the broadcast studios, without the use of extravagant settings. One of the items will almost certainly be Edric Connor's sung version of the Lord's Prayer.[4]

Perhaps Edric's most important television work involved his appearances in BBC programmes that promoted Caribbean music and dance. For example, as early as 1951, he took part in *Calypso Quarter*. Trinidad's calypsonian Lord Beginner was also featured. He had landed at Tilbury on the *Empire Windrush* on 22 June 1948, now recognized as the official commencement of post-war migration from the Caribbean to the 'mother country'. Also in 1951 Edric organized many concerts for the Trinidad All Steel Percussion Orchestra (TASPO) during their ten-week stay. They made their debut at the Festival of Britain celebrations at London's South Bank on 26 July. TASPO also appeared on television with Edric in *Caribbean Cabaret* (1951) with another popular calypsonian from Trinidad, Lord Kitchener, who had also arrived in Britain on the *Empire Windrush*. In a recording session held at the beginning of 1951, Kitchener recorded 'London Is the Place for Me', the song he had composed during his journey from Trinidad and which he performs in a memorable newsreel film made on his arrival at Tilbury. Another Trinidadian who appeared in *Caribbean Cabaret* was Boscoe Holder, together with his Caribbean Dancers. Holder had arrived in Britain in 1950 with his wife Sheila Clarke, their dancing troupe and a set of steel drums. They also appeared together on BBC television in *Bal Creole* (1950).

Yet another Trinidadian who made a big impact on post-war television was the chart-topping pianist Winifred Atwell. She made a number of appearances in variety shows and early 'pop' music programmes. In 1956 she approached the BBC and asked for permission to play Grieg's Piano Concerto on television. She was heartbroken when they turned her down. They said it would look like a gimmick. However, in 1957 they gave her permission to play the music of George Gershwin in a special tribute to the composer called *Rhapsody in Blue*. Meanwhile, at the height of her popularity in 1956, the BBC's new rival, ITV, offered her her own series, *The Winifred Atwell Show*, in which she was supported by Morecambe and Wise. In 1957 the BBC wooed her back for their version of *The Winifred Atwell Show*, thus making her one of the few artists to have their own series on *both* television channels.

Other African-Caribbeans who took part in early post-war programmes included the Jamaican trumpet soloist and band leader Leslie 'Jiver' Hutchinson and Cyril Blake and His Calypso Band. From Britain there was pianist Reginald Foresythe, band leader Ray Ellington and singers like Ida Shepley. In 1947 the Jamaican string bassist Coleridge Goode took part in one of the first jazz programmes, *Jazz Is Where You Find It*. After the service was resumed in 1946, visiting African–American stars who made appearances in the new medium included the opera singer Todd Duncan (1947). He had created the role of Porgy in George Gershwin's *Porgy and Bess*. The legendary Josephine Baker popped over from France to make an appearance in *Café Contintental* (1948) and Dorothy Dandridge was seen in *Starlight* (1951), three years before she was Oscar-nominated for her role in *Carmen Jones*. In 1952 Katharine Dunham and her dance company appeared in excerpts from their show, broadcast direct from the Cambridge Theatre in London. Two months later they were seen in *L'Agiya*, described as 'a story of love, hate, superstition and black magic in the lovely Caribbean island of Martinique'.

Unfortunately, before the introduction of videotape, no technology existed to record any of these early transmissions, though a couple of early BBC demonstration films featured Nina Mae McKinney (*Television Demonstration Film*, 1937) and Elisabeth Welch (*Television Is Here Again*, 1946). However, during the *Black and White in Colour* research project, one of the earliest known BBC telerecordings was rediscovered. It featured Adelaide Hall in *Variety in Sepia* (1947). This had been filmed (on 35mm) from a television screen by the BBC as an 'experimental telerecording', but this historic footage remained forgotten for over forty years until rediscovered by Stephen Bourne in the BBC's television archive in 1990.

The Coronation of Elizabeth II in 1953 boosted the popularity of television hugely, and soon over half of the population owned a set. Technically it became more sophisticated and widened the scope of the kinds of programmes which could be made. A second channel – ITV – began broadcasting on 22 September 1955 and set out to be more popular and less highbrow than the BBC, which was forced to respond by becoming more populist in order to compete.

On ITV, variety shows like *Sunday Night at the London Palladium* helped to nurture home-grown stars like Shirley Bassey and Cleo Laine, though American stars kept coming. Talents as diverse as Eartha Kitt, Duke Ellington, Sarah Vaughan, Harry Belafonte, Sister Rosetta Tharpe, Nat King Cole, Lena Horne, Billie Holiday, Paul Robeson and many others appeared on British television throughout the 1950s. But there was a downside to this, as Pearl Connor, then working as an agent for black artistes in Britain, acknowledges:

> the American media and the American projection was so enormous that British people were comatose under its influence. The whole gimmick was if you were American they accepted you. Black Americans had *Ebony* magazine and their own media working for them ... But we in England did not have our own media promoting us – *West Indian Gazette* came later. *The Voice* more recently. So we always had to wait to see if the *Daily Telegraph* or the *Guardian* would take note of what we were doing. We suffered a lot because of this bias.[5]

In 1957 the BBC created the daily news magazine *Tonight*, which featured the Guyanese singer and actor Cy Grant performing a 'topical calypso' almost every night for three years. His appearances in *Tonight* made Grant a household name. In 1941 he had joined the RAF as a navigator in Bomber Command, and was a prisoner of war in Germany for two years. After the war he studied law, but decided on a stage career

Cy Grant (1960)

instead. By the time he made his *Tonight* debut, he had just established himself as one of Britain's most promising actors. Earlier in 1957 he had given a critically acclaimed performance in the television drama *Home of the Brave* for Granada, and co-starred with Richard Burton and Joan Collins in the film *Sea Wife*. However, though *Tonight* made him famous, his association with the programme almost put an end to his acting career:

> *Tonight* made me very popular. I started doing lots of cabaret. However, I don't think they saw me as anything other than a calypso singer, someone very expendable. I don't think anyone appreciated that I had anything else to offer ... there was a terrible price to pay. I had been an established actor, but I never got asked to play dramatic parts any more.[6]

When the BBC launched its television service before the war, there were only 300 receivers available to pick up their first transmissions. But the new medium soon began to catch on with the public and, according to television historian John Caughie, 'Television drama was a central component of the early schedules, both pre-war ... and immediately post-war.'[7] In 1938 the BBC cast the Guyanese actor Robert Adams in a television version of Eugene O'Neill's *The Emperor Jones*. It was the first time a black actor had played a leading role in the new medium. When the BBC relaunched its television service after the war, Adams was cast as Jim Harris in O'Neill's *All God's Chillun' Got Wings* (1946). His sister was played by the Jamaican-born Pauline Henriques:

> It was tremendously exciting for me, partly because of the stature of Eugene O'Neill and partly because of the play itself. Although it had one or two black characters in it who were stereotyped, it had some very strong parts for black people. Robert Adams had the opportunity to show his range of acting. And I was lucky as well, because I played his rather bluestocking sister who is very keen on putting over the black point of view, that it is important to be courageous and very proud of your blackness. I identified very strongly with that. I think *All God's Chillun' Got Wings* was a very important thing for the BBC to do at that time. After all, it was the 40s and a very different world then for black people. I think the BBC pioneered something in giving us a play of that stature to act in.[8]

Pauline also recalls the experience of doing live television drama at this time:

> I thought television was wonderful because theatre came into the sitting rooms of viewers, but for an actor it was a tremendously difficult thing to do because everything was transmitted live from Alexandra Palace. There was no videotape in those days. Nothing was pre-recorded. Also, we only had one television camera and it was static. It was fixed to the studio floor and didn't move! So we, the actors, didn't have any flexibility. There was also a huge sea of cables all over the studio floor, and I was terrified I would trip over them. We had to remember to keep in shot all the time, and yet a sort of magic came out of this chaos.[9]

When Robert Adams was cast as the Prince of Morocco in *The Merchant of Venice*, transmitted on 1 July 1947, he became the first black actor to play a Shakespearian role on television. Unfortunately, during the live transmission of the play, Adams forgot one of his lines, panicked and fainted. Another member of the cast, Margaretta Scott, remembers how she improvised:

television went out live and, if you made any boo-boos, you had to get out of them. There was one memorable time when we were doing *The Merchant of Venice* in 1947 with me playing Portia. There was a splendid black actor playing the Prince of Morocco, which was memorable in itself, because he was the first black British actor to play in Shakespeare. The scene came where the Prince of Morocco meets Portia and he fluffed a line, then fell in a dead faint at my feet. I was left saying 'Help, ho! The Prince!' and so on. There were always surprises.[10]

The BBC continued to offer important dramatic roles to black actors throughout the 1950s. Gordon Heath starred in several major plays, including *Deep Are the Roots* (1950), *The Emperor Jones* (1953), *Othello* (1955) and *For the Defence* (1956). Eartha Kitt was seen in a *Sunday Night Theatre* presentation of her Broadway stage success *Mrs Patterson* (1956). John Elliot's *A Man from the Sun* (1956) featured Errol John, Nadia Cattouse and Cy Grant in a ground-breaking drama-documentary about African-Caribbean settlers in post-war Britain. Bertice Reading was seen in excerpts from the Royal Court's production of Carson McCullers's play *The Member of the Wedding* (1957). Writer Ted Willis confronted racism in several early episodes of the popular police drama series *Dixon of Dock Green*, and the African-American William Marshall starred as The Lord in an ambitious *Sunday Night Theatre* version of Marc Connelly's *The Green Pastures* (1958).

The Green Pastures was an American play which re-enacted scenes from the Bible using black actors. It was first staged on Broadway in 1930, filmed in Hollywood in 1936 and broadcast by the BBC in two radio versions in 1945 and 1956. According to the cast list in the *Radio Times*, there were sixty-three black actors in the production and, for Nadia Cattouse, the role of the schoolteacher, Mrs Deshee, was particularly rewarding:

> Mrs Deshee doesn't exist in Marc Connelly's original. In his play the character is a man, a schoolteacher who creates the atmosphere for the story in the schoolroom with the children. When the BBC made the television version, the role changed sex, and I was asked to play her. I can't remember the name of the person who was responsible, but this is an example of someone at the BBC remembering me, and wanting to use me.[11]

Nadia remembers the rehearsals for *Green Pastures* took place in Notting Hill at the time of the race riots:

> we were rehearsing *The Green Pastures* in a schoolroom in Notting Hill. The riots had started. One afternoon we noticed a gathering of about a dozen

white youths outside on the street looking very threateningly towards the building, and then the numbers started to grow. The BBC were informed about this and they were concerned that we were in danger. Decisions were quickly made and a bus arrived to get us out. The entire cast were asked to get on it, whether we lived in Notting Hill or not. However, one of the senior members of the cast, an elderly actor called Rudy Evans, refused to get on the bus. He told the man from the BBC that he lived nearby and was going to walk home. If any white boys tried to attack him, he would deal with them! I shall never forget that fearless old man. He was from that generation who had been here from before the war. He said something like, 'I walk in the cloak of righteousness. They will not harm me,' and the BBC man said, 'Yes, I understand, but please get on the bus.' But Rudy refused. The bus took us to Hammersmith tube station and we had to make our own way home from there. The next day the BBC found us an alternative rehearsal room in Ealing.[12]

On ITV, racism was explored in *Thunder on Sycamore Street* (1957), starring Earl Cameron, and *Armchair Theatre* presented the third television version of *The Emperor Jones* (1958), this time with the African-American opera singer Kenneth Spencer in the lead. Also in 1958, Kenneth Spencer, Gordon Heath and Errol John headed the cast of *Cry, the Beloved Country*, and Ted Willis's stage drama *Hot Summer Night* was presented by *Armchair Theatre* in 1959. A second version of *The Member of the Wedding* was presented as a *Play of the Week* production in 1960 with Vinnette Carroll in the lead. By 1961 many popular drama series and soaps on ITV were beginning to feature black actors, including *Emergency – Ward 10*, *Probation Officer* and *Danger Man*.

However, with the exception of Eartha Kitt's play *Mrs Patterson*, which had been co-authored by the African-American Charles Sebree and Greer Johnson, who was white, all of these dramatic productions were written by whites. There were few openings for black dramatists in television at this time, but a breakthrough was made when the Trinidadian Errol John adapted his play *Moon on a Rainbow Shawl* for ITV's *Play of the Week* series in 1960. Sadly, no recording of John's acclaimed television adaptation exists, and this has been the fate of most British television programmes in the age of unrecordable transmission. But what has survived in Britain's television archives provides fascinating glimpses of black entertainers and drama in the formative years of British television.

For example, apart from the telerecording of Adelaide Hall's appearance in 1947, up to 1961 other recordings of performing artists include Winifred Atwell, Cy Grant, Harry Belafonte, Duke Ellington, Shirley Bassey, Billie Holiday and Leontyne Price. A recording of Charles Holland's *Otello* exists from 1959, as well as Paul Robeson discussing his appearance at Stratford in *Othello* in the arts programme *Monitor* (1959). Surviving dramas include *Othello* (BBC, 1955), *Mrs Patterson* (BBC, 1956), *A Man from the Sun* (BBC, 1956), *The Emperor Jones* (ABC, 1958), The *Green Pastures* (BBC, 1958) and *Hot Summer Night* (ABC, 1959).

Perhaps the most interesting archive 'holding' – and one that deserves greater recognition – is *The Big Pride*. In the 1950s the Guyanese writer Jan Carew and his Jamaican wife, Sylvia Wynter, were part of an important generation of African-Caribbean poets and novelists who lived and worked here. In 1961 they were commissioned to adapt their BBC radio drama, *The University of Hunger*, for ITV's *Drama '61* series. Based on events that actually happened in Guyana in 1958, it tells the story of three men who break out of prison and try to escape, not only from their past but also the harsh reality of their lives. Said the *TV Times*: 'In their struggle to do this they find themselves as men and become part of a legend, part of a song.' However, the recording that was made of this compelling drama, retitled *The Big Pride*, remained forgotten until Stephen Bourne persuaded

William Marshall and Johnny Sekka in *The Big Pride* (1961)

69

the National Film and Television Archive to acquire the worn, torn negative, restore it and make a new viewing copy. It is a unique visual record of the work of two important black dramatists, for very few examples of the early television plays of African-Caribbean writers have survived. Among those lost for ever are three by Trinidadian Errol John: *Moon on a Rainbow Shawl*, *The Dawn* (1963) and *The Exiles* (1969).

The cast of *The Big Pride* included William Marshall, Nadia Cattouse, West Africa's Johnny Sekka and Trinidadian Barbara Assoon. The producer was Herbert Wise. Thirty-six years after its first transmission, *The Big Pride* was shown at the National Film Theatre in 1997. Herbert Wise attended the screening with several surviving cast members, including Nadia Cattouse and Tommy Eytle. To the surprise and delight of the audience, just ten minutes before the screening, Jan Carew arrived from America to introduce the event:

> So, thirty-six years after *The Big Pride* appeared on TV you have resurrected it with the help of the British Film Institute! In the early '60s I was under contract to ATV to write three plays a year, and *The Big Pride* was the first. I adapted it from *The University of Hunger*, a stage play on which Sylvia Wynter and I collaborated. We had originally adapted the stage play for the BBC's Third Programme. Subsequently, I adapted the radio play for TV, and Sylvia added a couple of female characters, who were not in the original. *The Day of the Fox*, in which Sammy Davis Jr and Zia Mohyeddin starred, was the second play. And then there was *Exile from the Sun*, a play based on the unusual life story of a black Brazilian artist I had met in Paris. Everything was set for *Exile* to go into production (I still have copies of the shooting script) and Leo McKern agreed to play the lead, but there was a strike at the ATV studios and shortly afterwards I left Britain. That third play was never produced.[13]

At the end of 1961, Jan Carew's *The Day of the Fox*, another play in the *Drama '61* series, was screened. Sadly, no recording has survived. In 1962 the Carews settled in Jamaica.

NOTES

1 Bruce Norman, *Here's Looking at You: The Story of British Television 1908–39* (London: BBC, 1984), p. 151.
2 Elisabeth Welch, interview with Stephen Bourne, in Jim Pines (ed.), *Black and White in Colour: Black People in British Television Since 1936* (London: British Film Institute, 1992), p. 22.
3 John Cowley, 'London is the place: Caribbean music in the context of empire 1900–60', in Paul Oliver (ed.), *Black Music in Britain: Essays on the Afro-Asian Contribution to Popular Music* (Milton Keynes: Open University Press, 1990), p. 64.

4 *Radio Times*, 21 June 1946.
5 Pearl Connor, interview with Bourne, in Pines (ed.), *Black and White in Colour*, p. 40.
6 Cy Grant, interview with Isaac Julien, in Pines (ed.), *Black and White in Colour*, p. 47.
7 John Caughie, 'Before the golden age: early television drama', in John Corner (ed.), *Popular Television in Britain: Studies in Cultural History* (London: British Film Institute, 1991), p. 25.
8 Pauline Henriques, interview with Bourne, in Pines (ed.), *Black and White in Colour*, p. 27.
9 Pauline Henriques, interview with Stephen Bourne, Brighton, 4 August 1989.
10 Margaretta Scott, quoted in Brian McFarlane (ed.), *An Autobiography of British Cinema* (London: Methuen, 1997), p. 517.
11 Nadia Cattouse, interview with Stephen Bourne, London, 8 August 1989.
12 *Ibid*.
13 Jan Carew, letter to Stephen Bourne, 10 June 1997.

7

Robert Adams and Orlando Martins

Men of Two Worlds

Robert Adams was once Britain's leading black actor but, like many black achievers in British history, he is now forgotten. After appearing in a succession of stage productions and films, he founded the Negro Arts Theatre in 1944. This was one of the first attempts to create a black theatre company in Britain. Two years later Adams co-starred with Eric Portman in *Men of Two Worlds*, playing the first leading role ever given to a non-American black actor in a British film. For a time Robert enjoyed celebrity status in Britain, but it was short-lived. By the 1960s his acting career had declined to such a degree that he was reduced to playing nothing more than a glorified 'extra' for director Joseph Losey in the prison drama, *The Criminal*.

The son of a boat builder, Adams was born in Georgetown, British Guiana, around the turn of the century. In 1920 he won a government scholarship to be trained as a teacher at Jamaica's Mico Teachers' Training College, from which he graduated with honours. While teaching in British Guiana, he produced and acted in amateur stage productions. After his arrival in Britain in the 1920s he was forced to earn a living in low-paid jobs, such as labouring, before a sports promoter encouraged him to become a professional wrestler. Consequently, Adams became well known in British and European wrestling circles as 'The Black Eagle', and achieved the distinction of becoming heavyweight champion of the British Empire. Away from the sporting world, he was a founder member of Dr Harold Moody's League of Coloured Peoples in 1931. Moody was its first president, and the LCP based itself at his home in Queen's Road, Peckham. This is now marked with a blue plaque in Moody's honour.

Adams started appearing in films as an extra in 1934. Early supporting roles included the cabin boy Mesty in *Midshipman Easy* (1935), a comic role as Paul Robeson's pal Monty in *Song of Freedom* (1936) and the one-eyed, evil African chieftain Twala in *King Solomon's Mines* (1937). In *Old Bones of the River* (1938), a comic adaptation of some of Edgar Wallace's short stories, Adams sent up Paul Robeson's Bosambo in *Sanders of the River*. In 1940 he worked as Robeson's stunt double in *The Proud Valley* and in 1941 he appeared in a Colonial Film Unit production called *An African in London*. After playing the Nubian Slave in Gabriel Pascal's 1945 screen version of George Bernard Shaw's *Caesar and Cleopatra*, Adams found himself elevated to movie stardom when he was cast in a leading role in the melodrama *Men of Two Worlds*. He played Kisenga, a composer and concert pianist who, after spending fifteen years touring Europe, agrees to return to his village in Tanganyika to assist the district commissioner in persuading the villagers – including his family – to leave the area to avoid a sleeping-sickness epidemic. In spite of Thorold Dickinson's sensitive documentary-style direction, which at times gave the film great emotional power, *Men of Two Worlds* failed because of its condescending view of Africans. Nevertheless, at the time of the film's release in 1946, most critics considered this 'ground-breaking' film a sincere attempt to explore themes concerning the battle of science against superstition, and of modern medicine versus the power and influence of the African witch doctors.

Eric Portman and Robert Adams in *Men of Two Worlds* (1946)

When Dickinson was originally casting the film in 1943, he had Adams in mind for the part of the witch doctor, Magole. However, after considering, then rejecting, the Guyanese conductor Rudolph Dunbar for the role of Kisenga, Dickinson gave the part to Adams. The West African actor Orlando Martins was assigned the role of Magole. Racism reared its ugly head when Dickinson approached the National Gallery to film the opening sequence of Kisenga playing at a lunchtime concert. But Dame Myra Hess, the famous pianist who organized and gave concerts at the gallery during the war, refused permission, declaring that no black man had ever been permitted to play at any of her concerts. As a result, Dickinson had to reconstruct the National Gallery in a film studio.

By the end of shooting, Dickinson was reported to have said of Adams: 'his was less performance than behaviour'. However, Adams received nothing but praise from the critics. Said A. E. Wilson in *The Star*: 'Robert Adams, with his stalwart figure, his pleasant personality and his resonant voice, is particularly striking as Kisenga.' Dilys Powell in the *Sunday Times* noted his 'moving piece of acting' and Joan Lester in *Reynolds News* remarked on the 'fine voice and dignity which he brought to the screen'. Adams himself said in an interview at the time:

> If all my screen parts were as dignified, human and moving as the one in *Men of Two Worlds*, then one might soon be able to influence cinemagoers in the right direction. And if they see Negroes playing cultured, intelligent people often enough, they will begin to realize that the coloured man is not necessarily a superstitious, hymn-singing buffoon ... The most powerful of all vehicles of education has been, and still is, the screen ... Hollywood has much to answer for, but British studios have had the courage to make a step forward. In *Midshipman Easy*, *Song of Freedom*, *The Proud Valley*, and a few others, Negroes were not exactly jungle types. And now further progress has been made in *Men of Two Worlds* ... Out of the suffering of the last war, people have learned to have a measure of understanding; and we wish earnestly that this spirit of co-operation and helpfulness will persist.[1]

Adams began his stage career in 1935 and three years later played the lead in Eugene O' Neill's *The Emperor Jones* at Cambridge's Arts Theatre. In 1939 he gave an impressive performance as the Caribbean strike leader in *Colony* for the left-wing Unity Theatre. Towards the end of the war he founded the Negro Arts Theatre and, with the support of the Colchester Repertory Theatre, staged Eugene O' Neill's *All God's Chillun' Got Wings*. One critic, quoted in the January 1945 newsletter of the LCP, declared: 'I have seldom seen a better performance than that of Robert Adams. This was power on the stage, a power which caught all the light and shade and poetry of the play and made it quiver and burn with life.' In interviews Adams spoke of his plans to stage work by black writers, as well as ballet and dance. He planned to extend their work by touring America and the British Empire under the auspices of the British Council, but his venture was short-lived. Britain was not ready to accept – or support – a black theatre company. Meanwhile, in 1946, the Unity Repertory Company invited Adams to appear in another production of *All God's Chillun*, and in 1948 he played Bigger Thomas in *Native Son*, based on Richard Wright's acclaimed novel. This repertory production was staged at London's Boltons Theatre. However, an opportunity to play Othello for the Old Vic did not materialize, as Adams explained:

Some years ago I was approached to play Othello for the Old Vic. Everything was apparently satisfactory, then suddenly a continental was given the chance to do it. While he brought a much needed virility to the part, his lack of knowledge of English was obviously a drawback, his power was alright but his inflections were ludicrous. Yet what was the explanation for rejecting me? I was told that I had not sufficient Shakespearian technique.[2]

However, in spite of his successes, by the 1950s Adams's acting career was in decline. He had already considered law as an alternative career, and qualified as a barrister in September 1948. In a letter to a friend dated 28 November 1948, Adams explained:

I read for the Bar for several reasons. The Stage as it exists for the Negro is a most precarious type of existence. If one manages to succeed on the Music Halls like HUTCH then one may if one lives carefully look forward to a somewhat secure old age. But the position is different for the Dramatic Artiste, and that is my Field. The parts are few and far between and when one reaches Stardom the position becomes more difficult still. Apart from this the main objection is the Negro stereotype which seems to be the standard for the Coloured Artiste. When one raises objections one immediately hears that one's head is getting too big. So, knowing the difficulties, I have set as my Artistic Goal the centralization of Negro and coloured talent – dramatically – both of the West Indies and Africa in this country ... I think in terms of owning a Theatre and having a Dramatic School etc. but the task is such a big one and is meeting with such opposition that it is breaking my heart. When I was in the League of Coloured Peoples and working with Dr Moody it was I who passed on to him the idea of the Cultural centre, but after his death [in 1947], and my dissociation from the League I have to continue alone to get the idea over ... I asked Mr Creech Jones for help in terms of a Scholarship to the West

Indies to study certain conditions and to interest local talent and local help but so far he has not even condescended to see me; I tried to get some help from the Colonial Development Fund but again no success has attended my efforts. But I will not be beaten. Booker T. Washington was once in the same position ... Perhaps one day when I shall have succeeded the Government may then realize how useful the idea is both as a contribution to the stabilizing and continuance of Empire relationships, and to improved human relationships and understanding.[3]

In spite of his success in *Men of Two Worlds*, Adams was not employed as an actor by the British film industry for five years. When he returned to the screen in 1951, it was to play second fiddle to the music-hall comedian Arthur Lucan in a low-budget comedy called *Old Mother Riley's Jungle Treasure*. This was Lucan's penultimate Old Mother Riley film. The long-running series had exhausted itself, and ended the following year. In *Jungle Treasure*, Adams played Chief 'Stinker', and this sorry spectacle included a sequence in which he assisted some villains in stirring up voodoo worshippers in the African jungle.

After a long break from acting, in 1958 Adams returned to London's West End stage in Eugene O' Neill's *The Iceman Cometh*. He also made a number of appearances on television, including *The Green Pastures* (BBC, 1958) and Errol John's *Moon on a Rainbow Shawl* (ITV, 1960). His final screen appearance was a far cry from his role in *Men of Two Worlds*. For his role as a prison inmate in *The Criminal* (1960) he received a screen credit, but he was little more than a glorified extra, appearing just long enough for the audience to observe a sad, disillusioned, tired old man. According to his friend, Peter Noble, he was 'disheartened by not having any follow-ups to *Men of Two Worlds*',[4] and he returned to Guyana, where he took a job as headmaster of a school, and also worked in the government's information department. It is believed Robert Adams died in Guyana in 1965.

It is possible that Adams's contemporary, Orlando Martins, holds the record for being the black actor who has had the longest film career in Britain. He started as an extra in 1926, and made his last appearance in 1971, just before he retired. He was proud to be an ambassador for his country, Nigeria, and later said in his biography, published in 1983, 'I am very very happy to say that I am one of the pioneers, if not *the* pioneer African film star.'[5]

Martins was born in 1899 in Lagos, Nigeria, West Africa, the son of Emmanuel Akinola Martins and Madam Paula Idowu Soares. His paternal grandfather, a freed Portuguese slave, was a wood seller who lived to the age of one hundred and twenty. Educated at the Eko Boys' High School in Lagos, he left in 1916 to work as a book-keeper for a French firm.

Orlando Martins (1946)

During the First World War his grandmother became a prisoner of war when the Germans held the Cameroons, and it was her suffering at German hands that led Martins to give up his job in Africa and travel to London in 1917, hoping to join the British Navy. Too young to get into the Navy, he managed to join the Merchant Marine instead, where he served until the end of the war.

Settling in London in 1919, he made an early theatrical appearance in 1920 when the Diaghilev Ballet, led by Anna Pavlova, arrived in London and recruited Orlando to appear as a Nubian slave. He later recalled: 'I hated the part, but as I was young and hungry, I had no other choice.'[6] Afterwards, he survived by taking a variety of jobs. He was a porter at Billingsgate fish market; a wrestler known as 'Black Butcher Johnson'; a snake-charmer with Lord John Sanger's Circus; night watchman; kitchen porter; road sweeper; and, after making his debut in *If Youth But Knew* (1926), an extra in silent films.

In 1928 he joined the Mississippi Chorus of the musical *Show Boat* at the Theatre Royal, Drury Lane, and later toured Britain with the production. Martins also acted on stage in a couple of plays with Paul Robeson: *Stevedore* (1935) and *Toussaint L'Ouverture* (1936). In 1939 he alternated the lead with Robert Adams in *Colony* for the Unity Theatre. During the war Martins was engaged in important war work for four years, and consequently he was unable to continue his acting career. Returning to the screen in 1945, he gave a fine performance as Jeremiah, the International Brigadier, in *The Man from Morocco*. He was then cast as the influential witch doctor Magole in *Men of Two Worlds* . These two roles established Martins as one of Britain's most sought-after character actors. In 1948 he was described by Peter Noble in *The Negro in Films* as

> a tall, powerful figure of a man with a deep bass voice, friendly, hospitable, and with a grand sense of humour. He is keenly interested in the foundation of a Negro Theatre in London. As he points out: 'If this ever comes into being it will mean not only that Negro talent in every theatre art can be shown to the world, but a continuity of employment for this talent which is now going sadly to waste.'[7]

One of Orlando's most memorable roles was Blossom, the Basuto warrior, in *The Hasty Heart*, which he played on the London stage in 1945 and in the screen version in 1949 with Richard Todd. Other London stage appearances included *Cry, the Beloved Country* at St Martin-in-the-Fields, Trafalgar Square (1954), and *The Member of the Wedding* at the Royal Court (1957). He made his first appearance on television in 1937 and, among many other roles, played the runaway slave Jim in *Huckleberry Finn* (BBC, 1952) and John Kumalo in *Cry, the Beloved Country* (ITV, 1958).

In British films of the 1950s Africa was used as nothing more than a colourful, exotic backdrop for white settlers or adventurers. They had titles like *Where No Vultures Fly* (1951), *West of Zanzibar* (1954), *Simba* (1955), *Safari* (1956) and *Tarzan and the Lost Safari* (1957). Almost without exception these films provided Martins with employment, though he was invariably typecast as a friendly African native. However, when *Where No Vultures Fly* was chosen as the 1951 Royal Film Performance, critic Thomas Spencer in the *Daily Worker* attacked the film for presenting 'Britain's colonial empire in Africa as a jolly land of paternal officials and "loyal" Africans ... although it allows dignity to its wild animals, the film refuses to regard Africans as anything but comic'.[8] Martins did not consider it beneath him to appear in these films. They paid the rent. But at least one film journal drew attention to the possibility of broadening his range, as this extract from *The Cinema Studio* in October 1951 reveals:

He is, indeed, a character far removed in real life from *Where No Vultures Fly*, and getting to know and understand him is to want to see him given parts in films more in keeping with the real Orlando ... Orlando's talents, together with a delightful sense of humour, could be employed by a film producer without any attempt at propaganda but merely as entertainment to show the negro as a warm, sensible, charming human being in our modern way of life.[9]

Unfortunately, film producers seldom allowed Martins out of the jungle. The rare exceptions included *Good Time Girl* (1948), in which he played Kolly, the nightclub doorman, and *Sapphire* (1959), in which he appeared as a barman in a nightclub. Martins's other screen credits included *The Nun's Story* (1959), *Sammy Going South* (chosen as the 1963 Royal Film Performance) and *Mister Moses* (1965), but few of his film roles gave him any real scope as an actor. In 1959 Martins returned home to Lagos, and thereafter accepted only occasional acting assignments. Towards the end of his career he appeared in two films by Nigerian writers: Wole Soyinka's *Kongi's Harvest* (1970) and Chinua Achebe's *Things Fall Apart* (1971). In 1970 the British Actors' Equity Association awarded Orlando an honorary life membership in recognition of his long career in British films. In 1981 Martins was included in Nigeria's honours list, and attended a ceremony in February 1982 to receive the medal of Membership of the Order of the Niger (MON) from the President, Alhaji Shehu Shagari. In 1983 he was presented with the National Award in Theatre Arts by the Society of Nigerian Theatre Artistes at an impressive ceremony at the University of Calabar. Orlando died in Lagos in 1985 at the age of eighty-five, and was buried at the Ikoyi cemetery in Lagos.

NOTES

1 Robert Adams, interviewed by Peter Noble, *Film Quarterly*, Spring, 1947, pp. 16–18.

2 Robert Adams, 'Colour prejudice in art', *Film Reel Review* (Glasgow: Film Reel Review, 1948). Courtesy of Peter Powell. The 'continental actor' referred to by Adams is probably the Czechoslovakian Frederick Valk, who played Othello for the Old Vic at London's New Theatre in 1942.

3 Robert Adams, letter to Mr Greenidge, dated 28 November 1948. Courtesy of Val Wilmer.

4 Peter Noble, letter to Stephen Bourne, 27 October 1982.

5 Takiu Folami, *Orlando Martins, the Legend: An Intimate Biography of the First World Acclaimed African Film Actor* (Lagos, Nigeria: Executive Publishers, 1983), p. 73.

6 *Ibid.*, p. 21.

7 Peter Noble, *The Negro in Films* (London: Skelton Robinson, 1948), p. 178.

8   Thomas Spencer, 'Not vultures – colonists. Royal film insults Africans', *Daily Worker*, 6 November 1951.
9   'Let him blossom out ... as Martins!', *The Cinema Studio*, October 1951, p. 35.

FURTHER READING

Chaim Litewski, 'The acceptable face of British colonialism: *Men of Two Worlds*', unpublished MA thesis, 1983.
Peter Noble, (ed.), 'Why not a Negro theatre?', in *British Theatre* (London: British Yearbooks, 1946).
Jeffrey Richards, 'Emergent Africa: *Men of Two Worlds*', in *Thorold Dickinson: The Man and His Films* (Beckenham, Kent: Croom Helm, 1986).

8

Edric Connor
A Man for All Seasons

I n post-war Britain Edric Connor was a major celebrity on radio and television, and a special hero in Trinidad, the country of his birth. He was also a storyteller, writer, film-maker, dancer and actor – in West End plays and musicals, in Hollywood movies, as well as the first leading black performer in Shakespeare at Stratford-upon-Avon. He was also a much-loved and respected ambassador for the arts and culture of the Caribbean. With his wife, Pearl, he also supported and encouraged younger, inexperienced black actors. Together, in the mid-1950s, Edric and Pearl organized an agency which represented nearly 90 per cent of non-white actors working in Britain, and later, in the early 1960s, they formed the Negro Theatre Workshop. Through this, Edric and Pearl gave opportunities for valuable experience to serious-minded new-comers.

The son of a shoemaker and small farmer, Edric was born in the village of Mayaro, Trinidad, in 1913. At sixteen he won a scholarship from the Trinidad government railway to study engineering at the Victoria Institute, Port of Spain, where he won the Stephen gold medal for mechanical engineering. In his spare time he studied Caribbean folk singing. During the war he worked on the construction of the American naval airbase in Trinidad and saved enough money to move to Britain. In 1944 he left Trinidad, intending to continue his engineering studies, but took with him some notes on Caribbean folk music. He had already presented a series about the subject on Radio Trinidad, and on his journey to Britain he carried letters of introduction to the BBC. Two weeks after his arrival he made his debut on BBC radio in *Calling the West Indies*, a programme for listeners in the Caribbean. His appealing voice and charming personality made a deep impression, as Pearl remembers:

Towards the end of the war, and immediately after, the British government made an effort to show some appreciation for all the people from the colonies who had contributed to the war effort. Those little Caribbean islands had all stuck their necks on the block. Some of our young men had gone and died. My own brother joined the Royal Air Force and flew a Lancaster bomber. So the British government wanted to show some appreciation. There was an open-door policy. They weren't locking us out, yet. But it didn't last. By the 1950s we had become second-class citizens.

The BBC were also interested in helping to promote and assist some of the third-world people, and the Caribbean people. So Edric came to Britain at a good time. Doors were open to him. He didn't have to kick too hard. At that time there weren't many black people appearing on radio and television, and so it was relatively easy for Edric to attract attention.[1]

One of Edric's earliest appearances on BBC radio was in a production of Jerome Kern and Oscar Hammerstein II's *Show Boat*, in which he played Joe and sang 'Old Man River' (1944). He also helped to introduce Trinidad folk music and calypso to Britain. From 1945 to 1947 Connor was featured in the popular music series *Serenade in Sepia* with Evelyn Dove, a contralto of West African and English parentage. Its success led to a television version in 1946. Edric was also keen to develop his acting skills. In 1947 he accepted an invitation from Sir Stanley Marchant, Principal of the Royal Academy of Music, to play The Lord in a drama students' production of Marc Connelly's *The Green Pastures*. Afterwards they presented him with a bible as a tribute. He also gained valuable acting experience in productions with the Rose Bruford School of Speech and Drama in London. Rose Bruford helped him with his acting studies, and the Board of Governors of her school awarded him their first Honorary Diploma.

When Edric returned to Trinidad in 1948, he was welcomed home with open arms and celebrated as a hero. A park was named after him in Mayaro, the village of his birth, and a large crowd attended his recital of American, European and Caribbean songs in the dance hall of the Prince's Building:

> Connor's powerful baritone and technical skill succeeded in making him audible all over the hall ... It is true, as he reminded us, that his voice was somewhat tired by a week's work under pressure, but the dramatic quality of the songs and the natural actor's ability which he possesses brought out all the fire and power of his voice.[2]

During that visit, Pearl was given the responsibility of taking care of Edric throughout the celebrations. She was born in the village of Diego Martin, outside Port of Spain:

I had a powerful family, in that my father was a headmaster, my mother was a teacher and they were the ward officers of the district, and registrars. But the person who most influenced me was Beryl McBurnie. She was probably the most famous Trinidadian, responsible for the projection of our culture and the arts. She was an inspiration to generations of young Trinidadians. She was instrumental in arranging scholarships for some of her dancers, and educating all who came within her ambit in national pride, which permeated everything she did. She also started the Little Carib Theatre, which provided me with my first acting experience. Beryl taught us how to dance, and to appreciate our own art and music. She tried to build up the personalities of our people. When I was a member of the Little Carib Theatre, Edric came back to Trinidad. He was looked upon as a local hero. I was selected with another girl to accompany him as couriers, even though he knew Trinidad very well! We admired him, of course, and were very proud to be with him. That's how I first met him.[3]

When Pearl arrived in Britain in 1948 to study law, she met Edric again, and romance blossomed. They were married in London on 26 June 1948:

Edric was about six foot two. A relaxed, very handsome man. A very quiet man. He was a contained, disciplined person. Charming and soft-spoken. He was rarely agitated. He always gave the impression of being at ease. He was an independent man who believed in pulling his weight. He was always well dressed, he looked after himself, he believed that he was an ambassador for Trinidad. When I first met him I knew him as a singer and later, after we married, I got to know more about his career. He was an avid student. A self-made person. He read widely. He had a great collection of books on all sorts of subjects. He embraced literature, music and so on. He was self taught. But as soon as he realized the need for expertise in developing his voice he went to America and studied there. Privately, of course. In England he did the same. He was always learning. Always practising and developing his art. He was a perfectionist and believed in what he was doing. He wanted to be the best.[4]

With her new husband, Pearl met and befriended some of the great names in the world of the performing arts in post-war Britain:

Edric had his heroes and he was a great admirer of Paul Robeson. We all admired him, and thought he was one of the greatest artists, and a great man. We knew about his history. Edric hero-worshipped him. Paul was Edric's role model and Edric wanted to be like him. So, not long after we were married, when Paul came to England in 1949, Edric brought him to the house for tea. I remember thinking my teaset wasn't up to scratch, so I

Edric and Pearl Connor (1958)

had to rush out and buy a new china teaset! On important occasions, or for a celebration in our culture, we have to have something special, and I wanted a new teaset. For me that was important, but I don't think Paul Robeson even noticed, he was so busy talking to Edric!

Paul dominated our sitting-room. He was a very big man. Huge and towering. Edric was big too, but he looked small against Paul. I always remember that. We all looked up to Paul, ideologically and physically. Like Edric, he had great charm with a soft and gentle nature. The feeling between the two men was mutual. Paul liked this young man. Edric was fifteen years younger and he knew what was happening in our world, the black world, in America and throughout the world. Edric wanted to hear about the civil rights struggle in America, and what Paul was doing. Paul admired him for that and, when he came to our house, it was a great honour he paid to Edric, and Edric never forgot it. So we became friends with the great man. About ten years later, in 1958, director Tony Richardson wanted to present a black actor for the first time at the Stratford Memorial Theatre, and he invited Paul to play Gower in Shakespeare's *Pericles*. But when Paul turned the part down, he recommended Edric for it. So Edric became the first black actor to appear in a Shakespeare season at Stratford-upon-Avon. It was a beautiful role, too.[5]

Invited by Glen Byam Shaw, then director of the Shakespeare Memorial Theatre, to stage a production at Stratford, the innovative young director Tony Richardson chose *Pericles*. It proved to be one of the high points of his career in the theatre. Richardson staged the production on what resembled a vast ship and cast Gower, the chorus/narrator of the play, as a black man. He also set Gower's lines to music, as Richardson later recalled:

I hit on the idea of having Gower's lines set to music (by the splendid, now almost forgotten and underrated Roberto Gerhard) and sung. In the course of trying to cast Gower, I suddenly thought of Paul Robeson. Robeson had been ostracized, maligned and discriminated against for years, and it seemed a wonderful opportunity to make restitution for some of the suffering he'd endured, and a wonderful role for him to make a comeback in ... He was tempted, but not totally well, and finally he couldn't make it. But the offer had tempted Paul enough to make him decide to come to Stratford next year, as Othello.[6]

In 1947 Edric was featured in a Pathé film short performing 'Water Boy', but it was not until 1952 that he made his film acting debut in *Cry, the Beloved Country*, based on Alan Paton's novel about apartheid in South Africa. Edric was cast in a supporting role as John, the selfish brother of the minister, the Reverend Stephen Kumalo (Canada Lee). During the next decade, he played featured roles in a number of British and American productions, including the harpooneer Daggoo in John Huston's *Moby Dick* (1956), *Fire Down Below* (1957), *The Vikings* (1958) and as Balthazar in Nicholas Ray's *King of Kings* (1961). Several were filmed on location in Africa and he also worked as the adviser on African music for *The Heart of the Matter* (1953), based on the novel by Graham Greene. Filming in Africa had a special meaning for him, as Pearl explains:

All the films based in Africa intrigued him. He wanted to go there. He felt Africa was part of his history and ancestry. We all did, in the Caribbean. We were all holding on to that. When he played the part of the African chief, Ushingo, in *West of Zanzibar* [1954], he was on location in Kenya during the time of the Kikuyu uprising, and he came back with a lot of stories about that. A few years later he went back to play Waitari, the African leader, in John Huston's *The Roots of Heaven* [1958]. But the one that really impressed him was *Cry, the Beloved Country*, which took him to South Africa for the first time. During the making of that film he met Alan Paton, Canada Lee and Sidney Poitier. This was one of Sidney's first big films. And they all came back to our home here in London. It was a great gathering place for these people. They were all friends. There was also a young actor in the film called Lionel Ngakane, playing Absalom, who came here from South Africa. He worked as an actor in this country, and later turned to directing. So Edric was absolutely riveted by this experience, and the situation in South Africa, because all the black American and British actors in the film had to become 'honorary whites' when they got there. They were not allowed to enter South Africa as black men. They were not allowed to stay in the hotels. They had to live with some Indians outside the city when they worked there. That was a terrible shock. It was the first time we became familiar with the situation in South Africa. We didn't know very much about it before. It hadn't filtered down to the Caribbean.[7]

In 1955 Edric played the Reverend Stephen Kumalo in a BBC radio version of *Cry, the Beloved Country*, with Gordon Heath as the young priest, Msimangu, and Elisabeth Welch in a rare non-singing role as his sister, Gertrude. In 1956 Edric was featured in a West End stage musical called *Summer Song*. Also in the cast was Thomas Baptiste, a young singer and actor from Guyana:

I remember Edric with great affection, admiration and a certain amount of sadness because, in the time he lived, he was a very important artist in this country, but he wasn't really appreciated. He was a great performer. He had wonderful presence. He looked somewhat like a majesterial Jomo Kenyatta: tall, bearded, with square shoulders. And he sang magnificently. His voice was unique. It had a timbre like nobody elses except, perhaps, Paul Robeson. So when I worked with him, I learned a great deal. I also learned something that has become important in my life. Edric always wanted to succeed, to prove that he was as good as anybody else. I suspect he felt that he had to be twice as good as his contemporary British artists. But where he failed was not to realize he had the right to fail, and I think that's a pity. In that area I benefited from him because, for myself, I know I have the right to fail. I must have failed hundreds of times! But not Edric. He felt if he did anything which did not work out positively, it was a reflection on his people. Black people. And I don't think anybody should carry that burden or responsibility on their shoulders. You can only do what you can as well as you can. But he was a great artist and should be remembered.[8]

Throughout his career, Edric was always trying to find ways to promote the music of the Caribbean. For instance, in 1951 he organized many concerts for the Trinidad All Steel Percussion Orchestra during its ten-week stay, including its debut at the Festival of Britain celebrations at London's South Bank. In 1953, when he appeared in the West End play *The Shriek*, Edric inserted the popular calypso 'If you want to be happy and live a king's life, never make a pretty woman your wife' into the script. Though his role in the film *Moby Dick* was small, Edric made a very important, but easily overlooked, contribution. Daggoo is required to sing a sea shanty to inspire the men in their boats during the whale hunt. From his own repertoire, Connor chose 'Hill an' Gully Rider', a 150-year-old Jamaican folk song by an anonymous composer. Pearl remembers how Edric was fully aware that it would be recognized by Caribbean people in the audience:

'Hill an' Gully Rider' is about the undulating land in Jamaica, but it was the undulating sea of *Moby Dick*, the ocean where they were looking for the whale, where Edric introduced the song. And it is a lyrical, lilting song, a beautiful thing that the director John Huston loved straight away. And Edric was always trying to do that, introduce Caribbean music into the films he worked on, and letting people know about our songs. So Huston allowed him to have an input, which was very good for Edric, and good for the film, also, I should think.[9]

Though Edric succeeded in almost everything he set out to do, Pearl reveals that some doors remained firmly closed:

He took the opportunity to go to America and train in opera. He had this marvellous baritone and in America he learned about technique. But in those days they had no room for people like Edric. It wasn't even thought about at that time, that a black actor from the Caribbean could ever perform in the opera houses of Britain. Yet, though he sung the roles of Amonasro in *Aida* and King Boris in *Boris Godunov* in Europe, Edric was never asked to sing at Covent Garden. It was very frustrating for him.[10]

Connor also wanted to become a television producer and director at a time when no black person could be found behind the camera, except as a scene shifter. In the wake of the 1958 Notting Hill race riots he put forward an idea to the BBC for a series of fifteen-minute television films called *Edric Connor Sings*, in which he and others would sing calypsos and Caribbean folk music, filmed against an authentic Trinidad background. Edric understood the power of the television medium, and believed he could offer the British public what he called a 'true picture of the people of the West Indies and their culture'. Pearl recalls: 'He trained with the BBC. This gave him a qualification but, after he completed his training, he wasn't given the opportunity to direct. Not one BBC assignment came his way.'[11] Determined to become a film-maker, in the early 1960s he directed a series of short films about the Caribbean which he funded himself with help from the British Film Institute. They included *Carnival Fantastique* (1960), about the famous Trinidad carnival. The following year the government of Nigeria commissioned him to direct *Bound for Lagos*. Connor was Britain's first black film director, but he faced opposition from people in the film industry who categorized him as a singer, and would not take him seriously.

In 1956 Pearl and Edric founded the Edric Connor Agency, which later became known as the Afro-Asian Caribbean Agency. For twenty years the agency represented artists, writers and performers from the Caribbean, Malaysia, India and Africa:

After the war, Edric was looked upon as a father figure in Britain's black community so, when performing artists came from the Caribbean, they came straight to our London home. In those days there were very few places where they could meet. Edric and I had a very large living-room with a fire, and this would be used a meeting place. I would say that 90 per cent of African, Asian and Caribbean people who wanted to join the acting profession came to us for help and advice. We'd let them sleep on the floor until they could find a place to live. Calypsonians, dancers, Lord Kitchener himself. All those people came to us. Edric was a generous man, and felt committed to helping these people. He was a giver. So Edric and I decided to do something for them, and we became the first agency to represent them. In those days we joked about casting directors in Britain. We said they employed us by standing outside Baker Street station and seeing who had the thickest lips, the biggest nose and the largest bum! Edric and I were determined to change that. Also they kept inviting black stars and actors over from America, like Harry Belafonte, Eartha Kitt and William Marshall, because they had glamour and celebrity status which gave them the edge on Britain's black performers. We had no media attention. No press coverage. No general promotion. In Britain our actors had to make it on pure merit and friends. We even fought with Equity to give more chances to British black actors because they kept bringing over Americans. We had a very difficult time convincing casting directors that our black actors could act.[12]

In the early 1960s Edric and Pearl were instrumental in forming the Negro Theatre Workshop, a company of thirty black actors. The company is best known for their productions of Wole Soyinka's *The*

Road at the Theatre Royal, Stratford, part of the 1965 Commonwealth Arts Festival, and *The Dark Disciples*, described as 'a blues version of the St Luke Passion'. In 1966, when *The Dark Disciples* was produced for television by the BBC in their *Meeting Point* series, George Browne (Jesus) and Bari Jonson (Judas) headed a largely unknown cast. The production was staged in the famous church of Bow Bells, the blitzed St Mary-le-Bow, in the City of London, and shown on BBC1 on Palm Sunday, 3 April 1966. Sadly, no recording of this historic production has survived.

Edric Connor suffered a stroke and died on 16 October 1968. As a Trinidadian performer in Britain he had been a trailblazer, an artist touched with greatness, and an inspiration to those who followed. Pearl remembers that Edric was determined to succeed in everything he did, despite the obstacles:

> I would think coming to this country right after the war, as Edric did, and getting into BBC radio, and moving among the people, he did a great deal of good for our own community. Setting standards. He saw himself as a self-appointed ambassador for his country, Trinidad. We were very nationalistic back then. We believed we had a country worthy of recognition. Those were the things that attracted me to him.
>
> Most of all it was his generosity that set him apart. He supported many charities, in the days when it was not fashionable to do so. If you supported a charity back then, you did it because you wanted to, not because you wanted to appear in the newspapers or on the telly. You did it privately. This shows you what Edric was made of, as an artist, as a Trinidadian, as a black person in this country. Don't forget we black people were being judged all the time. So all the time we felt we had to show our best. But also that we were human. We're made of the same stuff. If you cut us, do we not bleed? I think Edric was conscious of himself, and he had a sense of destiny, but he died much too young. He hadn't achieved everything he wanted to do. But he moved into this country and took every opportunity he had here, in America, in Africa, to make a lasting mark so that those who came after him would know that it was possible. Possibilities was what he was about, that if you had the chance, you could take it and make good.[13]

In 1971 Pearl married Joseph Mogotsi, leader of the prestigious black South African singing group The Manhattan Brothers. Together, Pearl and Joe have planned and organized tours throughout the world for black South African singers, dancers, musicians and actors. However, in 1976, for personal reasons, Pearl decided to close the agency she had formed with Edric. Kind, generous and warm-hearted, 'mother' Pearl has dedicated her life to fighting for the rights of black artists in Britain, as well as promoting black arts for almost half a century. In 1998, during the

BBC's *Windrush* season, she was interviewed in a short television profile of Edric in BBC2's *Black Firsts* series.

Today, Pearl Mogotsi is still a force to be reckoned with, and is deeply concerned that the achievements of black artists, especially in Britain, are not remembered: 'In Britain there is no record of the contribution we have made to the performing arts. Edric did good work, but it is lost in time and space. There is no memory in Britain for us. There is a hole in the ground, and we fall into it.'[14]

NOTES

1 Pearl Connor Mogotsi, interview with Stephen Bourne, London, 26 July 1993.
2 *Trinidad Guardian*, 15 February 1948, p. 11. Courtesy of Ray Funk.
3 Connor Mogotsi, interview with Bourne.
4 *Ibid.*
5 *Ibid.*
6 Tony Richardson, *Long Distance Runner: A Memoir* (London: Faber and Faber, 1993), p. 100.
7 Connor Mogotsi, interview with Bourne.
8 Thomas Baptiste, interview Stephen Bourne, London, 17 August 1993.
9 Connor Mogotsi, interview with Bourne.
10 *Ibid.*
11 *Ibid.*
12 *Ibid.*
13 *Ibid.*
14 *Ibid.*

9

Winifred Atwell
Honky Tonk Woman

In an episode of *Coronation Street* shown in 1964 Frank Barlow throws a party for his friends in the Rover's Return. The champagne flows, the party begins to swing and Len Fairclough suggests to Ena Sharples: 'How about you having a little tinkle on the piano, darling, a touch of the Winnie Atwells.' A brief – and easily missed – acknowledgement of the Trinidadian piano player Winifred Atwell, it's nonetheless significant. At the time this episode was transmitted, Atwell was – just as much as the residents of 'The Street' – a folk hero for Britain's working classes, and an important part of popular culture in post-war Britain. Indeed, in the 1950s, Atwell was one of our most popular entertainers. In the bleak years after the Second World War, her cheerful personality and honky-tonk music brightened many working-class homes. A knees-up was not complete without Winnie's records being played, and they sold in their millions. In 1954, when Winnie topped the British pop charts with 'Let's Have Another Party', she became the first black recording artist to reach number one. By then she had also become the first artist from Britain to have three million-selling hits. Between 1952 and 1960 she had no fewer than eleven top-ten hits and, to date, she remains the most successful female instrumentalist ever to feature in the British pop charts. At the peak of her popularity her hands were insured at Lloyd's for £40,000 – a vast sum in the early 1950s – and her fan club had over 50,000 members. One of the many fabulous legends surrounding Winifred was that she had built a house in Hampstead in the shape of a grand piano!

And yet today Winifred Atwell is almost forgotten. There are several reasons for this. By the mid-1950s she faced competition from other successful (white) pianists, including Russ Conway and Mrs Mills. Though she attempted to keep up with the advent of rock and roll – in

1957 she recorded the medley 'Let's Rock 'n' Roll' – it hastened the end of her career in the charts. A few years later, in the early 1960s, her popularity declined as tastes in popular music changed radically – a generational shift in attitude and expectation that has obscured a great deal of what came before. It is questionable whether she broke down any racial barriers, but she was one of the most successful and best-loved entertainers of her time, as well as undeniably one of the first African-Caribbeans to become a celebrity in an era when black performers in Britain had more chance of success if they were American. Clearly, Atwell's numerous television appearances throughout the 1950s, including her own series on both channels – ITV (1956) and BBC (1957) – boosted her record sales, enhanced her celebrity status, and established her as the first home-grown black star of British television. But television – especially in the age of live and unrecordable transmission – has no memory. Here today, gone tomorrow, all memory of Winifred Atwell on the box has slipped away.

The daughter of a chemist, she was born in Tunapuna, near Port of Spain, Trinidad, in 1915, according to her 1947 marriage certificate, where she gives her age as thirty-two. She began playing piano at the age of four and, within a couple of years, she was giving Chopin recitals at charity concerts, as her mother, Sarah, later remembered:

> I was a district nurse and dad was a busy druggist in Tunapuna, Trinidad. So often we had to leave Winnie on her own. But she never got into mischief as she would play the piano for hours. At six Winnie could play the piano as well as the organ in church, but we had no piano on which she could practise. We'd saved 500 dollars to buy our house, but when dad and I saw how much Winnie needed a piano, we spent the money on a new piano instead. It was not until 1943 that we were able to build our own house. There isn't a sacrifice I wouldn't make for my daughter. Winnie doesn't say it in words, but I know in her heart how glad she is that her piano helps her to make her mummy happy.[1]

As a young woman, Winifred worked in her father's chemist shop, and he insisted that she took a degree in pharmacy. But in her spare time she entertained her friends, and continued to take part in charity concerts. After performing in Trinidad's Services Club during the war, Winifred went to New York to study piano technique with the celebrated classical pianist Alexander Borovsky. In 1946 she came to Britain, determined to become a concert pianist. Her heart always lay with the classics. Her tutor at the Royal Academy of Music was Professor Harold Craxton, and his son, Michael, recalls those early days of hope and promise:

Father liked her sunny, charming personality, and she was always very cheerful. He had great respect for her musicianship and there was a very good rapport between them. Sometimes, before a big concert, she would come to father for advice. Father wouldn't have given her the time that he did if he didn't feel that she was going to be a considerable talent on the concert platform. If she had continued as a classical pianist she would have been seen more often on the concert platform in this country, but she decided to pursue the honky tonk style of piano playing which amused my father very much! She had considerable musicianship and also wrote books on musical training.[2]

Winifred studied music during the day, and earned a living by working in the evenings playing piano in dance halls and clubs. In 1947 she married Reginald 'Lew' Levisohn, who gave up his stage career as a variety performer to become her manager. Encouraged by Lew, Keith Devon and his associate, the impresario Bernard Delfont, the shy, former child prodigy was groomed for stardom. In 1948 Devon booked her into a Sunday charity concert at the London Casino in place of a star who had fallen ill. Winifred was almost completely unknown before the curtain rose but, after captivating the audience with ragtime music, she found herself taking several curtain calls. Delfont signed her to a long-term contract and sent her on a tour of provincial music halls. After a few months, Delfont showed his faith in his protégée by booking her into the London Casino as part of an all-star variety bill. She played boogie-woogie, ballads and 'swing' numbers and won over the audience with her charm. The story of her battered, broken-down piano became legendary. Winifred discovered it in a Battersea junk shop and bought it for less than £3! It became known as Winifred Atwell's 'other piano' and travelled with her to the nation's variety theatres, to radio, television, recording studios and eventually, in 1952, to the top of the bill at the London Palladium, as record producer Norman Newell recalls:

Winnie was around at the right time. Immediately after the war there was a feeling of depression and unhappiness, and she made you feel happy. She had this unique way of making every note she played sound a happy note. She was always smiling and joking. When you were with her you felt you were at a party, and that was the reason for the success of her records. What was amazing about Winifred Atwell was the fact that she was such a brilliant musician. She played many classical works, but half-way through her stage act she'd turn to the audience and say, 'Now I am going to bring on my *other* piano', and somebody wheeled it on, an old piano which had a very honky-tonk sound. Then she sat down and played all the tunes that were totally different from the classics she had played in the first half of her act. It was

Winifred Atwell (1957)

always a joy to work with Winifred Atwell because she was happiness personified.[3]

On the night of 3 November 1952 Winifred made an unforgettable appearance in the first Royal Variety Performance for the new Queen Elizabeth II. To a rapturous reception Winifred closed her act with a number she had composed specially for the occasion, 'Britannia Rag', which reached number five in the pop charts. After her appearance in the Royal Variety Performance, Winifred was often invited to Buckingham Palace to play for the royal family at private parties. Also in 1952, Winifred's recording of 'Black and White Rag', written in 1908 by ragtime composer George Botsford, was a big hit. Years later her recording was used as the signature tune for BBC television's popular, long-running snooker series *Pot Black* (1969–84).

Among those observing Winifred's climb to fame were three young black women who settled in Britain after the war, and entered the performing arts. Nadia Cattouse first heard about Winifred when she was serving with the ATS:

When I was in the army in the 1940s we called our leave times 'home away from home' and we would stay with people who had come from our country of origin. I stayed with Mr Rupert Arthur and his family who were also from Belize. They lived in Benedict Road in Brixton. He told me about Winifred Atwell, who lived just down the road. They were friends with her. She wasn't famous then, just starting out. After I left the army I returned home to British Honduras. But when I came back to England a few years later, I was amazed to find Winifred Atwell's name in lights outside theatres alongside the likes of Arthur Askey and Frankie Howerd. She had become a big show-business personality. Off stage she was a true Trinidadian. Well-educated, middle-class but full of warmth and fun. She fitted in with the English. You had to in those days if you were going to make it. She also succeeded because her husband, Lew Levisohn, had the right contacts, and the 'push'. Through him she became a star, and she must have wanted it, because she told people she would put her head in a lion's cage for him. That's how much she loved him.[4]

Fellow Trinidadian Pearl Connor was, with her husband Edric, at the heart of a growing and active community of Caribbean performing artists in London, and remembers Winnie well:

Winnie came from a really conservative family. She was a quiet, dignified lady. She played that piano very well, but she wasn't playing honky tonk when she first came to Britain. That was unheard of! When she showed how expert she was, Winnie married Lew Levisohn, an entrepreneur, a promoter, and he brought her out of herself. On-stage, with Lew's support and direction, she changed completely. She became a different person. All that stuff with the honky tonk, pounding away at the Palladium, that was somebody else. Off-stage she became that quiet lady again. It was quite an experience seeing Winnie make these changes. She wasn't somebody who talked loud, or shouted, so everything she did on stage was an act. And when you saw her on stage you'd think she was an uninhibited extrovert. Though some of us Trinidadians knew her, and her family, she never got mixed up in the general movement of assisting our people, or exposing herself to politics. She wasn't that kind of person, anyway. She kept herself to herself right to the end of her life. But she broke down barriers in her own way with her expert piano playing. And people forget she made a wonderful recording with a Trinidadian steel band, the Pan Am North Stars, called 'Ivory and Steel'. She was a great credit to us all. We were very proud of her.[5]

When the singer and actress Isabelle Lucas arrived in London from Canada in 1954 she approached Winifred to ask for advice. She remembered being invited to her home in Hampstead, and meeting her parents:

95

In Canada black people didn't know what Winifred Atwell looked like, so we assumed she was white. You can imagine how shocked we were when we found out she was black. In those days it was unheard of for a black woman to be given so much attention and have so much success in Britain. When I came to Britain in 1954, she was the only black woman I had heard about who lived here. I didn't come here from the Caribbean so, on my arrival in this country, I didn't have any black friends or contacts. When I came to Britain and entered 'show business' I had no one to advise me about how to present myself on stage or at auditions. In those days there were no beauty salons for black women in this country. Black women styled their hair in their kitchens. I needed advice on how to straighten and style my hair, but I didn't know any black women in Britain. I had only heard about Winifred Atwell. So one day I looked her up in the London telephone directory, and found her listed! I rang her, and to my great surprise she answered! I explained my predicament, and she invited me to her home in Hampstead. It was as easy as that! I met her lovely parents, whom she had brought to this country from Trinidad, and Winifred gave me some hair straightening irons. A few years later, in Brixton, she opened one of the first hairdressing and beauty salons for black women. Winifred was so helpful and nice. Though she was a big star, she didn't look down her nose at anyone, or put on airs and graces. She was very down-to-earth, and charming.[6]

Winifred Atwell never made a secret of the fact that her heart lay with classical music. Despite her success with ragtime and honky tonk, she never lost sight of her original ambition to become a concert pianist. In 1954 her exquisite recording of Rachmaninov's '18th Variation on a Theme by Paganini' reached number nine in the pop charts. On 28 November 1954 Winifred packed the Royal Albert Hall as a soloist, accompanied by the London Philharmonic Orchestra. She played the Grieg Piano Concerto and George Gershwin's 'Rhapsody in Blue'. Said music critic Sidney Vauncez: 'The evening was a roaring success, and when the last tempestuous cadenzas had faded away, a radiant Winnie reappeared on the platform, clasping a lovely bouquet, to acknowledge the wild applause surging from every part of the dome-shaped hall.'[7] This unique relationship with the audience was recognized by Sir Harry Secombe, who co-starred with Winifred, Alma Cogan and Beryl Reid at the London Palladium in the hit revue *Rocking the Town* (1956):

Winnie had this ability to communicate with audiences. When she played the piano and looked up to give that sparkling smile, audiences loved her. She was also a great person to be with. She spread happiness around and we felt better for being in her company. I remember a party at Alma Cogan's house one night when Winnie played 'Clare de Lune' for us. We were spellbound. Some of us didn't know that she had been classically trained.[8]

At the height of her popularity, Winifred made her film debut playing a guest role in the comedy *It's a Grand Life* (1953), starring the Lancashire comedian Frank Randle and the glamorous Diana Dors. Shy and self-conscious when she is introduced, Winifred relaxes as soon as she starts playing the piano. It was her first, and last, appearance on the big screen. However, it is a little-known fact that, off screen, in 1956, Winifred played the piano for John Mills in the lively musical comedy *It's Great to Be Young*. But Winifred, in spite of her fame and popularity, did not receive any screen credit for her contribution to this film.

In spite of her success, by the end of the 1950s the writing was on the wall. Tastes in popular music were changing rapidly and Winifred's manic style of piano playing, with its famous 'tinny' barroom sound, went out of fashion. Happily, Winifred had become well known abroad and her first Australian tour in 1958–9 lasted thirteen months. In fact, her popularity in Australia was so great that when her record sales began to fall in Britain she spent more and more time there with her husband, returning only now and again to Britain for a club date or television appearance.

Though never a political activist, Winifred made her anti-segregational views known on a tour of Australia in 1961, when she revealed how infuriated she was by the exclusion of aborigines from her concerts:

> She said that at Moree, in New South Wales, it was not until she was near the end of her programme that she learned that aboriginals in the audience had been forced to sit apart from white listeners on hard wooden benches. At Rowen, in North Queensland, she said aboriginals had been refused admittance to the theatre where she appeared. At her request the management had finally left the doors of the theatre open so that the aboriginals could watch and listen from outside. She listed this as the worst example of segregation she had found in Australia. Of the Moree incident she said: 'Had I known about it before, I would have had second thoughts about appearing.'[9]

However, nothing could have prepared Winifred for the racism she encountered in 1969 before entering New Zealand for a concert tour, because this time it was directed at her. New Zealand's Immigration Department insisted that she show them her return ticket to Australia before entering the country. Two years later Winifred was granted permission to live in Australia – as an immigrant:

> Pianist Winifred Atwell has been given permission to settle down in Australia as an immigrant. She has been told this officially in spite of the

country's 'White Australia' policy. An Australian immigration official said yesterday that she had been granted residence because she was 'of good character and had special qualifications.' Immigration Minister Mr Phillip Lynch said: 'We will not stand in the way of an international artist of such repute.'[10]

Winifred tolerated this because she had grown to love Australia, and Britain did not want her any more. However, her happiness was not to last. In 1978 Lew died and she never completely recovered from the shock of losing the man to whom she had been married for over thirty years. Three years later she was finally granted Australian citizenship but died from a heart attack in Sydney on 27 February 1983.

In 1957 Winifred looked back on her career:

> I am so grateful for my lovely memories: the excitement of receiving letters commanding my appearance in three Royal Variety Shows ... the evening just before Christmas of 1956, when I played for Her Majesty at a private party, when the Queen requested 'Roll Out the Barrel' and a 15-minute encore ... playing with [conductor] André Kostelanetz ... the Sydney and London Symphony Orchestras ... duets with the Governor of Trinidad, the Lord Mayor of Sydney (Australia), and with my dear friend Liberace ... all are wonderful milestones in my Memory Lane. But in the final reckoning – I am happiest when, having played a television show or made a broadcast, I read the letters of my friends all over the country. Mama always says, 'Whatever you do, try and bring a little happiness and light into a dull life.' I hope I can always do that with my piano.[11]

NOTES

1 Mrs Sarah Atwell, *TV Times*, 24 May 1957.
2 Michael Craxton, interview with Stephen Bourne, London, 20 July 1993.
3 Norman Newell, interview with Stephen Bourne, London, 12 August 1993.
4 Nadia Cattouse, interview with Stephen Bourne, London, 1 January 1997.
5 Pearl Connor Mogotsi, interview with Stephen Bourne, London, 26 July 1993.
6 Isabelle Lucas, interview with Stephen Bourne, London, 25 November 1996.
7 Sidney Vauncez, 'On and off the record', *The Weekly Sporting Review*, 28 October 1959.
8 Sir Harry Secombe, interview with Stephen Bourne, London, 17 August 1993.
9 'Miss Atwell furious – segregation in Australia', *Guardian*, 8 November 1961.
10 'Winnie makes a big entry', *Sunday Mirror*, 4 February 1971.
11 Winifred Atwell, *Top Record Stars Annual* (1957), p. 43.

10

Gordon Heath
A Very Unusual Othello

In 1950 Gordon Heath made a record-breaking tour of Britain for the Arts Council in an innovative version of Shakespeare's *Othello*, staged by the theatre critic and producer Kenneth Tynan. He was the first black actor since Paul Robeson to play the role in Britain. Accompanying Heath on the tour was a Jamaican-born actress called Pauline Henriques, who later recalled:

> Tynan wanted to take *Othello* to the theatreless towns of Britain. We toured for six months through the Midlands, North England, Scotland and Wales, playing in school halls, church halls and, if we were lucky, a full-size theatre! Tynan decided on a most original presentation of the play ... He cast Gordon Heath as Othello. He was a slim, sensitive American actor who was really a folk singer, but he had a lot to give the theatre. We were all amazed that he had the range to play the part but he was a very good and a very unusual Othello. Tynan also decided to cast *Othello* with a black Emilia, and that's where I came in.[1]

Five years later, when Heath was cast as Othello again, this time in Tony Richardson's celebrated BBC television production, Britain's leading black actor, Robert Adams, was incensed. Heath recalled in his autobiography that he played the role

> practically over Mr Robert Adams's dead body. Mr A had been *the* Negro actor in the British Isles on the strength of several films and a number of supporting roles on stage. He was also a barrister and my London agent said he had managed to issue a challenge on the floor of the House of Parliament to my being employed and cast as Othello when, he asserted, there were actors, British subjects, with adequate talent to do as much or more. The authorities consulted the BBC casting director who assured them that they

had auditioned the black actors, including Mr A, in the UK and none of them came near to their requirements – either G. Heath or no one. Mr Adams's claim was disallowed.[2]

A magnificent cast also included Paul Rogers as Iago and Rosemary Harris as Desdemona, and the telerecording that exists of the transmission, broadcast live on 15 December 1955, reveals an elegant and understated performance by Heath. Since that time, only a handful of black actors

Rosemary Harris and Gordon Heath in *Othello* (1955)

100

have portrayed Othello in British film and television, and these include opera singer Charles Holland in a BBC version of Verdi's *Otello* (1959), Cy Grant in a schools production for Associated Rediffusion in 1969, BBC2's version of the Royal Shakespeare Company's production with Willard White and Ian McKellen as Iago (in 1990), and Laurence Fishburne in the 1995 film version with Kenneth Branagh as Iago. In *Sight and Sound*, Geoffrey Macnab described Fishburne as

> Impressive. His Othello is a saturnine, imposing figure, with a more or less permanent scowl fixed to his face ... he is suitably authoritative when it comes to barking out orders to his underlings, and speaks the verse, especially the more lyrical passages, quite beautifully.[3]

However, when Laurence Olivier, in blackface, re-created his flamboyant National Theatre performance for the screen in 1965 (a performance which earned him an Oscar nomination), dramatist John Osborne described it as ' unspeakably vulgar'. In 1981 there was controversy when the producer/director Jonathan Miller failed to cast a black actor as Othello in his popular *Television Shakespeare* series for BBC television. Originally the distinguished African–American actor James Earl Jones was coming to Britain to play the part, but Equity refused to give him permission. Instead, Anthony Hopkins played Othello as a light-skinned Arab. Understandably, many of our own black actors were upset, including Rudolph Walker, who later complained:

> That whole episode was particularly painful not only for me, but also for a lot of black actors in this country. The BBC bluntly refused to use any of the black actors in this country, saying that we were just not good enough. There was something rather unsavoury about that.[4]

Gordon Heath was born in New York City, and his early stage roles included Shakespeare's Hamlet for the Hampton Institute in 1945. Later that year he made his Broadway debut in *Deep Are the Roots*, the critically acclaimed drama by Arnaud d'Usseau and James Gow about racism in America's Deep South. Heath played Brett Charles, an American army officer who returns home to the estate on which he has been raised. While serving in Europe during the war he has been treated as an equal, but at home he is forced to confront the virulent racism of the Deep South again. In 1947 Heath visited London's West End with the production, and received more critical acclaim. After deciding to base himself in Europe, he lived with his lover, Lee Payant, mostly in Paris, where a more liberal attitude to homosexuality existed. In Britain homosexuality was a criminal offence until partially decriminalized in 1967.

From 1949 Heath and Payant ran a popular Left Bank café called l'Abbaye, and entertained customers with their folk singing. One of their friends, Leslie Schenck, remembers:

Heath discovered that the French were colour blind. He loved it. In 1949 Gordon's partner Lee Payant joined him in Paris. They'd been having a relationship in America for seven years. Lee was a wonderful guy. A sweetheart. He gave up his life for Gordon. They had a great deal of love for each other and they both liked Paris. It was such an exciting place in those days and, when it came to race and your private life, you were left completely alone. If homosexuality was against the law in Paris, they turned a blind eye. So Gordon taught Lee a few chords and songs, and they stayed in Paris, singing duets in l'Abbaye, a 'club' they eventually took over. It became an institution.

Of course, now and again a white southerner would visit l'Abbaye and cause a scene. One evening, when I was at l'Abbaye with a friend, a little old lady from the Deep South pointedly asked Gordon to sing 'Old Black Joe'. Gordon told her firmly – in his urbane, highly civilized Laurence Olivier way – 'I'm sorry, but I don't sing that.' Horrified, the old lady responded, 'You wouldn't dare talk like that to me if we were back home.' Said Gordon, 'Well, this is Paris, this is my bar and, what's more, if you're not careful I'll have you thrown out.' My then-companion asked Gordon, 'Shouldn't you have been nice to her, won her over, and taught her a lesson?' Gordon replied, 'Hell, I'm not interested in giving lessons to such people. All I want is for them to let me get on with it.' Gordon and Lee were together for a very long time, but when Lee died in 1976, it was a terrible blow for Gordon. In fact he decided he couldn't continue with l'Abbaye.[5]

In 1950 Heath returned to Britain to re-create the role of Brett Charles for a BBC television version of *Deep Are the Roots*. This was followed by leading roles in other British television plays, including Eugene O'Neill's *The Emperor Jones* (BBC, 1953), *For the Defence* (BBC, 1956) and *Cry, the Beloved Country* (ITV, 1958). In 1954 he narrated Halas and Batchelor's acclaimed animation film of George Orwell's *Animal Farm*, and in 1956 he took part in a reading of black poetry at the Royal Court with Earle Hyman and Cleo Laine. A few years later, in 1963, Heath and Laine, with Vinnette Carroll and Brock Peters, made a recording of black American poetry called *Beyond the Blues*. In 1959 he gave a memorable performance as the arrogant lawyer in the film *Sapphire* (1959).

In 1961, Heath starred in *Les Laches vivant d'espoir* for the French writer, director and producer Claude Bernard Aubert. Intimate relationships between black men and white women were rarely seen on the screen at this time, and this was something of a breakthrough. Daniel J. Leab describes the film as

a love affair between a French girl and an African student in Paris. They are well-matched, but their romance nearly founders under the pressure of race hatred. This film, called *The Colour of Love* in England, is symbol-ridden and marred by some *nouvelle vague* techniques ... the atrociously dubbed American version, *My Baby is Black*, was exploited on the worst possible level.[6]

When Heath visited America it always came as a shock to be treated like a second-class citizen in his own country. As for his acting career, he was offered very few roles worthy of his attention and he eventually became a theatre director in Paris. He also directed occasional productions for the University of Massachusetts.

In America in the 1950s, when Heath was working in Britain and France, Sidney Poitier rose to fame in Hollywood. Perhaps if Heath had stayed in America after his success on Broadway in *Deep Are the Roots*, he might have been offered the roles Poitier played. But his friend Leslie Schenck did not believe that Heath would have enjoyed that kind of international fame and popularity:

Gordon preferred to remain a free agent ... He loved the theatre, and a great cross he had to bear was that there were not enough roles for him to play, but he didn't make this a crutch as some people do, not at all. He just got on with his life and made the best of things. He didn't let it destroy him.[7]

Heath died in Paris on 28 August 1991 from an AIDS-related illness. He was undoubtedly one of the most talented and respected actors to emerge in the early post-war years.

NOTES

1   Pauline Henriques, interview with Stephen Bourne, in Jim Pines (ed.), *Black and White in Colour: Black People in British Television since 1936* (London: British Film Institute, 1992), p. 30.
2   Gordon Heath *Deep Are the Roots: Memoirs of a Black Expatriate* (Amherst: University of Massachusetts Press, 1992), p. 143.
3   Geoffrey Macnab, *Sight and Sound* Vol. 6, Issue 2, February 1996, p. 52.
4   Rudolph Walker, interview with Bourne, in Pines (ed.), *Black and White in Colour*, p. 80.
5   Leslie Schenck, interview with Stephen Bourne, London, 20 September 1995.
6   Daniel J. Leab, *From Sambo to Superspade: The Black Experience in Motion Pictures* (London: Secker and Warburg, 1973), p. 216.
7   Schenck, interview with Bourne.

11

Earl Cameron

A Class Act

Throughout the 1950s and 1960s Earl Cameron added a touch of class to a number of British film and television productions. He is, perhaps, best remembered for his appearances in the films *Pool of London* (1951), *Emergency Call* (1952), *Simba* (1955), *The Heart Within* (1957), *Sapphire* (1959), *Flame in the Streets* (1961) and *Guns at Batasi* (1964). But he also made an impact on television in such plays as *The End Begins* (1956), *A Man from the Sun* (1956), *Thunder on Sycamore Street* (1957), *A World Inside* (1962), *A Fear of Strangers* (1964), *The Death of Bessie Smith* (1965) and *Wind Versus Polygamy* (1968), as well as a number of 'cult' favourites like *Danger Man*, *The Andromeda Breakthrough*, *Doctor Who* and *The Prisoner*. Actress Nadia Cattouse often worked with Earl: 'we [black actors in Britain] had the highest regard for Earl. We all liked and admired him. He worked all the time, and gave each role tremendous dignity and humanity.' In 1979 Earl left Britain and settled in the Solomon Islands with his family. Fifteen years later, following the death of his wife, he returned to Britain and resumed his acting career. In 1999 he received a Lifetime Achievement Award from the Bermuda Arts Council. The following is taken from interviews conducted by Stephen Bourne and Richard Dacre in London in 1997:

I was born in Pembroke, Bermuda. My father was a stone mason but he died very young, when I was five, so my mother took jobs in hotels, that sort of thing, to keep the family together. I was the youngest of six children. When I grew up, Bermuda was a very comfortable little island and a very easy place to live. I remember the first time I went to the cinema – I must have been about five or six – to see a silent film at the Odeon Hall. I came out and every time I saw a white man I shouted, 'He was the man in the film!'

In the 1930s I joined the Merchant Navy, and often travelled to New York. This was great, because in New York I saw Paul Robeson in some of his films. I also went with my Bermudian pals to places like the Apollo on 125th Street in Harlem. At the Apollo we saw Count Basie, Duke Ellington, Ella Fitzgerald, Billie Holiday, Earl Hines. They were all there, all the big bands, all the big stars. The two places that meant anything to us Bermudians were the Apollo Theatre and the Savoy Ballroom. In New York black artists like Basie, Ellington, Ella and Billie were accessible to black people, but in London it was different. People like Hutch and Snakehips, who worked at the Café de Paris, were fairly exclusive to white audiences. There was a difference. But in London during the war I became friendly with some members of Snakehips's band.

I arrived in London in October 1939 on a ship called the *Eastern Prince*, but it was impossible for a black person to get a job. My first job was in the Charing Cross Hotel as a dish washer and even then they were reluctant to take me on. After growing up in the comfort of Bermuda, I was not prepared for the hardships of London and the war. I was here all through the Blitz, but I coped with the war extremely well. When I arrived I did not know London at all, so I was not aware of established black communities in places like the East End. However, I had arrived in London with two other black guys, and we were good pals, so I wasn't alone. I lived in the West End, and didn't have trouble finding digs, because the landladies were also foreign – French, Italian.

In 1941 I was working in the kitchen of the Strand Corner House and fed up with menial, casual jobs. One day a friend of mine called Harry Crossman gave me a ticket to see the revival of *Chu Chin Chow* at the Palace Theatre, in which he and five other black guys had walk-on parts. They were dressed in exotic costumes and I thought to myself, 'Hell, I can do what you're doing.' So I asked Harry how I could get into *Chu Chin Chow*, but he said all the parts were cast. Two or three weeks later I met Harry in Jig's Club, a meeting place for Africans and West Indians in Wardour Street, and he said, 'Earl, your big chance has come. Russell didn't turn up, and the director, Robert Atkins, has told me to find someone to take his place. If you come with me, I'll introduce you to him.' Robert Atkins looked me up and down, said 'You'll do', and that night I was on stage! In the dressing-room I met the other black guys including Jimmy Holmes, Tunji Williams from Nigeria and a very nice old man called Napoleon Florent. We called him 'Nap'. He had appeared in the original version of *Chu Chin Chow* during the First World War. He was a decent man, a fine man, and I had the highest respect for him. He had a great sense of humour. And that night I went on stage for the first time, my knees buckling like mad, sweat pouring down, but I was determined to get through it! All those eyes watching me. I don't know why I didn't faint! But all I was thinking about was that lousy job in the Strand Corner House that I had escaped from!

Once I was in *Chu Chin Chow*, a transformation took place! I called myself a 'theatrical', an actor, and I was luckier than most because my Bermudian accent sounded American. This helped, because in 1942 I appeared in an American play by Robert E. Sherwood called *The Petrified Forest* at the Globe. I played Joseph, the chauffeur, and I had a few lines. The guys from *Chu Chin Chow* were amazed. 'You got *lines!*' they said in disbelief. From time to time I worked as a film extra, and in 1946 I screen tested for the director Thorold Dickinson for *Men of Two Worlds*, but I was unprepared, and didn't get a part.

I had no training as an actor, but in 1947 my friend, the singer Ida Shepley, introduced me to Miss Amanda Ira Aldridge [1866–1956], a singing teacher and composer who was prominent in the music world in England. She lived in Kensington Palace Gardens and was the daughter of the famous black American Shakespearian actor, Ira Aldridge [1807–67]. Miss Aldridge was about eighty at this time but still giving elocution lessons and instructing people in voice projection. She was light-skinned, rather short and stocky. She was a lovely, well-spoken, delicate and dignified lady with a tremendous sense of humour. She could laugh about most things. She was a courteous, beautiful human being, but not wealthy. I had the highest regard for her, and we got on extremely well. She helped me tremendously and I continued having lessons with her for at least two years. She told me all about her father, and showed me pictures of him. She did not like Herbert Marshall, who later published a biography of her father [*Ira Aldridge: The Negro Tragedian*, 1958]. She didn't have a high opinion of Paul Robeson, either. She had given Robeson elocution lessons when he was preparing for his first appearance as Othello at the Savoy Theatre. She helped him greatly but, in later years, she was hurt when he failed to give her any credit.

There were places in London that operated a colour bar. Now and again I would come up against it. When I was understudying Gordon Heath in *Deep Are the Roots* at the Wyndham's Theatre in 1947, I went into a pub with two black friends in Shaftesbury Avenue and they wouldn't serve us! So we had a big argument with the landlord. We told him we weren't leaving. So he called the police and, when they arrived, they pushed us out! *Deep Are the Roots* was a fine American play about racism in the Deep South, and it did me a lot of good, because whenever a repertory theatre wanted to stage it, they would cast me in Gordon Heath's part because he had gone to live in Paris after the London run. I did seventy different repertory productions over a period of four or five years as well as a radio version for the BBC in 1949. It gave me tremendous experience of English theatre. There was hardly a town I didn't appear in.

In 1951 Zoltan Korda, the director, interviewed me for a part in his screen version of Alan Paton's *Cry, the Beloved Country*. Korda said, 'Tell me, are you a good actor?' I said, 'Yes.' So he introduced me to Alan Paton, but I had a feeling that he didn't think I was right for the film, probably because I wasn't dark enough to play an African. Korda arranged for me to have a screen test for the part of the priest, but I did something very stupid. Determined to get the part, I became preoccupied with darkening my skin, to convince Alan Paton I could look like an African. I spent some time at a place in Camden Town trying to get some sort of tan under a light. It didn't make any difference at all. In doing so, I didn't learn the part very well. I'd had only one screen test before, for *Men of Two Worlds*, and I should have prepared myself better. After the test, two or three weeks went by, and I heard nothing from Korda. So I called him and he said, 'Look. You came to my studio and you didn't know your lines. It is unforgivable for an actor not to know his lines. Good morning.' That taught me a lesson! Sidney Poitier got the part.

Sidney and I became friends. We have acted together occasionally and in 1973 he directed me in *A Warm December*. Sidney is a hard-working person. I admire him because, when he arrived in Hollywood, the only black people he saw in the studios were the shoe-shine boys. Today, of course, he is still a big star, and has directed eight or nine films. All those heavy odds against him!

I was touring in a terrible play called *13 Death Street, Harlem* and desperate to get out. So I contacted a girl I knew who worked for a film company and I asked her if there were any openings. She suggested that I call Ealing Studios who were casting a film called *Where No Vultures Fly*. But I was told that the production wasn't ready to start. However, they had seen my picture in *Spotlight*, and wanted me to see the director Basil Dearden, who was looking for a black actor to play Johnny, the merchant seaman in *Pool of London*. A meeting was arranged and I got on well with Dearden. He sent me the script, and I was thrilled. The story follows the adventures of a crew from a merchant ship who come ashore for a weekend. One of them, a Jamaican called Johnny, befriends a white girl and this was the first time a British film had shown a racially mixed relationship. It was a fabulous part and Johnny appeared all through the picture! Several black actors had tested for it, including Neville Crabbe and Cy Grant. But, after my bad experience with Korda and *Cry, the Beloved Country*, I was determined to do well in the screen test. Eventually I got the part, and Susan Shaw was cast as the white girl.

Susan Shaw and Earl Cameron in *Pool of London* (1951)

So, after trying for several years to get into films, I ended up with this delightful part. I would say it is still the best part I've had in films. The amount of fan mail I received was amazing. People felt sorry for me. They thought I really was that lonely Jamaican guy wandering around London looking for friends!

I got to know the director, Basil Dearden, very well. He was a very nice man. He did *Pool of London* with his partner, [producer] Michael Relph, but at that time Michael Balcon, who ran Ealing Studios, was not happy about including the racial theme. But Dearden and Relph insisted and, I suppose, this started them on the road to making the so-called 'social problem' pictures, including *Sapphire*.

The director, Brian Desmond Hurst, was a very touchy man. When he directed me in *Simba* with Dirk Bogarde, I upset him. He overheard me tell the actor Sydney Tafler that I thought *Simba* was 'fair'. His face turned red and he looked at me and said something I would not accept from anybody. He called me a 'bloody nigger'. Sydney looked at me as if to say 'forget it'. He could see me getting angry. So I just walked away. I said nothing. It wasn't a very happy film. Brian Desmond Hurst and Dirk Bogarde didn't get on very well, either.

After appearing in *Pool of London* I had ambitions. I wanted to play big parts in films. But, unlike Sidney Poitier in America, I didn't quite make it into that league. I didn't become a box-office attraction like Dirk Bogarde or Kenneth More. This was partly due to the fact that black film actors in this country were not given any promotion. Our names did not appear on film posters. I lost count of the times we met with Equity to try and stop black Americans being brought over to take roles in British films and television. This happened because casting directors didn't believe we – black British actors – could act. But, in spite of this, I did work consistently throughout the 1950s and 1960s.

I enjoyed making *Sapphire*. It was a very good film and received the British Academy Award for Best British Film. It was good to be directed by Basil Dearden again. Maybe *Sapphire* happened because of the racial tensions in Notting Hill in 1958. But I knew Janet Green, who wrote the screenplay, and I don't think she was influenced in any way by what happened in Notting Hill. The film is not about that. It's a whodunit thriller with a race angle.

Flame in the Streets dealt with racism in a contemporary setting. Like *Sapphire*, it gave cinema audiences an opportunity to see black people as real people. John Mills, who played the union leader whose daughter wants to marry a black man, was absolutely brilliant in it. I am sure commercial films like *Sapphire* and *Flame in the Streets*, which reached mass audiences, helped raise their consciousness. They knew that racism existed, but they didn't see it exposed. And when they did, certain people felt ashamed about it. So, to an extent, those two films helped make people aware of what life was really like for black people in this country at that time.

I remember chatting to Roy Baker, the director of *Flame in the Streets*. He said, 'Look, I'll be very honest, I don't know many of your people,' as he put it, 'and I'd be grateful for any tips you can give me.' I had read the script by then, and there was a lot of domestic stuff in the film, and some directors didn't know how working-class black people lived, and they showed their houses with twenty people living in one room. I told Roy this didn't happen. I told him that films and television plays tended to show people from the Caribbean or Africa being dirty, which was just not true either. I advised him to visit some of the homes in the area where we were filming, and see for himself how black people lived. I wanted him to give some reality to the story, rather than the stereotypical view.

I remember being on location in Camden Town one night, standing around waiting to be called for a scene, when suddenly a guy came from nowhere, punched me to the ground and ran away! So I got up, a bit bruised. We had no idea who he was, but I suppose he must have been a member of the National Front or something similar, and resented the film being made.

I should have been in the first James Bond film, *Dr No* [1962]. I went to see Cubby Broccoli and Harry Saltzman about the part of Quarrel and I was pretty much on the damn film. Then Saltzman said, 'You're a very good actor but you are not right for this part,' so I didn't get it. Three years later I played James Bond's chauffeur in *Thunderball*. It wasn't much of a part. I just drive James Bond around the island. But whatever comes along, you play it. Who wants to be typecast! Anyway, I had seven glorious weeks in Nassau. I didn't have much to do in the film, but it was a lovely location!

I remember one of the first television plays I appeared in was *The End Begins* [BBC, 1956]. I played the lead, a wonderful part. It was written by Ray and Jean Rigby, and I had already acted in the original stage version at the 'Q' Theatre with Margaret Tyzack. It was about a group of survivors of a nuclear bomb. It was a live transmission, a nightmare to do. Nerve-racking. You couldn't afford to dry at all! Another drama I remember very well was Leon Griffiths's *A Fear of Strangers* [ATV, 1964]. I played a musician, a saxophone player, and during a gig in a small town somewhere in England, I have a one-night stand with a white woman. But the following morning she's found dead. Stanley Baker played a psychologically disturbed policeman who tries to force a confession out of me. But during the interrogation I show that I am tough too, so we're at each other's throats the whole time. It was a very good, strong two-hander. Errol John's *The Dawn* [BBC, 1963] was interesting because we didn't have many black writers in television. Errol had written *Moon on a Rainbow Shawl*. He was a very talented actor and writer, but he was inhibited and sensitive. I think he should be given greater recognition for his work. I acted in other television plays by black writers including John Hearne's *A World Inside* [BBC, 1962] and Obi Egbuna's *Wind Versus Polygamy* [BBC2, 1968].

My experiences of theatre, television and films has been wonderful. I've enjoyed every minute of it. Some things I did well, some things I didn't. I don't look at myself as a great actor. Others can judge that. But acting has never been my number one priority in life.

FURTHER READING

Linda Bellos, 'Windrush special: a portrait of Earl Cameron', *Black Filmmaker*, Vol. 1, No. 3, 1998, pp. 8–9.

12

'London Is the Place for Me'
Nadia Cattouse, Errol John and
A Man from the Sun

When writer Caryl Phillips was interviewed about his television adaptation of *The Final Passage*, he claimed that it was the first time television had dramatized the experiences of people from the Caribbean in post-war Britain.[1] Not so. In 1956 the BBC had depicted the lives of newly arrived Caribbean settlers in *A Man from the Sun*. However, in spite of the wealth of material available, including novels by George Lamming (*The Emigrants*, 1954) and Samuel Selvon (*The Lonely Londoners*, 1956), it is hardly surprising that Phillips blamed British television for putting up a wall of silence around the subject. It was a silence that lasted for forty years. The subject was not explored in television again until 1996 when Channel 4 commissioned the two-part dramatization of Phillips's novel *The Final Passage*, first published in 1985. For Caryl Phillips, who was born in St Kitts in 1958 and came to Britain with his parents at the age of twelve weeks, this was a major breakthrough in providing African-Caribbeans with a television drama they could relate to:

I hope they feel proud to see a part of their story that has been written out of British history, I mean totally ignored. This country has a serious historical failure of memory, and I hope they feel they can look at it and say, that's part of my life ... I hope they feel connected to Britain; that it provides them with an umbilical cord to feel that this society is the place they've invested their lives in, because they have. It needs to be acknowledged ... They're going to get no one who says we value your contribution to this society because it's been absolutely crucial to the development of Britain in the last fifty years. What do they get? They get morons like Paul Condon [Commissioner of the Metropolitan Police] telling them their children are muggers ... So I want that generation to know, no, your contribution to this country has been remarkable. That's the generation I want to speak to first – the generation that came over ... I'm also interested in speaking to their children ... because I want them to understand that as much frustration as they're suffering in this society ... it's not their parents' fault.[2]

In 1956, when John Elliot scripted and produced *A Man from the Sun*, he was genuinely concerned about the attitudes of the British towards Caribbean settlers, aware that some were welcoming, while others were hostile. Elliot felt he needed to explore

> the clash between this mythical Britain and the actual grotty real Britain, which West Indians would face when they got here ... I spent the summer [of 1956] researching in Brixton and in other parts of London where there were West Indian populations. I just nosed around, sinking into the background, talking and listening to people, going to parties, to church, to work, and generally being a fly-on-the-wall ... So I went round and tried to find out what everybody thought, and I turned it into a script which ... was rather in the tradition of the pre-war GPO movies ... I started writing the script for *A Man from the Sun* in midsummer of 1956, and we had the show live on the air by November ... there had been no real attempt to do programmes about race relations in this country – even in the documentary field there had been very little on the subject ... it proved to be a bit of a landmark.[3]

To his credit, Elliot succeeded in portraying working-class black people as they really were, and highlighting some of the situations and conflicts they faced on their arrival here, as Pauline Henriques, who was cast as Mrs Zacharius, recalls:

> we were portrayed as real people, not as stereotypes. It gave a voice to black people who, unlike myself, had recently arrived in Britain. It was a very good, very lively play that had a lot of strands woven into it. It was a play for the day, right for the time, and I felt it was a very exciting thing for the BBC to do.[4]

A Man from the Sun tells the story of Cleve Lawrence (Errol John), a skilled carpenter from Jamaica, who arrives in Britain hoping to find work. At the beginning of the play, Cleve arrives at Southampton Docks, one among hundreds of new arrivals, most of them in a state of chaos and confusion. Nadia Cattouse, who appears as Nina, Cy Grant's common-law wife, explains:

Sometimes the man came first, sometimes the woman, but always the children came *after* their parents. I met many women who just came, with no experience of life outside the island they had left, and they would just ask somebody for guidance, take a bed wherever. Next day they'd walk along the street and, when they met a black person, they'd ask questions like 'Where are you living?' And then they would just walk into a shop or a factory all over the country and ask for a job. That was really amazing and I was very close to a lot of those women at that time when I was helping them. I remember one night there was a party of seventeen women who had arrived at Victoria. I tried to find them a night shelter, without success, so I took all of them to my home and let them bed down on my floor! But they were so indomitable and quietly just got on with finding a secure, safe home for their children.[5]

When Cleve eventually locates his cousin Alvin Jarvis (Cy Grant) in London, he is told a few home truths about the 'mother country'. Says Alvin, 'You think England's your mother country, but over here you are a foreigner.' Bewildered, Cleve replies, 'But we're all British citizens.' Explains Alvin, 'You're a British citizen in Jamaica, but here you're a coloured man.' Alvin's neighbour (Claud Collier) also opens Cleve's eyes to the reality of living and working in 'grotty' Britain:

I work on the buses. I'm a conductor – is my job. An' mostly people they're nice. But sometimes you know they give you the money like this, so as not to touch your fingers. An' if they do touch you they wipe their han' on their trouser afterwards like this.[6]

Says 'Daddy' Zacharius (André Dakar, aka Rudolph 'Rudy' Evans), an elderly 'father figure' in the black community, 'There is no colour bar in the law, but in people's hearts.'

The cast of *A Man from the Sun* reads like a directory of African and Caribbean actors and actresses then working in Britain. Apart from Nadia Cattouse, Claud Collier, André Dakar, Pauline Henriques, Errol John and Cy Grant, other speaking roles were taken by George Browne, Earl Cameron, Neville Crabbe, John Harrison, Joseph Layode, Sonny McKenzie, Pearl Prescod, Mark Shurland, Gloria Simpson and Keefe West. Joan Hooley made her television debut in a small role as a 'bridesmaid' and went on to appear in the soaps *Emergency – Ward 10* and *EastEnders*. Pauline Henriques remembers the freedom John Elliot allowed the cast in their interpretation of his script:

There hadn't been anything else like that written about black people for television and John Elliot's script was very alive and real. The cast picked up the spirit that Elliot had put into it. He was very concerned about getting it right, so he allowed us a lot of freedom in our interpretation of the play. [7]

Though *A Man from the Sun* succeeded in revealing some of the harsh realities of life for Britain's newly arrived settlers, Nadia Cattouse remembers another reality she faced during the making of the drama-documentary:

> When I played Cy Grant's common-law wife in *A Man from the Sun*, the props woman came to the studio floor and on to the set, which was the room Cy and I were supposed to be living in. I watched as she messed up the bed clothes, and made the room look as sleazy as possible. This was how she thought people from the Caribbean lived! So just before we went on the air, when no one was looking, I went in, straightened the bed clothes, and made the room look neat and tidy. It was a live transmission, so there was nothing she could do about it![8]

The daughter of Albert Cattouse, a civil servant who later became Deputy Prime Minister of British Honduras, Nadia was born in Belize City, British Honduras (now Belize). During the Second World War, as the labour shortage intensified, volunteers from Commonwealth countries were called for. Nadia was one of many women from the Caribbean who volunteered, coming to Britain in 1943:

> We arrived in Britain on a ship packed with US servicemen. I can remember my first impressions of London were in the middle of an air-raid. I couldn't understand why everyone was being so cool about it. Eventually I went to Edinburgh for special training as a signals operator. We worked in shifts sending and receiving messages by morse key and radio telephones. I was also a part-time PT (physical training) instructor with the ATS. [9]

After leaving the ATS, Nadia went to a teacher-training college in Glasgow and, having qualified in 1949, returned to British Honduras:

> We were one of the families always involved in public affairs. We became teachers, policemen, parsons, politicians. But I discovered I disliked what went with being a teacher there. I was expected to be a paragon of all the virtues and I couldn't accept that. When I tried to leave, I was called unstable. The Director of Education felt my duty lay with my people – a sort of 'You will be the woman behind the man'. But I think you can contribute wherever you are in the world. Sometimes, if you go home, you contribute less. Any talent you have can shrivel up with restrictions.[10]

Nadia Cattouse (1960)

Returning to Britain in 1951, Nadia was accepted for a place on a social sciences course at the London School of Economics. During her two years of study, she paid her way by working in kitchens, as a telephone receptionist, as a pollster for Gallup, as well as acting and singing:

At first I did acting and singing for fun, and to help pay my way through college. I remember joining the Commonwealth Students' Drama Group and working on amateur productions with people like Errol Hill and Errol John, who were both from Trinidad. I had never thought about becoming a professional actress and singer. My love of performing had started back home in British Honduras, but there was no way that we could become professional, so I never even considered it. But when we did productions in school, I was always picked out to do things. I remember we had a Canadian missionary at our high school who cast me in a production of *Pride and Prejudice*, and I enjoyed it, but I never had any ambition to become a professional actress. When I came to Britain, I carried on performing as a hobby, really. Eventually it crystallized into a professional career.

While studying at the London School of Economics, I was seconded to work for the Colonial Office, looking after Caribbean migrants who were arriving here, helping them find accommodation and work, things like that. Eventually I returned to the LSE to complete my course, but three months short of a degree I accepted an invitation to tour Britain in a variety show. That's how I made my professional debut. In the first half of this show I impersonated the girl from The Platters, and in the second half I was Lena Horne![11]

Nadia's television career began in 1954. Interesting parts occasionally came her way, such as the Russian lieutenant in *Caviar to the General* (1955) and Nina in *A Man from the Sun*, but there was always a downside:

In those days, when the BBC were casting a black actor and actress as husband and wife, they always tried to find a couple who matched each other's colour. If they didn't match they instructed someone in the make-up department to paint one of us dark so that we did match. I remember my sister calling me up after seeing me in a television play and saying, 'I wouldn't have recognized you if it weren't for your earrings!' All kinds of strange attitudes existed. I had a half-brother who was doing bit parts and I remember watching him killed three times in a Bob Hope film called *Call Me Bwana* [1963]. Somebody obviously believed we all look alike and the audience wouldn't notice. First, he was gunned down, then he was speared, on the third occasion he was killed in a stampede. Then we had to deal with those directors and writers who had this fixed idea in their head that, if you were American, you were streets better than anyone who came from the Caribbean. Our accents bothered them and they were constantly telling us to place our emphasis on a different syllable, that kind of thing. This would make us so self-conscious that we could never think ourselves into a role. We were always conscious of the demands of the director, or whoever, that we speak in a different way. So we sometimes felt we were losing control of the performance we wanted to give. I experienced a lot of that, but we never spoke out because we were afraid of not working again. Also, time costs money in this business, and we were constantly under pressure to finish a production on time. Instead, we used our intelligence to guide us through without upsetting anyone, or rocking any boats.[12]

But there was a positive side, too. Nadia acknowledges a small, but important, group of white producers and writers at the BBC who succeeded in making programmes for radio and television with black casts or themes:

John Gibson was a producer from Northern Ireland who was involved in radio drama. We did a lot of Caribbean plays for him, including *Christophe* in 1958, about Henry Christophe, the Black King of Haiti. Then there was Betty Davies, who came in the wake of John Gibson. We understood some people in the BBC renamed her 'Black Betty', because she was always producing plays with black actors in the cast. If it wasn't for people like them, we wouldn't have worked. They helped make things happen for us. I acted in a radio version of David Garnett's *The Sailor's Return* for the BBC in 1955 with Tony Britton and often broadcast for the Caribbean Service in radio plays by Caribbean dramatists like Sam Selvon, Jan Carew and Sylvia Wynter.[13]

In the 1960s Nadia enjoyed international acclaim as a folk singer, and was – briefly – the first black woman presenter of BBC radio's *Woman's Hour*.

Though *A Man from the Sun* remained the only British television drama about the lives of Caribbean settlers in post-war Britain until *The Final Passage*, there was one other television drama produced, three years after *A Man from the Sun*, which was never transmitted. *My People and Your People*, a 'West Indian Ballad Opera', was written by a white producer, D. G. Bridson, with 'additional dialogue and material' by the Jamaican writer Andrew Salkey. It started life on BBC radio and was broadcast on the Home Service on 22 July 1959. The cast included some of the best-known Caribbean actors working in Britain at that time: Edric Connor, Cy Grant, Pauline Henriques, Corinne Skinner-Carter, Pearl Nunez (Pearl Connor) and Nadia Cattouse. Cattouse remembers the production:

> D. G. Bridson wrote a musical play based in Notting Hill about a brother and sister arriving from the Caribbean. The action took place just before, during and after the riots. I played the sister, Kathy, who has a romance with a white man, Ian, played by Ewan MacColl. The music was Caribbean and arranged by Ewan MacColl and his wife, Peggy Seeger, and Tommy Eytle played his guitar. All the choral singing had been arranged by Pearl and Edric Connor with a West Indian choir. They rehearsed in a different place. One of the songs introduced in this play became very famous. It was 'The First Time Ever I Saw Your Face' which Roberta Flack later recorded and made world famous. Ewan sang it to me in the play. He had originally written it for Peggy. Afterwards, I was asked to join a folk group. Of course, when I agreed to do that, I became entirely removed from the world of radio and television acting.[14]

Nadia recalls that a television version of *My People and Your People* was pre-recorded by producer Christian Simpson and the BBC's Langham Group, with the same cast except for Ewan MacColl (John Cairney replaced him), but the production was never shown. D. G. Bridson later explained why:

> it emerged as something of a shambles. It certainly lacked all trace of the polish that he [Christian Simpson] would have given it, granted a fair chance. More important to me, it lacked all trace of the sometimes frightening authenticity which I had been able to give it on radio. I was not surprised when the production was finally written off and scrapped: I was merely relieved.[15]

On reflection, Nadia Cattouse feels that productions like *A Man from the Sun* and *My People and Your People* were made possible in the 1950s because

> there was goodwill by some white producers and writers to create drama for us. The arrival of migrants from the Caribbean, and the mark we made on this country, was captured by John Elliot in *A Man from the Sun* and later, on radio, by D. G. Bridson in *My People and Your People*. Others ignored us, or said things like Enoch Powell, which put a threat over us. In the 1960s, Powell's speeches led to hostility and attempts to either pretend we weren't here, or make sure we weren't visible.[16]

Regrettably, the radio version of *My People and Your People* was not recorded by the BBC. However, though *A Man from the Sun* was transmitted live, a telerecording was made by the BBC and, for preservation purposes, given to the National Film Archive. More than thirty years later, on 14 November 1989, a private screening of that telerecording took place at the British Film Institute. This brought together John Elliot and two of the actresses who appeared in the production: Nadia Cattouse and Pauline Henriques. It was the first time Nadia and Pauline had seen *A Man from the Sun* and, until they were contacted, neither had realized that the production had survived. Three years later, on 1 July 1992, *A Man from the Sun* was shown for the first time on television since 1956, when BBC2 included it in their *Black and White in Colour* season. However, by 1998, when Britain celebrated the fiftieth anniversary of the arrival of *Empire Windrush*, this ground-breaking television drama had been forgotten again.

Perhaps the most memorable scene in *A Man from the Sun*, and the one that has made the most lasting impression, is Errol John's appearance at the end. Writing a letter to his mother in Jamaica, shortly after his arrival in Britain, he begins, 'Hello, dear Mama; after this little time things is not too bad. I'd like to send you some money but I not got a job jus' yet. England's a wonderful strange place, but it's my home now, for better or for worse.'[17]

Errol John (1958)

Errol John was born in the Gulf of Paria, Trinidad. The year before he was born, his father, George John, was a member of a cricket team that played so well in Britain that Trinidad had to be recognized for Test status. After leaving school, Errol earned his living as a journalist and commercial artist. His real ambition, though, was to be an actor and in 1946, to gain experience, he co-founded with Errol Hill an amateur theatrical group, the Whitehall Players, in Port of Spain. For them he acted, designed, directed and wrote three one-act plays, and the company, also known as the Company of Players, had a profound influence on theatre development in the Caribbean. In 1950 Errol left Trinidad for Britain as a guest of the British Council and made a number of stage appearances. Pauline Henriques remembers Errol with affection:

> I immediately recognized his lovely personality and tremendous voice. But he was a rather shy, reserved, retiring person who found it difficult to be

with a group of actors who were taking the job of acting seriously, but also enjoying it and being very joyous about it. This wasn't Errol's scene. He found it quite hard to do that. I can remember encouraging him to try and come out of his shell and to enjoy acting – because black actors have this ability to bring a sort of inner joy and vivacity to the roles that they play. I tried to encourage this in Errol and I was right there behind him, doing a good counselling job on him. I think it gave him a good start.[18]

Errol began his film and television career as a bit player until a breakthrough occurred in 1956 with his role as Cleve in *A Man from the Sun*. In 1957, as a writer, he won the *Observer* Drama Competition (beating 2,000 competitors) with his play *Moon on a Rainbow Shawl*. He had written this in 1955 during a period of dissatisfaction with his acting career. One of the competition judges, Kenneth Tynan, described it as a 'hauntingly, hot-climate, tragi-comedy about backyard life in Trinidad'. The play was first performed when Errol adapted it for BBC radio as *Small Island Moon*. Broadcast on 27 May 1958, the cast included Errol (as Ephraim), Barbara Assoon, Robert Adams (as Charlie), Sylvia Wynter and Lionel Ngakane. A recording of this production has been kept by the BBC's Sound Archive. Later that year, when the first stage production of *Moon on a Rainbow Shawl* opened at the Royal Court Theatre on 4 December 1958 with the African-American Earle Hyman as Ephraim, it was not well received. However, when Errol adapted it for television as a *Play of the Week* production (ATV, 1960), taking the leading role of Ephraim again, television critic Peter Black showered praise upon it: 'Evidently television brought out some quality that the theatre missed. Casper Wrede's vivid production showed it to be unmistakably a work of unusual, tough, perceptive, and touching charm, filled with characters fresh and full of life.' [19] Unfortunately, this production has not survived in the archives. When *Moon on a Rainbow Shawl* was first seen in America as an off-Broadway production in 1962, directed by George Roy Hill, it received more praise from the critics. This time, James Earl Jones played Ephraim, and the cast also included Vinnette Carroll and Cicely Tyson. The *New York Times* said, '[Errol John] writes with such warmth and understanding that the problems and characters of a mean backyard in Trinidad assume a validity for a multitude of teeming, troubled places on this planet.'[20]

Meanwhile, Errol continued to work as an actor in British television and his many appearances included two plays with Gordon Heath (see Chapter 10): *For the Defence* (BBC, 1956) and *Cry, the Beloved Country*, as the young priest Msimangu (ITV, 1958). He also played a small role in the film *The Nun's Story* (1959) with Audrey Hepburn. A few years later Errol accepted offers to appear at the Old Vic in productions of Shakespeare's *The Merchant of Venice* (1962, as the Prince of Morocco) and *Othello* (1963). Unfortunately, the latter production was a disaster. Gordon Heath, who had played Othello for BBC television in 1955, felt Errol was too 'lightweight' for the role. John Elliot agrees: 'Errol was essentially a film and television actor, what I call a "close-up" actor. He didn't have the voice training to reach a large audience in a theatre. Perhaps that was one of the causes of his disquiet.'[21]

It was John Elliot who produced a television drama written by Errol for the BBC. In *The Dawn* (1963) Errol also took the leading role of an American Harvard graduate and writer who is sent to Africa to get a story about black nationalism. The following year, Errol had one of his best screen roles in *Guns at Batasi*. As Boniface, an African lieutenant who is responsible for a military coup, he gave a superb performance in a complex role. But such opportunities were rare. On reflection, it is regrettable that Errol did not play important roles in other British films of the 1960s. For example, he would have been perfect as Sylvia Syms's boyfriend in *Flame in the Streets* (1961) and the schoolteacher Mark Thackeray in *To Sir, With Love* (1967). Needless to say, he continued working in television, appearing in such popular series as *Danger Man* (ITV, 1964) and *Man in a Suitcase* (ITV, 1968).

In 1967 John Elliot cast Errol as John Steele, a Jamaican lawyer, in a six-part series for the BBC called *Rainbow City*. Recalls Elliot, who collaborated on several scripts with Trinidadian Horace James:

> About ten years after *A Man from the Sun*, I was approached by the Head of Programmes for BBC Birmingham to do a series about West Indians in this country ... There was a very strong feeling at the time that West Indians should be given the chance to be treated as people ... whose possibilities and talents were much greater than they had been allowed to show. And so with Errol John playing our chief character, we made him a professional man, a lawyer with a white wife, living in a racially mixed community in Birmingham. This was different, a shift of gear from how these things had been presented before ... I wrote it together with Horace James, a splendid, ebullient actor and writer, who had an inside view of something which I can only see from the outside.[22]

In 1969 Errol wrote *The Exiles*, his second original television drama, this time for BBC1's *The Wednesday Play* series. In *The Exiles*, Errol vividly sketched the lives of three highly literate and articulate Trinidadians who are dissatisfied with Britain, but equally ready to admit that they would be no more comfortable in Trinidad, or even Africa, which they might look to as an alternative home. Regrettably, like Errol's earlier *Moon on a Rainbow Shawl* and *The Dawn*, this television production no longer exists. Either it was transmitted live and not recorded, or recorded and wiped.

After appearing in *The Nun's Story*, Errol pursued a career in Hollywood and made occasional appearances in supporting roles, including *Assault on a Queen* (1966) with Frank Sinatra. In 1972 Sidney Poitier made his directorial debut with a Western called *Buck and the Preacher*, in which he also starred opposite Harry Belafonte. Errol found himself cast in a small supporting role, but he has no lines. It is embarrassing to see this fine actor being wasted as nothing more than a 'glorified extra'.

From time to time, Errol continued to surface on British television. Then, in 1986, he directed the first British stage production for nearly thirty years of *Moon on a Rainbow Shawl* for Philip Hedley, theatre director of the Theatre Royal, Stratford East. Hedley was committed to staging work by black dramatists, and creating opportunities for black actors:

> A serious turning-point in my commitment to Black theatre came under the tutelage of Errol John, author of *Moon on a Rainbow Shawl*. I remember my first meeting with Errol in my flat. He was a handsome, intense, sharply intelligent man with a burning ambition, which was to direct a production of his play ... [in 1958 it] had been directed by a highly regarded White, West End director. Errol was so angered by this unreal and sentimental production that he'd sworn he wouldn't allow another production in Britain until he could direct it himself ... the obvious breadth of Errol's humanity overcame my doubts. [23]

Joanne Campbell was cast as Mavis in this production, the role played by Barbara Assoon in the 1958 Royal Court Theatre production. Joanne recalls Errol's directing style:

> Errol John was a reserved, disciplined man. He was also a true gentleman. I loved working with him. For our production of *Moon on a Rainbow Shawl* Errol insisted that we have Barbara Assoon and Errol Jones brought over from Trinidad to be in the cast. In rehearsal Errol John encouraged the younger actors to learn about Trinidad from the older actors. He was interested in the younger actors, and how we were growing and developing. Errol rehearsed the play like a film: for instance, he gave us, the actors, the kind of attention and detail of a film. He would come very close to us, like a camera. Directors soon have an intuition, and become technically proficient but, for me, a director who is also an actor has more intimate energy. They are 'in' the scene with you. But it was interesting working with a *black* director who had acting experience. Errol brought an essence of film to

theatre. Two years later, Errol gave permission to London's Almeida Theatre to stage the play again on condition he direct. So he was hurt and angry when the Almeida asked Maya Angelou instead. Errol never bad-mouthed people. He always found something positive to say, but it was difficult to know what he thought about Maya. He wasn't angry with her, just with the lack of respect shown to him.[24]

Shortly after the Almeida Theatre production of *Moon on a Rainbow Shawl* closed on 4 June, Errol died in London on 10 July 1988. In his obituary in the *Independent*, Philip Hedley described Errol as a man who

> got a reputation for being 'difficult', which is often the case with actors who ask intelligent questions of directors, or who are prepared to take a stand on principle. He was a respected, highly professional artist and a very proud man, with many qualities which justified his pride.[25]

Pearl Connor regrets that he did not receive the acclaim he deserved:

> Errol became more and more frustrated about not achieving what he thought he would achieve ... He was a very versatile man, a brilliant actor and a talented writer ... He had the sort of achievements which, when they happen to a white actor, mean that person receives a great deal of recognition. But that didn't happen for Errol and eventually he was brought down to his knees, with the frustration of not getting things done. His talent was always there but the ability to project it wasn't. He virtually dropped out altogether ... Isolated, lonely, feeling forgotten and dejected, he died alone in his bed – he was found by his landlady. It was a tragic end to one of our most talented artistes.[26]

NOTES

1 Maya Jaggi, 'The final passage: an interview with writer Caryl Phillips', in Kwesi Owusu (ed.), *Black British Culture and Society: A Text Reader* (London: Routledge, 2000), pp. 157–168.

2 *Ibid.*

3 John Elliot, interview with Therese Daniels, in Jim Pines (ed.), *Black and White in Colour: Black People in British Television Since 1936* (London: British Film Institute, 1992), pp. 88–9.

4 Pauline Henriques, interview with Stephen Bourne, *ibid.*, p. 30.

5 Nadia Cattouse, interview with Stephen Bourne, London, 8 August 1989.

6 *A Man from the Sun* camera script, p. 21. Courtesy of John Elliot.

7 Pauline Henriques, interview with Stephen Bourne, Brighton, 4 August 1989.

8 Cattouse, interview with Bourne.

9 Caroline Lang, *Keep Smiling Through: Women in the Second World War* (Cambridge: Cambridge University Press, 1989), p. 36.

10 Kenneth Passingham, 'Nadia: fighting off that great black cloud of despair', *TV Times*, 11–17 August 1970.

11 Cattouse, interview with Bourne.

12 *Ibid.*

13 *Ibid.*

14 *Ibid.*

15 D. G. Bridson, *Prospero and Ariel: The Rise and Fall of Radio – A Personal Recollection* (London: Victor Gollancz, 1971), p. 256.

16 Cattouse, interview with Bourne.

17 *A Man from the Sun* camera script, p. 63.

18 Henriques, interview with Bourne, in Pines (ed.), *Black and White in Colour*, pp. 29–30.

19 Peter Black, unidentified press cutting.

20 *New York Times*, date unknown.

21 John Elliot, letter to Stephen Bourne, 11 February 1996.

22 Elliot, interview with Daniels, in Pines (ed.), *Black and White in Colour*, p. 89.

23 Philip Hedley, 'A theatre director's journey to the obvious', in Tunde Ikoli, *Scrape Off the Black* (London: Oberon Books, 1998), p. 10.

24 Joanne Campbell, interview with Stephen Bourne, London, 4 January 1997.

25 Philip Hedley, *Independent*, 19 July 1988.

26 Pearl Connor, interview with Bourne, in Pines (ed.), *Black and White in Colour*, p. 41.

FURTHER READING

Vivienne Francis, *With Hope in Their Eyes* (London: Nia, an imprint of The X Press, 1998).

Hammersmith and Fulham Ethnic Communities Oral History Project, *The Motherland Calls: African Caribbean Experiences* (1989); *'Sorry No Vacancies': Life Stories of Senior Citizens from the Caribbean* (1992) in collaboration with the Notting Dale Urban Studies Centre; and *A Ship and a Prayer: The Black Presence in Hammersmith and Fulham*, edited by Stephen Bourne and Sav Kyriacou (1999).

Sam King, *Climbing up the Rough Side of the Mountain* (London: Minerva Press, 1998).

Mike Phillips and Trevor Phillips, *Windrush: The Irresistible Rise of Multi-Racial Britain* (London: HarperCollins, 1998).

Tony Sewell, *Keep on Moving: The Windrush Legacy* (London: Voice Enterprises Ltd, 1998).

Onyekachi Wambu, *Empire Windrush: Fifty Years of Writing About Black Britain* (London: Victor Gollancz, 1998).

13

Lloyd Reckord and Lionel Ngakane

Actors with Movie Cameras

In 1958 the Jamaican actor Lloyd Reckord gave a memorable performance on the London stage in Ted Willis's controversial play *Hot Summer Night*. It was produced at the New Theatre in Shaftesbury Avenue at the height of the so-called 'Angry Young Man' period. Willis later claimed in his autobiography that it was the first drama to confront racism in Britain: 'the play garnered rave notices. "Red Hot Summer Night" was a typical critical response. Another less pleasant reaction came in the form of some hate mail in which I was dubbed a "nigger lover" and "white coon".'[1]

In Willis's hard-hitting drama, the liberal attitudes of Jack Palmer (John Slater), a white working-class trade union leader are put to the test when his daughter, Kathie (Andree Melly), falls in love with a Jamaican. Lloyd was cast as the Jamaican, Sonny Lincoln, an angry young *black* man – rarely seen on the London stage – who confronts the trade union leader with a few home truths. He later recalled:

> I can't remember receiving any flack over the play's controversial inter-racial relationship. The newspapers made a big deal of it. There was a full-page picture and headline saying 'First time on London stage, Black man kisses White girl', that sort of nonsense ... But I can remember one incident which occurred during one of the Saturday matinee performances. It was rather pathetic. It was during the scene when I kiss Andree Melly. A frail, rather timid and very gentle voice called out from the stalls – 'I don't like to see white girls kissing niggers'. There was dead silence in the theatre, and we went on with the play.[2]

Lloyd became involved in amateur theatricals in Jamaica before he left

125

for Britain in 1951 to study at the Bristol Old Vic Theatre School. In 1954 he directed an early version of his brother Barry Reckord's play *Della* at a small London theatre. Back in Jamaica in 1956, he started the Actors' Company, for which he directed and acted in foreign plays, including Arthur Miller's *The Crucible*, and a number of original Caribbean plays. Returning to London, he appeared with Cleo Laine at the Royal Court Theatre in his brother's play *Flesh to a Tiger* (1958), which was quickly followed by *Hot Summer Night*. In 1959 a television version was produced by the dynamic Canadian Sydney Newman, famous for his popular *Armchair Theatre* series. Slater, Reckord and Melly re-created their stage roles.

After *Hot Summer Night*, Reckord found himself typecast as, he said, 'nice young West Indians in love with English girls'. On television these included a second version of Eugene O'Neill's *All God's Chillun' Got Wings* (Associated Rediffusion, 1959) and his brother's play *You in Your Small Corner* (Granada, 1962). But the young actor wanted to direct. He wrote an impressionistic, semi-autobiographical twelve-minute short called *Ten Bob in Winter* and successfully applied to the British Film Institute for funding. Produced, directed and narrated by Reckord, this wry comedy of manners is set in the Ladbroke Grove area of London, and relates the experiences of African-Caribbean migrants as seen through the eyes of an unemployed student during a Christmas vacation. First shown in 1963, *Ten Bob in Winter* is now acknowledged as the first fiction film made by a black film-maker in Britain. Two years later Reckord's second short film, *Dream A40*, was released. Unlike his first film, this is a strange, but compelling experimental drama which explores a gay man's fears about his sexuality and physical attraction to another man. Recalled Reckord:

> I made it because I wanted to get into television production, but the film was entirely ignored, perhaps because I was too frank about homosexuality. The story came from a dream I had, and I built on that. It was a rather frightening dream. *Dream A40* is a frank statement on homosexual guilt. Instead of fantasizing about boy meets girl, I thought, well, let's try to be honest and make an interesting statement from my own experience. I didn't use black actors in the main parts, though I talked to a few of them about it. The black actors I spoke to would have had a more difficult time afterwards than the white actors for playing gays. Being gay in the Caribbean is less acceptable than Britain. Though homosexuality was illegal in Britain at that time, there was no law about making a film about gays, and I was interested in making a film that made a mark, that said something about the times we were living in, and the fear and guilt some gay men felt at that time. I was being defiant.[3]

Though Reckord made two impressive short films, he discovered that there was no place for a black director at the BBC at that time, as he later recalled:

> I remember going to the BBC and talking to a young director who had come in as a trainee. Originally he had been a young actor in the theatre and had worked with me as a walk-on at the Old Vic. Now, here he was, one of the BBC's latest recruits on a directors' programme. This sort of thing made me a little unhappy because, I thought, 'I haven't heard that so-and-so directed anything, or showed initiative by going out to make a film with his own money, which I have done twice.' Yet nobody, at any time, offered me a break as a trainee director in television. Soon afterwards I left Britain for good because I'd had enough.[4]

In 1968 Reckord returned to Jamaica and founded the National Theatre Trust, which has been described as 'a first-class company of actors performing a large and varied repertory of outstanding West Indian plays, the classics, and some of the best contemporary world drama'.[5] In the first two decades Reckord produced over forty such plays as well as introducing to Jamaican audiences a festival of Cuban films in 1971, and the Harlem Dance Theatre Company in 1973. His one-man show, *Beyond the Blues* – a collection of black writing from Africa, the Caribbean and the USA – toured successfully for many years, culminating in 1982 with performances at the National Theatre's Cottesloe Theatre in London.

When Lionel Ngakane first came to Britain from South Africa in 1950 to work as a journalist, he heard that Zoltan Korda was planning to direct a film version of Alan Paton's novel *Cry, the Beloved Country*. When Korda agreed to be interviewed by Lionel about the production, he was so impressed with the young man that he offered him a job as his personal assistant and technical adviser. He also gave him an acting role in the film. Lionel was cast as Absalom, the 'lost' son of the village priest, Reverend Stephen Kumalo (Canada Lee), who is imprisoned and executed for killing a white man. The scenes between Ngakane and Canada Lee in the prison are sensitively acted and they both give deeply felt performances. But off screen, Lionel's ambitions lay elsewhere. He wanted to become a film director.

Lionel was born in Pretoria, South Africa, where his parents worked as teachers. After moving to Johannesburg in 1936, his father set up a hostel for young delinquents with Alan Paton. It was around this time that Lionel's passion for cinema began when he saw his first film:

Lionel Ngakane and Canada Lee in *Cry, the Beloved Country* (1952)

I was seven years old when I saw my first film. There was an open-air cinema where a group of whites would bring films once a month: Westerns and Charlie Chaplin comedies. I didn't kick the habit even when I went to school and I used to go to the cinema every Saturday. I remember the first films with Lena Horne such as *Cabin in the Sky*. They were the first times that blacks appeared on the screen.[6]

One day Lionel's father came home with a 35mm projector as a present for his son. Lionel then collected small strips of film and projected them onto a wall at his home, upsetting his family when the film burned in the projector. At university in South Africa, Lionel studied political philosophy, geography and native administration (colonial and South African black administration), but these hardly prepared him for his job as Head of Wheels (maintenance) on the Johannesburg buses. As a freelance journalist, Lionel contributed to *Zonk* and *Drum*, two of South Africa's most successful black magazines, and it was as a journalist that he came to Britain, met Zoltan Korda and accepted his first acting role in *Cry, the Beloved Country*. Originally, Sidney Poitier had been considered for the role of Absalom Kumalo, but Korda cast Lionel after screen-testing both actors. Poitier played Reverend Msimangu instead, not realizing that the

128

South African authorities would only permit him to enter South Africa as Zolton Korda's 'indentured servant'. In 1981 he described this rude awakening in his autobiography:

> I was barely through customs when I noticed signs saying 'Bantu' and 'White'. Damn, I thought, nobody told me this. I got into a car with a representative from the film company for the ride into the city. I had visions of flopping down onto a comfortable bed as soon as I hit my hotel and sleeping for days. Little did I know. We drove for a long time, but I saw no signs of the city. Finally, we came to a little farm with a little house way out in the woods. 'What's this?' I asked. He said, 'This is where you're going to stay.' I said, 'Why? How come?' He gave me no response ... Canada Lee gave me a tour of the little house and the yard surrounding it before sitting me down in my room and easing me gently into the cold, stark facts of our situation. 'You know, we're officially here as indentured laborers. We are vouched for by Zoltan Korda.' Then he began to explain all the ramifications of South African society as it relates to black people. He said ... 'black people aren't allowed in the hotels. We're facing from twelve to sixteen weeks of work here, so let's do our work and get the hell out.'[7]

After filming *Cry, the Beloved Country*, Lionel returned to Britain and planned to become a film-maker, but he faced difficulties:

> Zoltan Korda encouraged me to become a film-maker, but I couldn't get any sponsorship from the South African government, or anybody else, and there were no film schools in this country. There were two film schools I could have gone to in Italy or Russia, but it was impossible for me to go to those countries because the South African government refused to give me a scholarship. Instead I bought a car, a 16mm camera, and experimented. To earn a living I continued working as an actor.[8]

For several years Lionel played supporting roles in British films made on location in Africa with titles like *Duel in the Jungle* (1954), *Safari* (1956) and *Odongo* (1956). But he felt these exploited Africa, providing nothing more than exotic backdrops for glamorous Hollywood stars like Dana Andrews, Jeanne Crain, Rhonda Fleming, Victor Mature and Janet Leigh. However, working on these films enabled the young actor to learn something about the technical side of film-making. In 1962 Lionel released his first film:

> The result of experimenting with my 16mm camera was a short film called *Sunday in London*, and this gave me the confidence to make a film by myself. I visited my home in South Africa and made a seventeen-minute documentary called *Vukani/Awake*, the first film about the political situation

in South Africa made from an African's point of view. Subsequently, it was shown all over the world during the anti-apartheid campaigns.[9]

For his second film, Lionel turned his attention to Britain. *Jemima and Johnny* was filmed in the early 1960s in the aftermath of the Notting Hill riots:

> During the time of the Notting Hill riots I was rehearsing in the area for a BBC television play called *The Green Pastures* and there were many black actors in the cast. Things got so bad outside with the rioters that the BBC had to arrange for us to be bussed out of our rehearsal room in Notting Hill with a police escort. I remember thinking I'd like to make a film about the relationship between black and white people in Britain, and the lack of understanding between them. I felt prejudice wasn't something you inherit. *Jemima and Johnny* cost me £5,000. It took me a year to raise that money and Peter Sellers gave me £1,000 of that. Derek Knight of Knight Films also helped me out by providing me with a production base. It was partly funded by the National Film Corporation and shot in 1963.[10]

Filmed in 35mm and black and white, with no dialogue, *Jemima and Johnny* is a charming short drama about the friendship between a black girl and a white boy, inspired by the French film classic *The Red Balloon* (1955):

> In 1964 it was the official entry for Britain in the Venice Film Festival, and won first prize for Best Short Feature Film. I was thrilled that we had won first prize representing Britain, and confident that I would make more films. But I never had one offer, or enquiry. I had high hopes, but people did not come to me. Years later I had this nagging feeling that, if I had been white, my career as a film-maker would have been different as a result of that prize.[11]

For several years *Jemima and Johnny* was shown all over Britain as a support to popular feature films like *Bonnie and Clyde* but, by the 1970s, it had disappeared from view. In the late 1980s it resurfaced and, thanks to June Givanni, then working as the head of the British Film Institute's African-Caribbean Unit, Lionel's film attracted attention with a screening on television by Channel 4 and distribution on video by the British Film Institute.

Aside from acting and film-making, Lionel became a founder member of two important institutions in African cinema – FEPACI (The Pan-African Film-makers' Federation) and FESPACO (The Pan-African Film Festival of Ouagadougou) – both of which represented Southern Africa and encouraging links between the African continent and Europe. June Givanni, speaking in 1994, described his ambitions for African cinema:

> In spite of the fact that he has been based in England, he has worked continuously for African Cinema. So it was no surprise that three months after South Africa's historic elections, he is poised to return with a strong plan of action. Internal problems in South Africa regarding cinema have to be addressed. A new National Cinema policy and the creation of a National Film School, are government initiatives he hopes to encourage and influence. Personally, his main task is to establish cinemas in the townships and to get worthwhile films onto the screens there. . . . The initiative has all the hallmarks of Lionel's philosophy as a self-taught and self-financed film-maker: if it's to survive and to be taken seriously then do it yourself, do it independently, do it commercially, but with integrity.[12]

NOTES

1 Ted Willis, *Evening All: Fifty Years over a Hot Typewriter* (London: Macmillan, 1991), pp. 145–6.
2 Lloyd Reckord, interview with Stephen Bourne, in Jim Pines (ed.), *Black and White in Colour: Black People in British Television Since 1936* (London: British Film Institute, 1992), p. 52.
3 Lloyd Reckord, interview with Stephen Bourne, London, 14 August 1991.
4 Reckord, interview with Bourne, in Pines (ed.), *Black and White in Colour*, p. 55.
5 *The Cambridge Guide to African and Caribbean Theatre*, edited by Martin Banham, Errol Hill and George Woodyard (Cambridge: Cambridge University Press, 1994), p. 214.
6 Lionel Ngakane, *Ecrans d'Afrique*, No. 11, 1995, pp. 11–12.
7 Sidney Poitier, *This Life* (London: Hodder and Stoughton, 1980), pp. 147–9.
8 Lionel Ngakane, interview with Stephen Bourne, *Black Arts in London*, No. 103, August 1988, p. 16.
9 Ngakane, interview with Bourne.
10 *Ibid*.
11 *Ibid*.
12 June Givanni, 'Return to the beloved country', *Black Film Bulletin*, Vol. 2, No. 2, Summer 1994, p. 3.

14

Carmen Munroe

Standing in the Light

On 20 February 1996 one of Britain's most successful black actresses, Carmen Munroe, was interviewed on stage by television presenter Brenda Emmanus at the Museum of the Moving Image in London. This was the fourth event in the *Black on White TV* television retrospective programmed for the National Film Theatre by Stephen Bourne. The interview has been transcribed and edited for this chapter. Before Carmen and Brenda appeared on stage, there was a screening of *Ted* (Anglia, 1972), in which she played a leading role as a nurse who helps rehabilitate a victim of a car crash, followed by extracts from *Rainbow City* (BBC, 1967), *Dr Who* (BBC, 1968), *General Hospital* (ATV, 1976) and *Encounters (A Song at Twilight)* (BBC, 1992), in which she played Paul Robeson's wife, Eslanda. Michael Abbensetts's play *Black Christmas* (BBC, 1977) and an extract from Channel 4's *Desmond's* had already been shown in a tribute to Norman Beaton on 6 February.

Carmen was born in New Amsterdam, Berbice, Guyana (then British Guiana). Her father, George Fitzgerald Steele, was a chemist who worked for the British government. Her mother, Maude Ernestine Plowell, taught piano. Carmen was educated in Smith's Church and Enterprise High School, graduating with the Cambridge University Senior School Certificate. She came to Britain in 1951, studied ophthalmic optics for a year, and then worked as a librarian in Tooting, South London. In 1957 Carmen joined the West Indian Drama Group, founded in 1956 by Joan Clarke, a Unity Theatre activist. The group was based at the West Indian Students' Union in Collingham Gardens, south-west London. Though not yet a professional actress, Carmen made an early stage appearance as Marthy Owen in the group's production of Eugene O'Neill's *Anna Christie*. This was produced by Joan Clarke and may have been the first time *Anna Christie* had been performed by an all-black cast. It was staged for the Unity Theatre in 1959.

Carmen made her professional stage debut in 1962 in Tennessee Williams's *Period of Adjustment* (Royal Court and Wyndham's Theatre) and later played several important roles in West End productions, including Alun Owen's *There'll Be Some Changes Made* (Fortune Theatre, 1969) and Jean Genet's *The Blacks* (Round House, 1970). When she played Orinthia, the King's mistress, in George Bernard Shaw's *The Apple Cart* (Mermaid Theatre, 1970), it was the first time she had been cast in a leading role that had not been written for a black actress. Since that time, Carmen has played an active role in the development of black theatre in Britain, including appearances in a number of productions by black dramatists: Caryl Phillips (*Strange Fruit*), Michael Abbensetts (*El Dorado*) and Edgar White (*Redemption Song*). In Lorraine Hansberry's *A Raisin in the Sun* (Tricycle Theatre and the Drill Hall Arts Centre, 1985) Carmen enjoyed a personal triumph as the matriarch Lena Younger. In 1987 Carmen again received critical acclaim as the charismatic Harlem gospel preacher Sister Margaret in James Baldwin's *The Amen Corner* at the Lyric Theatre. Said Giles Gordon in the *London Daily News* (18 March 1987), 'It is a complex performance of tragic magnificence, touching greatness.' In 1993, when she played Wiletta Mayer in Alice Childress's *Trouble in Mind* at the Tricycle Theatre, Rick Jones in the *Evening Standard* (14 October 1993) described Carmen as 'very much the star of the show. Her angry caricaturing of stereotypes in the third act is a brilliant *tour de force*.' For her performance in *Trouble in Mind*, she received a Best Actress award from the magazine *Time Out*. In 1995 Carmen appeared in Lorca's *The House of Bernarda Alba* at the Brixton Shaw Theatre and in 1996 she was seen in Lord Byron's *Cain – A Mystery* at the Barbican's Pit Theatre.

Carmen made her television debut in 1959 and, since that time, she has shown her versatility in numerous popular dramas and sitcoms, as well as impressive single plays. These have included John Hopkins's *Fable* (BBC, 1965), *Armchair Theatre* (*Love Life*) (ABC, 1967), *The Fosters* (LWT, 1976–77), *Crown Court* (Granada, 1976), *Mixed Blessings* (LWT, 1978-80), *Playhouse* (*By George*) (BBC, 1982), *Rumpole of the Bailey* (Thames, 1983) and *Screen Two* (*Great Moments in Aviation*) (BBC, 1995). Carmen has also acted in a number of important television dramas by black writers, including Barry Reckord's *Play for Today* (*In the Beautiful Caribbean*) (BBC, 1972), Alfred Fagon's *Shakespeare Country* (BBC, 1973), Horace Ové's *Play for Today* (*A Hole in Babylon*) (BBC, 1979) and three by Caryl Phillips: *The Hope and the Glory* (BBC, 1984), *Bacchanal* (*The Record*) (Channel 4, 1984) and *The Final Passage* (Channel 4, 1996). She was also seen in excerpts from *The Amen Corner* in *Mavis on 4* (Channel 4, 1987), in which Mavis Nicholson interviewed James Baldwin.

On 5 January 1989 Carmen was first seen in *Desmond's*, one of Channel 4's most successful and durable sitcoms. Co-starring Norman Beaton as the proprietor of a barber's shop in Peckham, south-east London, *Desmond's* was one of the few British television series to feature an almost entirely black cast. For five years (until it ended on 19 December 1994) this popular series won critical acclaim for its humorous exploration of the conflict between young British-born blacks and the values of the older generation who grew up in the Caribbean.

The following interview with Carmen Munroe and Brenda Emmanus is reproduced with kind permission of the National Film Theatre, London.

Brenda: When we were watching *Ted* you said, 'Oh, my God. I can't remember this. I haven't seen it.' Was it a shock for you?
Carmen: Yes.
Brenda: What went through your head as you watched?
Carmen: The big hair. I thought, 'God, she's got big hair.'
Brenda: You looked sexy, though.
Carmen: Is that what sexy is?
Brenda: Undoubtedly!

Brenda Emmanus and Carmen Munroe at the Museum of the Moving Image (1996)

Carmen: So now I know. I was pleased to watch it and I was pleased with what I did. I've learned since that a lot of the time we are afraid, not of our failures, but to stand in our light. And that is the reason I am here tonight. I couldn't possibly be present at a tribute. I didn't go off and climb Mount Everest by myself. I had people around me at the time who cared and wanted to see something happen of value. I thought *Ted* was of great value. It was funny in places. Very dated. But what was going through my mind was 'Go girl'.

Brenda: You once said that particular role was significant in that it gave you responsibility. It gave you a character of substance. Do you remember saying that?

Carmen: Yes, because *Ted* was probably the longest I'd been on the screen, in front of a camera. So from that point of view, yes, I had to sustain a part for a long period rather than come in, do my thing, add a bit of 'colour' to the scene, then leave. But in *Ted* one had to be believable over a long period. So that was the challenge for me. I had to make people believe she was a real person.

Brenda: Did your early life in Guyana have any influence on your career?

Carmen: Yes. Mostly from my mother. I only realized this in the last five years, how much she was responsible for the work that I do. She taught piano, but had a love of language. She read a lot, and imparted that to her children. She'd say, 'Fill your moments with something valuable.' And it was usually a book. A lot of West Indians will recognize what I am saying. It was always 'to the book. In there you will find the life you can possibly lead, the words that you need to live with, and live by in the future.' So from that point of view, yes, my Guyanese influence was through my mother.

Brenda: So did your desire to become an actress come from turning the pages of the book?

Carmen: Yes, I suppose 'actress' is the word, but it was more a desire to live as these people. Like the Lady of the Camelias. I died every night I went to bed.

Brenda: So you're a drama queen?

Carmen: Yes! Very quietly, though. Not upfront. In a little corner. Also, I wanted very much to dance. I watched work by Martha Graham. Later, I earned money dancing in cabaret here in London.

Brenda: You once said West Indians went to America to get rich, to England to be educated, and you chose England.

Carmen: Yes, because I was serious. When you returned to Guyana from America, you were well-dressed, glamorous, like the movies ...

Brenda: But America's the perfect place for a drama queen ...

Carmen: Well, I don't know. Even though I saw myself as a drama queen, there was this element of seriousness about life and there always was this feeling, when I grew up in Guyana, that you had to be serious. For your life you have to be educated, do something useful, and create something of value for mankind. So when I came to this country to work and study, that was real, that made a lot of sense to people back home. So I missed out on America.

Brenda: So you came here, worked as a librarian, and then joined a theatre group. Was that your introduction to acting?

Carmen: Yes. It was a great time. I joined the West Indian Students' Union. We met in this huge, wonderful building on the corner of Collingham Gardens, and students met other students. There were people from all walks of life. Mostly artists, and writers like Andrew Salkey and C. L. R. James. There was a lot of activity. It was marvellous. And if you couldn't get home, you put two chairs together and slept on them until morning. Also, we felt we were related to a bigger picture. When we came to England we quickly realized the Mother Country didn't know us, what we were, or what we were capable of. So we had this low expectation until we became part of the West Indian Students' Union, and began to raise our level of expectation. So we had this drive. We had to replace all the old attitudes with a new feeling. The feeling was that we were all away from home, so this meeting place helped us form relationships which were strong, very rich, supportive, caring and, above all, honest. I say that now because, today, honesty is missing, and I do regret it. And I'm talking about the acting profession.

Some of the actors I befriended included Leonie Forbes and Charles Hyatt from Jamaica. I also remember Horace James, who came from Trinidad. He would sit down, translate and transform Chekhov, and other classics, and take us all over Britain, performing wherever we could, in town halls, at universities. I remember travelling up to Leicester University, staying overnight, sleeping rough, and all the time being helped and pushed by people like Horace and Pearl Connor, who also came from Trinidad.

Brenda: So was it easy to take this work around the country?

Carmen: We made it possible. We didn't work for any money. We just knew we had to do it, because we felt there was a gap in the understanding of our culture, where we came from and who we were. We loved doing it. I also worked as a dancer with people like Boscoe Holder and toured up and down the country with Edmundo Ros and His Orchestra. Can you imagine doing limbo to an organ? In Scunthorpe? But I did.

Brenda: You mentioned Pearl Connor, who campaigned on behalf of black actors.

Carmen: She stuck her neck out. She made herself into an agent and handled actors, writers and models. She said, 'Our models don't work as much as your models, so if you're going to pay your models £4 an hour, our models have to have £5.' And she got it! That was the sort of woman she was.

Brenda: Your first professional stage appearance was in Tennessee Williams's *Period of Adjustment* in 1962.

Carmen: Yes, that's when I got my Equity card. I played a maid. She was called Susie and afterwards I decided, 'Well, I've played that maid, and she's the only maid I'm going to play.' There was nothing wrong with the maid, and I have nothing against maids, but I knew that if I allowed myself to continue to do this, I wouldn't be doing myself, the people who employed me, or the other artists any favours.

Brenda: Did you know exactly what you wanted to do?

Carmen: In a way, yes. There weren't specific roles, but there was an all-over role that I had to play. That was to improve myself, polish my life. And I could never separate myself from the whole picture at any time. I was always aware of what was necessary. I could see the whole picture. That was my plan. To understand how, with my life, I could improve, and to spread into all areas of my life.

Brenda: That was pretty unselfish thinking considering the lack of roles, and that you had to earn your bread and butter.

Carmen: Yes, but I've never seen my life or work in terms of competition. The only competition I am involved with is how I was yesterday, how I am today and how much better I can be tomorrow. You see, always you were working with people who were constantly working. Other indigenous actors. So there was always this feeling that you were playing a catch-up game. You were always so many steps behind. Not in principle, or in fact, but as it manifested in the work situation. You were always catching up.

Brenda: A lot of your early television work is missing.

Carmen: Not only is some of it missing, but most of it I haven't seen, because in those days I couldn't afford a television set! But having said that, I find it extremely embarrassing watching myself.

Brenda: Tell us about Jean Genet's *The Blacks*, in which you appeared with an all-black cast.

Carmen: It's a classic. A beautiful piece of writing. Very controversial and confrontational. This production encouraged me to push, and I enjoyed it because it was hard work, and challenging.

Brenda: You said in an interview that the late 1960s and early 1970s was a period of real creative excitement with lots of work.

Carmen: Oh, not just for me, but generally things were happening. New writers, West Indian writers, black writers. New work was coming on the

137

scene because we were breaking through and creating another dimension. We had ceased to adapt other people's work. We were doing our own work. You see, we were always expected to explain ourselves, to represent, which is frustrating, but necessary, because with every era, every period, you use the weapons at your disposal. It could have been better. Always when you look back, it could have been better.

Brenda: I have to ask you about John Hopkins's television play *Fable*, which you have described as a frightening play to have been in, and one of the most radical pieces of work you did at that time.

Carmen: It was exciting. Hopkins took the apartheid situation, turned it round, where the blacks were white, and the whites were black, and that was a dangerous thing to do. I was amazed he got it on. It wouldn't be shown now. They'd be worried it might stir up ideas of violence. But I think it should be shown to encourage people to have a debate.

Brenda: You have mentioned that there came a time in your career when you felt used and were just being cast to dress the set.

Carmen: I have said no to work in the past because I didn't think that I would be happy doing it, but when I said I felt used it was because I felt I did a good job, we all did, and then we were dropped and forgotten, and then every time we were given another opportunity, we felt we were being 'discovered' again. We had to play catch-up. Every job that I did I was 'discovered'. Sometimes black actors were cast who were not good. They were used because it was felt they would look good on the screen. It was a patronizing situation. People thought we were 'naturals' and didn't need experience or training. If you want slaves portrayed, you don't want an actor, you want a slave. And that is when I felt used, because nobody expected me to do anything. It's quite different when someone is making demands on you, giving you something to reach for.

Brenda: Surely with the lack of quality roles there must have been some competitiveness. When you were given a quality role, did you feel you had to be much, much better, and make a mark on the director?

Carmen: That wouldn't come because I am an African-Caribbean, that would come with what I wanted to do with the role. I would do the best I can, better than I've ever done. Shine. Create some kind of life. But I wouldn't do that because I feel I am competing with anybody else. As I say, I am always in competition with myself.

Brenda: Can I ask you about *General Hospital*?

Carmen: Oh, yes. Sister Washington. Jason Rose had been playing the African-Caribbean doctor in that and he'd been saying, 'Look, you have a ward full of nurses, and not one of them is black! That doesn't happen in any hospital.' Jason said to me, 'I'm going to talk to them. I think they should employ you.' And he did. And *they* did! So I found myself with this script and Sister said a few words. I thought, 'She's not going to just say a few words, she's going to *say* a few words!' And that's what I did! After lunch, Sister was given a name: *Washington*! At the end of recording my first episode I went to the bar with the cast, and someone came up to me and said, 'Would you like to do another episode?' And what I am saying in my head is, 'I am making you do that.' That was my mission.

Member of the audience: It is such a pleasure to see you on a screen this size, and to see how much the camera loves you. With black actors on the screen there is so much presence in the eye and the face that there's this constant tension between the trite things they have to say, and this incredible frame-filling image. For me, that is the most striking thing about watching you on a big screen, a great stillness, and such quality in your performance. It is beautiful to see. How do you, from your vantage point, see this ark of achievement, and do you think individuals brought this, or a groundswell of contributors?

Carmen: There has always been this ark. We're diminishing now. I feel disheartened every time I look at the screen and see something like *Pride and Prejudice* or *Sense and Sensibility* that will exclude most of the artists living in this country, minority ethnic artists. These things need to be done, but they come in waves, and everything has to be *Brideshead Revisited* or *Sense and Sensibility*. We're always having to come from behind.

Brenda: Does that exhaust you?

Carmen: Yes. The pain of being in it, that is what is exhausting.

Brenda: In the past you have spoken about a time in the 1970s when the work started to dry up. Can you tell us about that period.

Carmen: After the 1960s the directors who were exciting to work with left us and went to America. So, at auditions, I had to face new directors who were asking me questions like, 'What have you done?' New people were getting in on the act, but they knew nothing of what had come before. This happened mostly in television work.

Brenda: Do you feel you have a personal responsibility for the roles you accept?

Carmen: Yes, I do, because I don't want to embarrass myself or anybody else.

Member of the audience: What message would you give the young people today about the apprenticeship you have to serve, and how to stay with it?

Carmen: The only thing I would say is, 'Stay with it.' If you've got something you feel you want to do, something you want to create, stay with it. You have to have a sense of self, a centred self as opposed to being self-centred, you have to have goals. You don't need to shift them, and sometimes you will be thrown off course. To young people I would say,

'Keep your goal in your sights, whatever you want to do. All life is a struggle, but if you are thrown off too easily, then you didn't want it in the first place. Don't make youth a problem for yourself, the next job is the one.' I'm an eternal optimist. I harness all that I've learned, and take it with me on the road, because things will change.

Brenda: What do you think of the new generation, people like Trix Worrell, Isaac Julien, the Bibi Crew, the Posse?

Carmen: It's lovely to see it happening ... and I want to see it go on. You sitting here talking to me. I've never been interviewed by a black woman in my life!

Brenda: Now I'm embarrassed.

Carmen: Who did *you* see? What made *you* want to do this?

Brenda: The newsreader, Moira Stuart. Who inspired you?

Carmen: The books and the words. American actresses like Ethel Waters and Hattie McDaniel.

Member of the audience: But they played maids.

Carmen: Yes, but they were struggling actresses, and you have to work with the time that you live in. They had to play maids because you can't change anything from the outside, you have to be in it and change it from within.

Member of the audience: I am forty-seven now but I remember as a child seeing people like Paul Robeson and Marian Anderson when they visited the Caribbean. Marian Anderson made an impact all over the world and she influenced every black opera singer who came after her. So it is not true to say all our role models were maids, because Marian Anderson was not like that. However, we seldom see any positive role models from this country and, when we do, it is not easily available. I cannot find *Desmond's* on video. When I go into Blockbusters it is not there. Now that Norman Beaton has died, it is economic sense to have *Desmond's* on video on sale in W. H. Smith's so our children will have access to it.

Carmen: That is true, but we have young people doing something about that.

Brenda: Do you see television as a medium for radical change?

Carmen: There should be change everywhere. Not just television. We have to look at the whole picture or we will not know how to change it.

Brenda: You have had success and made changes through *Desmond's*, and you have been quoted as saying that the success of *Desmond's* was the fact that it was real, with black people in situations where they would be, saying things they would say, doing things they would do.

Carmen: It was new, exciting and good. It was appealing, entertaining and the characters were believable. You see, in the early days we felt we had to explain ourselves, which is not a bad thing, but today we can go out and say something else about the human condition. I may sound over-tolerant, but I maintain that we have to work with what we've got. The conflict and the pain comes when you overlook it, you've moved away and you're struggling, but you don't know what you're struggling with.

Brenda: But do we work within the mainstream, or go off and do our own thing? How do you see progress from here?

Carmen: We do both. We go off and do our own thing, and work with the mainstream as much as we can. We have the talent, and the numbers, to do our own work.

Member of the audience: What do you see are the luxuries of having survived in the business?

Carmen: The luxuries? I can tell you what is wonderful, I am not destroyed. I am still here and I can do it again if I want to. I've had the satisfaction of working with some wonderful people, and they're still my friends, and I watch it happening again with somebody else, and I can share my life with that person.

Brenda: Do you feel lucky?

Carmen: No. I've worked very hard. I think the biggest thing is being with the people I work with. Watching it happening for others. I'm happy being an actress.

Brenda: We'd like to thank you for being here.

Carmen: I just want to say this can't be a tribute, it's got to be a celebration with the people who are here tonight. It's the last thing I wanted to do, but my son read this to me yesterday, guidance from Nelson Mandela: 'You must not be afraid of your own life. Your life will light the way for other people.'

Brenda: Well, shine on Carmen Munroe!

FURTHER READING

Carmen Munroe, 'My life has become bigger', in Carole Woddis (ed.), '*Sheer Bloody Magic': Conversations with Actresses* (London: Virago, 1991).

Carmen Munroe, interview with Stephen Bourne, in Jim Pines (ed.), *Black and White in Colour: Black People in British Television since 1936* (London: British Film Institute, 1992).

15

Invisible Women

W hen Marianne Jean-Baptiste became the focus of media attention at the time of the Cannes Film Festival in 1997 it was not because she had landed a major role in a film, but for making accusations of racism. Within months of receiving BAFTA, Golden Globe and Oscar nominations for Mike Leigh's *Secrets and Lies*, the actress complained that she had been excluded from a celebration attended by Britain's newest film personalities. Simon Perry, Chief Executive of British Screen, had invited a group of young actors, including Emily Watson and Kate Winslet, to the festival, but there were no black actors on the list. Said Marianne:

> When I was told that British Screen had invited a group of young actors out to Cannes, I just burst into tears because I thought this is so unfair. It was a snub. What more do they want? If you think about it, I made history. Not only was I the first black British woman to be nominated for an Oscar, I was the first black British person. I see myself as British and I want to be celebrated by Britain . . . I don't want to sound like someone who has a chip on their shoulder. But if you keep quiet nothing will ever change and nothing will ever be done about it.[1]

The story of black actresses in British cinema is one of invisibility and yet those who have made an impression, such as Elisabeth Welch, Nina Mae McKinney, Cleo Laine, Shirley Bassey, Cassie McFarlane, Cathy Tyson and Marianne Jean-Baptiste, are constantly 'written out' by film historians.

Between the wars, African-American entertainers like Florence Mills and Josephine Baker captured Europe with their songs, beauty, elegance and style. Some of them even starred in British films, including Elisabeth Welch, whose career is surveyed in Chapter 5, and Nina Mae McKinney.[2] McKinney made an impressive screen debut in MGM's *Hallelujah!* (1929), Hollywood's first all-black cast production. The strikingly beautiful and talented newcomer was described as The Black Garbo, but there were

Marianne Jean-Baptiste (1996)

no follow-up roles. Like Josephine Baker before her, McKinney had to come to Europe to find work. In Britain she made a name for herself as a cabaret entertainer. In 1935 she starred opposite Paul Robeson in *Sanders of the River*, but her portrayal of the jungle exotic was unconvincing. All through the film she behaved as though she were on-stage at the Cotton Club. But at least she didn't take her role seriously, unlike co-star Robeson. In fact, it was McKinney who provided the film's few highlights, especially when she sang 'Congo Lullaby' to her baby daughter. Says Kenneth M. Cameron, 'The song may be un-African, but the sequence is a moving one whose dramatization of the love of a black woman for a black child obliterated the "savage" stereotype.'[3]

With the exception of Elisabeth Welch, black women who were

cabaret or stage stars made only rare appearances in British films of the 1930s, usually 'guest' appearances in musical sequences. These included the great American blues singer and composer Alberta Hunter in *Radio Parade of 1935* (1934), British-born cabaret star Mabel Mercer in *Everything is Rhythm* (1936) (later released in America as a 'soundie' called 'A Harlemesque Revue') and Jeni Le Gon, an American buck and wing, acrobatic and 'flash' dancer, in *Dishonour Bright* (1936).

In 1930s Britain there was a lot of work for black chorus girls, especially in West End nightclubs like Ike Hatch's Shim Sham Club, and the popular *Blackbirds* revues. But there was little work for them in British films. An exception was *London Melody* (1937), in which Anna Neagle – dressed in white – performed the racist 'Jingle of the Jungle' with a group of scantily clad black chorus girls.

During the war one of Britain's most distinguished stage and screen actresses, Flora Robson, blacked up for two important screen roles. In Hollywood she played Ingrid Bergman's African-American maid Angelique Pluton in the melodrama *Saratoga Trunk* (filmed by Warner Brothers in 1943, it was released in 1945), set in New Orleans in 1875. Robson was cast because Sam Wood, the director of the film,

> hated black people and this was one of the reasons for casting a white woman. Strangely, when Flora was made-up, he treated her as though she really were black. Gone were all the niceties he had used to charm her into accepting the role. For some of the scenes Flora had to drive to different locations and was shocked to find exactly how black people were treated. Policemen ordered her about and a crowd of soldiers shouted obscenities at her. She longed to pull back the collar of her blouse and show she was white underneath.[4]

By the time *Saratoga Trunk* was released, Robson had returned to Britain to play another black role, Cleopatra's slave Ftatateeta in Gabriel Pascal's lavish screen version of George Bernard Shaw's *Caesar and Cleopatra* (1945), first staged in Berlin and New York in 1906, and in London in 1907. Ftatateeta is nothing more than a grim, overbearing savage.

From time to time a small acting role surfaced for an occasional black actress. Thus, British cinema audiences saw – for the first and last time – Princess Kouka (from Sudan) as Paul Robeson's wife in *Jericho* (1937); Eseza Makumbi (from Uganda) as Robert Adams's sister in *Men of Two Worlds* (1946); Carmen Manley (from Jamaica) as Earl Cameron's wife in *Emergency Call* (1951); Vivienne Clinton (from Exeter) as Mary Kumalo in *Cry, the Beloved Country* (1952); Marjorie Fender as 'Tuppeny' in *One Good Turn* (1954), a Norman Wisdom comedy set in a children's home;

Trinidadian calypso singer Lucille Mapp as one of the nurses in *No Time for Tears* (1957); and Shari as the prostitute in *Tiger Bay* (1959). But the most famous black woman of 1950s British cinema has to be the one we never actually saw, other than as a corpse: Sapphire Robbins in *Sapphire* (1959).

Sapphire was a mixed-race music student who had passed for white, and this is revealed when two police officers inspect items of her clothing. Her true racial identity is discovered hidden in a locked drawer: 'colourful' items of underwear which Sapphire had worn under her tweed skirt. The film's director, Basil Dearden, explained this deliberate use of colour: 'My idea is to throw all this (the sombre winter backgrounds) into contrast with the sudden splashes of colour introduced by the coloured people themselves. The things they wear, the things they carry, their whole personality.'[5] Throughout the film black people are associated with 'splashes of colour', violence, sexual promiscuity and sleazy jazz music. In spite of strong competition (*Look Back in Anger*, *Tiger Bay*), it won the British Academy Award for Best British Film, a token gesture if ever there was one. But the film only succeeded in reinforcing the very racism it set out to expose and condemn.

In the 1950s two exciting young singers, Cleo Laine (from Southall in London) and Shirley Bassey (from Tiger Bay in Cardiff, South Wales) burst onto the British music scene but, in spite of their success, they failed to make the transition to movie stardom. In fact, Laine had to wait until she was over seventy to play her first screen acting role when she supported Judi Dench in BBC television's *The Last of the Blonde Bombshells* (2000). Though she was typecast as a jazz singer, Laine could have given Dench a run for her money if she had been given a more substantial acting role. It shouldn't be forgotten that Laine made her acting debut on the London stage just a few months after Dench. In May 1958 she debuted at the Royal Court in *Flesh to a Tiger*, written by the Jamaican dramatist Barry Reckord. Despite critical acclaim (the *Daily Sketch* described her performance as an 'astonishing debut'), Laine knew the score. In her autobiography she said, 'I had to play the waiting game until a director came along who wanted me ... except, of course, as an English rosebud.'[6] She's still waiting, and the British acting profession is the poorer for it. For a little while, Laine did have a handful of film assignments. For instance, in *6.5 Special* (1958) she sings a jazz number, accompanied by her husband John Dankworth and his orchestra, and in Joseph Losey's *The Criminal* (1960) she sings John Dankworth and Alun Owen's haunting 'Thieving Boy' over the opening titles. In 1963 she made an important – but overlooked – contribution to Joseph Losey's *The Servant*, starring Dirk Bogarde. The moody theme song, 'All Gone', written by Harold Pinter (who also wrote the film's screenplay – his first for the cinema) and performed by Laine in various atmospheric John Dankworth arrangements, is possibly the first use of a song lyric as part of a script. It is not only the film's warning voice of the gathering darkness surrounding two of its main characters, Susan (Wendy Craig) and Tony (James Fox) but it also draws attention to Tony's growing emotional and possible sexual dependence on his man-servant, Barrett (Bogarde).

It took until 1996 for Shirley Bassey to make her first on-screen film appearance when she played herself in *La Passione*, performing a camp cabaret waltz surrounded by gleaming red Ferraris. However, like Cleo Laine, Bassey has made important contributions to the soundtracks of British films. When Bassey belted out the theme song to *Goldfinger* (1964) she became forever associated with the James Bond films, and was an integral part of their success. Says Muriel Burgess:

> The title song for *Goldfinger* was a world hit. Shirley's voice, displaying all its incredible pitch and range, opened the film and set its tone. It was a dynamic performance ... Shirley became known internationally as 'The Goldfinger Girl'. Crowds of her fans gathered at airports all over the world, serenading her with the song.[7]

However, when Shirley sang 'Goldfinger' in Las Vegas in 1964, she was shocked by the reaction of the audience, who were surprised to find a black woman singing the James Bond theme. They had never seen her and assumed she was white.

Shirley sang on the soundtracks of two thrillers: *The Liquidator* (1966), starring Rod Taylor, and *Deadfall* (1967), starring Michael Caine, before returning to Bond themes. Her sexy and teasing rendition of the title song to *Diamonds Are Forever* (1971) provided her with another show-stopping concert favourite, but she bowed out after performing the unimpressive theme song to *Moonraker* (1979). The tradition of using black divas on the soundtracks of Bond movies has continued with Gladys Knight (*Licence to Kill*, 1989) and Tina Turner (*Goldeneye*, 1995).

Unfortunately, apart from *La Passione*, Bassey has never made an appearance on the big screen. Early in her career there was talk of her playing a small role in J. Lee Thompson's *Tiger Bay*, as well as starring opposite Sidney Poitier, but the closest she got to movie stardom was as director Carol Reed's first choice for the role of Nancy in *Oliver!* (1968), a screen version of Lionel Bart's popular stage musical, based on Charles Dickens's novel *Oliver Twist*. Presumably, Bassey was under consideration because she had had a hit in the British pop charts with her recording of Nancy's big number, 'As Long As He Needs Me'. The casting of Bassey in such an important musical role on the screen would have been revolutionary in 1968, but there were problems. Robert F. Moss reveals that 'Reed's first choice for this part was Shirley Bassey, but Columbia vetoed her because it was felt that a black Nancy would alienate [white] filmgoers in the American South.'[8] Nicholas Wapshott gives a slightly different version: 'Columbia vetoed the idea, believing that the murder of a black woman [at the hands of Bill Sikes] would cause unnecessary offence to American audiences, particularly to southern blacks.'[9]

Other black divas who popped up in British films of this period included Millie, the Jamaican reggae singer, who performed her chart hit 'My Boy Lollipop' in *Swinging UK* (1964). Later that year Millie co-starred with Elisabeth Welch in *The Rise and Fall of Nellie Brown*, an enchanting musical specially written for television. In 1975 the flamboyant American soul diva Tina Turner appeared as the Acid Queen in *Tommy*. This was Ken Russell's overblown version of the Who's rock-opera about a deaf, dumb and blind kid who becomes a pinball-playing messiah. Touching on adultery, sadism, male rape and drug addiction, Turner's 'turn' is horrible. The Acid Queen exists above a sleazy strip joint run by Tommy's sleazeball step-dad, Frank (Oliver Reed). With a red neon light constantly flashing, the scantily dressed, oversexed Acid Queen, waving a syringe in the air, attacks the defenceless Tommy, and introduces him to drugs. *Tommy* is racist (the Acid Queen) and homophobic (Uncle Ernie, a pervert who likes to 'fiddle about' with men), and Tina later admitted she should have known better:

> Then we came to my big scene, and this pair of twins walk in with a pink pillow – and there's this *huge* hypodermic needle on it! I was shocked – I didn't know anything about this. I said right out loud, 'My God, is this movie promoting drugs?' I don't know why I'm so naive about those things. I mean, even the name of my character – the Acid Queen – hadn't tipped me off. Ken Russell just laughed, though.[10]

Three years later the gifted and respected singer and composer Joan Armatrading also made a big mistake when she agreed to write and perform the title song to *The Wild Geese* (1978). Her biographer, Sean Mayes, describes the film as

> an undistinguished adventure piece about a group of white mercenaries (with a token black) rescuing a deposed African president ... The film is a tasteless exercise in commercialism and attracted controversy because of its perceived racialist implications. Unfortunately Joan failed to realize the kind of project in which she was involved, despite insisting on seeing a 'rough

cut' of the film beforehand. At the premiere she was heckled by a young crowd, shouting something to the effect that a self-respecting West Indian girl shouldn't be selling her ass by writing a theme song to a movie about mercenaries killing blacks. Interviewed the following afternoon, she said . . . 'it's a Boy's Own film in terms of adventure . . . But there is a message or moral, if you like – that we're all equal and should be able to live together.'[11]

It is sad that Patricia Ngozi Ebigwei felt it necessary to anglicize her – much prettier – Nigerian name to Patti Boulaye in order to be accepted by the British public. But that's what she was expected to do in the 1970s. In doing so, she won popularity and fame after a memorable debut on television's *New Faces* talent show in 1976, but her subsequent attempt to become Britain's answer to Diana Ross failed miserably. Her appearance in *The Music Machine* (1979), released at the height of the disco craze, did not help matters. Vastly inferior to Hollywood's *Saturday Night Fever*, it starred Gerry Sundquist, who was a good actor, but no John Travolta. Neither was Camden Town's Music Machine discothèque a substitute for New York's Studio 54. Adding insult to injury, television presenter Esther Rantzen made a 'guest appearance' as a disco judge, a clear indication of how desperate the film was. So *The Music Machine* deserved to fail, though Patti did not. Luckily, she survived long enough to enjoy success and popularity again as a cabaret entertainer, and on stage in *Carmen Jones* in the early 1990s.

Another singer whose film career ended before it had barely begun was the mixed-race Nigerian/British soulstress Helen Folasade Adu, popularly known as 'Sade'. In 1986 she agreed to appear as the nightclub singer Athene in *Absolute Beginners*. This musical version of Colin MacInnes's novel about life in Soho and Notting Hill of 1958 was an expensive flop and Sade's film career sank faster than Patti Boulaye's.

In addition to these brief appearances by singers, the British film industry offered cinema audiences sexy slave girls in films like *Up Pompeii* (1971); an occasional vampire (Marsha Hunt in *Dracula AD 1972*); an occasional exotic superstar (Eartha Kitt in *Up the Chastity Belt*, 1972); and the tragic Minah Bird, the 'only major black starlet in British sex films'.[12] Minah survived the 1970s, but her career did not. This had nothing to do with her being black. Along with other actresses in sex films she became unemployable in the 1980s when the arrival of video killed the market. A possible suicide cut short the life of Minah Ogbenyealu Bird in 1995. She was just forty-five.

During this period more substantial roles were given to Glenna Forster-Jones in John Boorman's critically acclaimed *Leo the Last* (1969), Sheila Scott-Wilkinson in *The National Health* (1973), Esther Anderson as Sidney

Poitier's love interest in *A Warm December* (1973) and Floella Benjamin in *Black Joy* (1977), but the less said about *Love Thy Neighbour* (1973), the better. In this 'spin-off' of the television series, Nina Baden-Semper re-created her role as Barbie Reynolds.

Hardly any British historical films have acknowledged the existence of black women. For instance, no one has attempted to film the life of Mary Seacole, the Jamaican nurse who was decorated by Queen Victoria for her work in the Crimean War. It was not until Shope Shodeinde was cast in *The Sailor's Return* (1978) that a black actress was given an opportunity to play such a role. James Saunders based his script for *The Sailor's Return* on the novella by David Garnett, first published in 1924. Set during the reign of Queen Victoria, it came within a very English tradition of doomed love stories (cf. Thomas Hardy), and tells the story of a sailor (Tom Bell) who returns to his West Country home with an African wife (Shodeinde). The film's director, Jack Gold, explained why making a film about a black person in a historical setting was important to him:

> by setting it in a period one has to try and clarify the situation. Every prejudice is openly stated but in a non-malicious way because there hasn't been time for malice to grow – it is the strangeness, the 'otherness' you were talking about – and what I am really hoping is that one would go back and cleanse one's mind of all the edifice of sociology, politics, crime etc. and actually try and see a black person as for the first time and what it is like to be a black person. I think that those are the parameters of the film.[13]

Although *The Sailor's Return* was well received at the 1978 Cannes, Karlovy Vary and London Film Festivals, a distributor could not be found, and the expected cinema release never materialized. Sold to television, *The Sailor's Return* was shown on ITV in 1980. Shope, who gave a wonderful performance, went on to make a number of stage and television appearances, including Channel 4's sitcom *No Problem!* (1983–5). But film roles eluded her and, when acting roles eventually dried up, she turned to modelling.

In 1986 Cathy Tyson won critical acclaim for her role as a prostitute in *Mona Lisa*, but, unlike her co-star, Bob Hoskins, she's still waiting for a good film script to come her way. Cathy revealed that after *Mona Lisa* nearly all the parts she was offered involved her taking her clothes off. Since that time, she has appeared in several popular television dramas, including two series of *Band of Gold* – but she's still being cast as a prostitute.

In the independent sector a new generation of black film-makers began to provide decent roles for black actresses. Menelik Shabazz's *Burning an*

Illusion (1981) gave newcomer Cassie McFarlane a fully rounded, complex character to play. For the first time, black women began to work as film critics in this country including Isabel Appio, who described the excitement the film created at the Commonwealth Institute's Black Film Festival in 1982:

> The most overwhelming audience turnout was for *Burning an Illusion* which had eager viewers spilling into the aisles. Females reacted openly, cheering Pat (Cassie McFarlane) through her journey as she sheds her 'colour TV and engagement ring' values, confronts her troublesome boyfriend, and discovers a more rewarding political identity. It was proved that night that there is a vast and receptive audience who at the moment is starved of films dealing with subjects with which they can identify.[14]

Cassie McFarlane may have received the 1982 *Evening Standard* Film Award for Most Promising Newcomer (presented by David Puttnam), but acting roles eluded her. In spite of her talent and ability (she was trained at RADA), by the mid-1980s Cassie had been relegated to a couple of lines as a nurse in an episode of the television series *The Bill*. However, by the end of the decade, she had turned her attention to the other side of the camera, studying film at the London College of Printing.

Other black British women of Cassie's generation began working as film-makers in the 1980s, mostly in the independent sector, and they have included Maureen Blackwood (*The Passion of Remembrance*, 1986); Martina Attille (*Dreaming Rivers*, 1988) and Ngozi Onwurah (*Welcome II The Terrordome*, 1995). However, though these films offered positive roles for black actresses, they coincided with some objectionable stereotypes in commercial cinema. These included Alphonsia Emmanuel's portrayal of Tony Slattery's oversexed girlfriend in Kenneth Branagh's terrible comedy *Peter's Friends* (1992) and Tamika Empson's equally oversexed, crazy teenager in *Beautiful Thing* (1996).

By the end of the 1990s the only black female movie star we could offer the world was Scary Spice in *Spice World*, though in 1998 Anjela Lauren Smith gave a memorable performance in *Babymother*. Though the film didn't propel her into movie stardom, Anjela gave a vibrant performance in this enjoyable melodrama with songs and attitude. She played Anita, a young mother of two who lives on a Harlesden council estate and aspires to be a dance-hall queen. To achieve her ambition, she dumps her 'babyfather', steals his money and sells her body to pay for an expensive session in a recording studio. Anita is far removed from Nina Mae McKinney's jungle exotic of *Sanders of the River* of the 1930s, indicating that, perhaps, British cinema had moved on in its depiction of

Cassie McFarlane and David Puttnam at the 1982 *Evening Standard* Film Awards

black women. But, in spite of *Babymother* having a black writer/director, Julian Henriques, reactions were mixed, especially in the young black community:

> To test *Babymother's* authenticity, we showed it to five real-life dancehall girls in east London – two of whom actually appear in the film – while they were getting ready for their own Saturday night out ... Neither Diane nor Jenna like the term 'babymother', but apart from that, the women follow the film intently – and vocally – and identify with almost everything that happens. *Babymother* has a stamp of gritty estate living, with its catfights, competitiveness and upfront rude-girl attitude ... But, for some of the film's critics, it is pandering to innacurate prejudices. 'These are black people the way white people in Channel Four [which partly funded the

film] want to see them, not how black people would,' insists a film-maker who was involved in the planning stages of *Babymother* before leaving the project. He is also unhappy about the film's depiction of scantily-clad young girls: 'It's flogging black ass and tits, and a lot of black people object to it.'[15]

NOTES

1 Marianne Jean-Baptiste, interview with Dan Glaister, *Guardian*, 15 May 1997, p. 3.
2 Stephen Bourne, 'Nina Mae McKinney', *Films in Review*, January–February 1991; and 'Black Garbo', *Pride*, April 1999.
3 Kenneth M. Cameron, *Africa on Film: Beyond Black and White* (New York: Continuum, 1994), p. 100.
4 Kenneth Barrow, *Flora: An Appreciation of the Life and Work of Dame Flora Robson* (London: Heinemann, 1981), p. 146.
5 Basil Dearden, *Kine Weekly*, 25 December 1958.
6 Cleo Laine, *Cleo* (London: Simon and Schuster, 1994), p. 150.
7 Muriel Burgess, *Shirley: An Appreciation of the Life of Shirley Bassey* (London: Century, 1998), p. 174.
8 R. F. Moss, *The Films of Carol Reed* (New York: Columbia University Press, 1987), p. 251.
9 Nicholas Wapshott, *The Man Between: A Biography of Carol Reed* (London: Chatto and Windus, 1990), p. 330.
10 Tina Turner with Kurt Loder, *I, Tina* (London: Viking, 1986), p. 175.
11 Sean Mayes, *Joan Armatrading: A Biography* (London: Weidenfeld and Nicolson, 1990), p. 90.
12 David McGillivray, *Doing Rude Things: The History of the British Sex Film 1957–81* (Sun Tavern Fields, 1992), p. 106.
13 Jack Gold, interview with Sheila Whitaker, *Framework*, Issue 9, Winter 1978/9.
14 Isabel Appio, *Caribbean Times*, 26 February 1982.
15 Carmen Russell, 'We're queens of the night', *The Big Issue*, 24-30 August 1998.

FURTHER READING

Lola Young, *Fear of the Dark: 'Race', Gender and Sexuality in the Cinema* (London and New York: Routledge, 1996).

16

Lesbians and Gays

Black lesbians and gays are practically invisible in British film and television. In the past, on the rare occasions they surfaced, they were invariably portrayed as objects of desire for white characters. However, it has to be said that one of the first films to include a black gay character, *The L-Shaped Room* (1962), was sympathetic in its treatment. Written and directed by Bryan Forbes, he adapted his screenplay from the novel by Lynne Reid Banks, first published in 1960. In Forbes's hands *The L-Shaped Room* is a fine example of the 'kitchen-sink' genre popular with British audiences at that time. In the film, Leslie Caron plays Jane, unmarried and expecting a child, who leaves her comfortable middle-class home for a room in a run-down boarding-house in Notting Hill. Among the residents she befriends are Mavis (Cicely Courtneidge), an over-the-hill music-hall entertainer who is also a cat-loving lesbian, Toby (Tom Bell), an aspiring writer, and Johnny (Brock Peters), a jazz musician from the Caribbean. Peters was 'imported' from Hollywood to play Johnny, yet another example of the casting of African-Americans in British film and television, a practice which has persisted for decades. Bryan Forbes handles the 'difficult' (for 1962) themes of single parenthood and gay sexuality with perception and frankness. He also inspires memorable performances from a superb cast. However, in Banks's novel Johnny is caricatured. For example, when Jane expresses her fear of the black boarding-house resident to Toby, he describes Johnny's 'white eyes rolling' and adds that he is 'naturally inquisitive. Like a chimp ... He could no more resist having a look at you than a monkey could resist picking up anything new and giving it the once-over.' Later, Toby reveals to Jane that Johnny is also gay: 'He wouldn't hurt a fly ... he's a first-class cook ... he does needlework too.'[1] However, when Forbes adapted the novel for the screen, he eliminated the racism and homophobia of Banks, and in the process, humanized the character.

Johnny shares an easy-going, relaxed friendship with Jane and Toby. Though he remains an outsider, on the margins, throughout the film, he is no more isolated than his friends. In the boarding-house he is fully accepted as a member of the constructed 'family'. Johnny is in love with Toby, but after he discovers Jane and Toby have slept together, he explodes at her in a jealous rage: 'I had a *good* friend in Toby. He always talked to *me* before.' Subsequently, by revealing Jane's pregnancy to Toby, Johnny is responsible for terminating the couple's relationship. But afterwards he apologizes to Jane and she, in turn, forgives him. They remain friends, but Toby stays angry with Jane till the end of the film.

Bryan Forbes fully intended to create a believable character who, like lesbian Mavis, is not a caricature:

> Brock Peters character was changed – again the gentle approach with a total absence of 'camp', for I have always felt that this is the obvious, easy route to take and much abused. Why did I present Brock as gay? Well, exact memory eludes me as it does most authors, but I guess I wanted a counterpoint – the role played by Tom Bell was somebody who could not face up to the truth of loving somebody who was carrying another man's child. I tried to people that house with a variety of people I knew existed at that time and in those circumstances, but it was never a conscious effort on my part to be 'different' – just, I suspect, an awareness that the public's perception was changing ... I, along with many others in the profession, were no strangers to the homosexual scene – but there was no prejudice as such – I have always judged people by their talents, not their race, religion or sexual leanings – that is to say I don't care whether somebody is a black, gay, Jewish extrovert – all I care about is whether he or she is a good actor. I think this is largely true of the profession as a whole ... [Johnny] came about because of a writer's instinct to explore all the facets of human behaviour rather than a determined effort to be daring.[2]

A few years later *Two Gentlemen Sharing* (1969) proved far less successful in its depiction of a black gay man. Based on the novel by David Stuart Leslie, published in 1963, this film was not given a theatrical release in Britain. Robin Phillips plays Roddy, an upper-class advertising executive, who agrees to share his flat with Andrew McKenzie (Hal Frederick), an Oxford-educated Jamaican law student with a desire to integrate with the white world. However, Andrew is a snob who has problems 'integrating' with anyone. He wears earplugs at a black disco and complains, condescendingly, to his Jamaican girlfriend, 'What's so good about this? A bunch of London transport porters jumping up and down.' By the end of the film, disillusionment, anger and bitterness have set in. Andrew has grown to despise Roddy's world, as well as the politics of Black Power revolutionaries. He decides to return to Jamaica. Roddy, on the other hand, is fascinated by 'Negroes', who, he believes, are 'sexually superior'.

In one scene at the disco Roddy's obnoxious, drunken friend Phil (Norman Rossington) pushes past Marcus (Ram John Holder), a tall, statuesque black queen. Marcus is puffing on a long cigarette-holder. 'Watch it, man,' he says to Phil, stroking his white silk shirt. 'This stuff is inflammable.' Phil ignores him, but finds himself attracted to the queen's companion, Amanda (Daisy Mae Williams), a young black woman wearing a tight-fitting miniskirt and pink wig. Making a beeline for her, Phil asks her for a dance, but Marcus interrupts, 'No, baby. We've just come to see the spooks enjoy themselves.'

In David Stuart Leslie's novel, Marcus is presented as Marcus Bimba, a prostitute and dancer in a show called *Banana Boat*. The author describes him in homophobic and racist terms as 'kinky', 'mincing' and 'slithering', with 'a face like an infatuated Disney serpent. No chin at all. Six foot three with a coy little fuzz of black curls like pubic hair.' Unable to resist 'a lavender-striped shirt with a pink tie', Marcus informs Roddy that 'Nice white folks make allowances for little me, because I'se just a simple coloured boy who don't know no better.'[3]

Marcus is a gay caricature in the screen version, too. Though elegant, he's predatory and determined to seduce Roddy. At the disco, Marcus approaches Roddy and exclaims, in a horrible whining voice, 'Hi, baby. Whatever you're looking for, you can find it here.' All the time he is licking his lips. When Roddy replies, 'I'm looking for two girls,' Marcus responds, in that same whining voice, 'Two girls? Do I look like two girls?'

Towards the end of the film, when Roddy throws a party in the flat, he becomes drunk and embarrasses himself in front of his guests. Feeling faint, he goes upstairs to his bedroom, and collapses. Predatory Marcus follows him, gently opens the bedroom door, joins Roddy on the bed and begins to stroke his face. Roddy wakes up and, horrified, draws away from Marcus. He asks him what he wants. Marcus replies, 'You've got a nice pad here. I was just thinking I might move in. Come on, baby, you've got room for me. There's nothing wrong with two gentlemen sharing.' In a drunken haze, Roddy punches Marcus in the face. On the floor, Marcus looks up at Roddy and says, 'Shucks, baby, you've got it bad.' The film ends with a policeman clearing the party guests from the house after complaints from neighbours. Roddy is left alone.

Marcus is a nasty character, and one of the worst examples of a particular kind of gay movie stereotype: the predatory queen. However, in *Two Gentlemen Sharing*, Andrew is an intriguing character, far removed from the safe and 'noble' image being projected by Sidney Poitier in Hollywood at that time in films like *Guess Who's Coming to Dinner?* (1967). But the film suffers from explicit homophobia and racism. When the Jamaican actress Esther Anderson, who was cast as Andrew's girlfriend, was interviewed in the magazine *Cinema X* in 1969, she commented:

> it was making fun out of West Indians in Britain ... the coloured boy who's playing a queer – it's so overdone, overplayed. Coloured people aren't going to like it and that boy, Ram John Holder, is going to get a bad time from his people. If he had played it quite normally and it only came out that he was queer, it would have been more effective and could have impressed people instead of them saying, as they will, 'oh, that faggot black boy'. I've never seen a Negro queer mincing like that. In fact, I've never met a Negro queer. That's why Ram John played it as he did, I suppose; the white man's impression of what a queer is. Oh sure, he's funny. He'll make you laugh. But he'll offend every coloured person in the audience. I heard that Quincy Jones refused to do the music for the film because of that scene.[4]

In *Girl Stroke Boy* (1971) writer-producer Ned Sherrin was responsible for putting another black gay man at the centre of a British film. It was based on David Percival's play *Girlfriend*, which had a short run in London's West End in 1970. In the film, Joan Greenwood plays Lettice Mason, a successful authoress – and mother from hell. 'Darling, I hope you will choose to do what you think is right, as long as you discuss it with me,' she tells her son Laurie (Clive Francis).

Lettice and her headmaster husband George (Michael Hordern) prepare a small dinner party to welcome Laurie home. He arrives at their snowbound country retreat with his flamboyant black partner, Jo (Peter Straker), but the Masons are unable to determine whether or not Jo is female. Jamaican-born Peter Straker, who had been a member of the original cast of the 1960s hit rock musical *Hair*, made his film debut as Jo. He was billed simply as Straker to preserve the ambiguous sexual identity of his character.

Lettice refuses to accept the possibility of her son being gay. 'In my day you wondered which man was going to ask you to dance, not which one was the man!' she exclaims; however, when Peter Straker appears as Jo, it is difficult for the actor to disguise the fact that he is playing an effeminate gay man, though he is supposed to be androgynous. Nevertheless, George believes Jo is a woman. Throughout the film, Laurie and Jo enjoy a tender, loving relationship. They are affectionate, warm and passionate towards each other. The two men kiss on the lips several times – unseen in films at that time – and Jo says to Laurie, 'We care for each other and show others we care.' Clive Francis and Peter Straker give convincing performances as the gay lovers and, together with Peter Finch and Murray Head in John Schlesinger's better-known *Sunday, Bloody Sunday*, also released in 1971, this film broke new ground in the portrayal of gay relationships on the screen.

However, unlike *Sunday, Bloody Sunday*, which was a critical and commercial success, *Girl Stroke Boy* received a hostile and homophobic reception from film critics which ensured that it was never seen again, except for one brief appearance on television in 1978 as a 'Saturday Adult Movie'. In the *Evening Standard* Alexander Walker called it a 'tedious, ill-made, appallingly-acted and directed piece of mindlessness',[5] while Richard Afton complained in the *Evening News* that 'it's difficult to understand how *Boy Stroke Girl* [*sic*] ever got made. It was one of the most stupid films I have seen. A one-word description would be putrid ... it disgusted me. Seeing men kissing each other and making love is not my idea of entertainment.'[6] However, this charming, funny minor gem of British cinema has stood the test of time, finally resurfacing, with great success, in the 1999 London Lesbian and Gay Film Festival. Ned Sherrin, writing in his autobiography, felt the criticism of the film was unjustified:

> The plot sounds sleazy but the play handled it tactfully and amusingly and the parents and the lovers ... gave elegant high comedy performances under Bob Kellett's direction. It has remained one of my favourite films and I could not understand the very severe press criticism it received. *Girl Stroke Boy* seemed to delight audiences until the press show, when dismay set in.[7]

For years black lesbians were invisible in British films, save for a fleeting glimpse of an 'extra' in the famous Gateways club scene in *The Killing of Sister George* (1969). Black lesbians and gays were also invisible on British television, though a handful surfaced towards the end of the 1970s. At this time, black gay men were portrayed as nothing more than objects of white gay sexual desire, and one of the first to appear was Sugar (Reg Tsiboe) in *A Hymn from Jim* (BBC2, 1977). This bizarre comedy thriller was written by Richard O'Brien for the *Premiere* series. O'Brien was famous for creating *The Rocky Horror Picture Show*, and in *A Hymn from Jim* he explores the strange world of Jim Tayo (Christopher Guard), a pretty but psychotic pop star. Having received yet another gold disc, Jim is anxious to be alone in his plush penthouse apartment for an interview with a journalist from a teen magazine. However, his lover Sugar, who has recently moved in, is furious when Jim tries to evict him. Sugar refuses to leave, and threatens to expose the selfish, hypocritical Jim to the teen magazine and his adoring fans: 'An interview? This is going to be an exposé. Me exposed in living colour.' Jim loses control and smashes his newly acquired gold disc over Sugar's head, killing him instantly. At the end of the story, revenge is taken by two black dudes. Pursuing Jim in their car, they cause an accident in which he is killed. Though Sugar's appearance had been brief (before the opening credits) the end reveals he had friends in the black underworld, willing to avenge his murder.

Coming Out (1979), written by James Andrew Hall for BBC1's popular *Play for Today* series, received mixed reviews. Richard Last in the *Daily Telegraph* called it a 'sympathetic view of homosexuality',[8] while Keith Howes, television critic for *Gay News*, blasted it for being 'incapable of tackling the "coming out" theme it had set itself ... This was the gay world seen through pebble-thick glasses with all the self-deprecation and mendacity that television viewers have been conditioned to expect.'[9] Howes felt that the play, though relatively frank and revealing about gay life, was negative in its attitude towards gay men in particular, and gay political action in general. The plot revolves around Lewis Duncan (Anton Rodgers), an 'Agony Aunt' who is faced with the prospect of having to 'come out' in public after publishing a pro-gay article in a non-gay magazine (under a pseudonym). In one brief scene we see him picking up Polo (Ben Ellison), a young black prostitute, in Piccadilly Circus.

Lewis is next seen naked in bed with Polo. They have just had sex, and Lewis is curious to know more about his bed partner. 'Black Polo's a good lay,' explains the young man. 'Clean sheets, no clap, get your rocks off in style.' He calls himself Polo because 'I'm cool and sweet, man, with a hole in the middle.' He says he earns £5,000 a week, doesn't pay tax, but tells Lewis angrily, 'I *earn* my money. I went with forty-two last week, and all of them dogs.' But Polo wants to prove to Lewis that he has a 'heart of gold' by offering him 'one on the house'. In spite of this gesture, Polo is as hard as nails, bitter and angry. He hates what he does, and probably despises himself too. Robert Cushman in the *Radio Times* felt that 'the hero's session with a black male prostitute was explosive ... not for anything it said, but for the mere fact of its appearing on a television screen'.[10]

Surprisingly, British television's first fictional black lesbian was not a prostitute, like Sugar and Polo, or any other kind of stereotype. In fact, Velma Small (Isabelle Lucas), who made a brief appearance in an episode of the sitcom *Agony* (London Weekend Television, 1979), is a beautiful, outspoken, maternal feminist. The episode, entitled 'Too Much Agony, Too Little Ecstasy', was shown just two weeks after *Coming Out*. Written by Anna Raeburn and Len Richmond, Velma gives agony aunt Jane Lucas (Maureen Lipman) some advice: 'You can keep men, as far as I am concerned ... Girl, if you're shipwrecked, you must swim for it.' Velma was described by Keith Howes in *Gay News* as Jane's 'fellow earth mother' and 'a relentlessly together bald black lesbian with two children, a girlfriend called Emmy, and a 24-carat heart'.[11] Needless to say, Emmy and the children existed off screen and Velma was never seen again.

In the late 1970s and early 1980s it was rare for black women to be seen in British television drama. With few exceptions, roles for black women were restricted to inmates of Stone Park, the prison in *Within These Walls* (London Weekend Television, 1974–8), nurses in St Angela's, the hospital in *Angels* (BBC1, 1975–83), or dope addicts with an insatiable sexual appetite. In 1979 Floella Benjamin complained about the situation in *Time Out*:

> 'It's so depressing,' she says. 'I've done three dramatic roles on television this year. In the BBC's *Waterloo Sunset* and *Angels* I played a prostitute. In LWT's *Kids* I played a good time lady who neglects her children. I've said to producers and directors why can't you give me other parts? They reply, 'It's not realistic my love. The public wouldn't accept it.'[12]

In 'Melody', a homophobic episode of *The Gentle Touch* (London Weekend Television, 1980), starring Jill Gascoine as a tough police officer, Vicki Richards appeared briefly as a black lesbian prostitute. She's also the girlfriend of a kinky white lipstick lesbian. A few years later, when Cathy Tyson (as Simone) starred opposite Bob Hoskins (as George) in the film *Mona Lisa* (1986), the black lesbian prostitute took centre stage. *Mona Lisa* was a huge critical and commercial success, and the teaming of Hoskins

Bob Hoskins and Cathy Tyson in *Mona Lisa* (1986)

and Tyson was truly inspired. Both actors give superb performances, and deserved the critical praise and awards showered upon them. Simone and George are one of the great double-acts of cinema.

However, some critics expressed concern about Simone. On his release from prison, George, a small-time loser, is employed in a vice racket, delivering porn videos. He also works as a driver/minder to Simone, a high-class call-girl. George has a heart of gold, and falls in love with the enigmatic, elegant Simone. He undertakes, at her request, a search for her friend Cathy (Kate Hardie), also a prostitute, who has disappeared. George eventually finds Cathy, but in doing so discovers, to his horror, that the two women are lovers. But does this 'twist' in the plot work, and is the film's treatment of the lesbian relationship sympathetic? Louis Heaton, film critic for *Chic*, a popular black British women's magazine of the 1980s, thought not:

> Cathy Tyson's Simone, though competently acted, lacks both credibility and character. Despite their obvious best intentions, the film-makers have given us yet another stereotyped 'hard' black woman whose hatred of men manifests itself in lesbianism. Prevented from showing warmth or weakness, or to explain how she came to this way of life, Simone remains as anonymous, enigmatic and one-dimensional as her famous namesake. [13]

And in an interview in *City Limits*, Cathy Tyson expressed her reservations about screenwriter David Leland's treatment of Simone and Cathy's relationship:

> I thought the surface of that was just scratched, they were just two pretty lesbians, and it's very erotic for men. I liked Kate Hardie's part, but I didn't have a lot to do with her on screen and we didn't develop the relationship enough. As an actor, no matter how small the part is, you've got to make the most of it, and I felt inhibited, there just wasn't much between us. So we held hands and we cried, that I could manage.[14]

In response to Tyson's criticisms, David Leland had this to say:

> Essentially *Mona Lisa* is about George. About his prejudices, his ignorance, his innocence ... George never leaves the action. The film does not explore the complexities of the relationship between Simone and Cathy. That was not the purpose or the intention of the film. It is just one more reality which assaults George ... Yes, Neil Jordan [director of *Mona Lisa*] and I are both voyeurs, there's nothing more we enjoy than tuning into lesbian relationships. This is why we wrote the film ... I've never met Cathy Tyson or talked to her, so I don't know where she got the notion that I thought

Simone and Cathy should be 'just two pretty lesbians' or that I found the notion erotic. I think that's for her to sort out. I do think she's very good in the part despite a whole series of appalling costumes ... By the by, I think that some of Fassbinder's films are wonderfully voyeuristic and very enjoyable they are too.[15]

When black lesbians and gays were not being portrayed as white men's sexual fantasies, other hideous stereotypes jumped out of the closet. One of the most embarrassing examples of the wrist-flapping queen surfaced on television in 1985 in the sitcom *In Sickness and in Health*. This was writer Johnny Speight's sequel to his famous – and controversial – *Till Death Us Do Part*. Once again, Warren Mitchell took the lead role as the East End racist and homophobe, Alf Garnett. His home help Winston (Eamonn Walker) is his worst nightmare: black, named after his hero Winston Churchill and gay (with a white lover). Alf refers to him as 'Marigold' but Winston hits back, taunting Alf with lines like: 'I'm British with a *gorgeous* tan. So eat your heart out.' Says Keith Howes:

> Alf Garnett didn't properly focus on gays until the arrival of his black home help in 1985. Winston was a semi-stereotype, but Speight's invention flagged after one or two appearances. Winston soon retreated into repetition and supportive huddles with Alf's daughter Rita. Predictably, Rita liked Winston, but only came to his defence when Dad attacked his colour and race, not his chosen sexual expression.[16]

Since Winston's appearances in *In Sickness and in Health* (1985–7), very few black gay men have surfaced in mainstream British film and television, and hardly any black lesbians. Among the exceptions are two feature films: *The Fruit Machine* (1988) and *Young Soul Rebels* (1991). *The Fruit Machine* was written by Frank Clarke, a working-class gay Liverpudlian, whose talent has been ignored by the British film and television industries. It is a film with a heart, and the relationship between innocent, sensitive Eddie (Emile Charles), the mixed-race gay teenager, and his rent boyfriend and protector, Tony (Tony Forsyth), is beautifully realized. When Isaac Julien's *Young Soul Rebels* was released in 1991, critics were sharply divided. They either loved it or hated it. 'I found it thoroughly engaging from start to finish,' declared Bernardine Evaristo in *Spare Rib*.[17] Alexander Walker, who hated *Girl Stroke Boy*, described it in the *Evening Standard* as 'badly made ... trivialising ... incomprehensible'.[18] But, whatever the critics felt about the film, it was an important landmark – the first British feature film made by a openly gay black director.

After graduating from St Martin's School of Art in the mid-1980s, Isaac joined Sankofa, a film and video collective funded by the left-wing Greater London Council and Channel 4. This group of black film-makers set out to challenge preconceptions about black identities in their films. One of their first feature-length productions was *The Passion of Remembrance* (1986), which included the first African-Caribbean gay couple in a British film. During the making of *Passion*, Julien saw the film *My Beautiful Laundrette*, the love story of Omar, a business-suited Asian, and Johnny, a white punk. It inspired the young film-maker who, for the first time, saw a relationship on the screen he felt he could identify with:

> I could relate to *My Beautiful Laundrette* even though I found the identities of Omar and Johnny very problematic. But to describe *My Beautiful Laundrette* as a realist text is also problematic because a lot of the film is fairly stylized. The scenes in *The Passion of Remembrance* between the black gay couple are homages to *My Beautiful Laundrette*. When we were shooting *Passion* we were going to cut the kissing scene but, after seeing *Laundrette*, I insisted on keeping it in. Sexuality is often seen by black people as a white disease. *The Passion of Remembrance* is trying to fill in the gaps.[19]

Three years later, Isaac directed the homoerotic *Looking for Langston* (1989), a short meditation on the African-American poet Langston Hughes, and he described his next project, *Young Soul Rebels*, as a 'stylized narrative film'. A thriller, it is set in London in 1977, the year of the Queen's Jubilee. When a young black gay man is found murdered in the local park, two black DJs, Chris (Valentine Nonyela) and gay Caz (Mo Sesay), find themselves caught up in a tangled web of suspicion, lust and music. *Young Soul Rebels* is a seductive film, and Julien's exploration of sexual and racial identities is unselfconscious. In all of his films, Julien has explored the theme of black masculinity, as he explained in an interview in *Gay Times* in 1991:

> Where I see myself different from a number of white gay activists is that I think they are interested in sex and sexuality as an emphasis. When I was involved very early on in the Black Lesbian and Gay Group, we were very interested in issues of policing and gender. These kinds of debates were related to debates around black masculinity and I think generally this is a debate that takes a far more fundamentally important position in black politics than it takes in gay politics. I don't know how a gay political discourse takes on these questions of black masculinity. I think black communities are written off as homophobic. So there is no work except what we've been doing in Sankofa, and the work being produced by the Black Audio Film Collective. *Young Soul Rebels* continues that investigation around the construction of black masculinity.

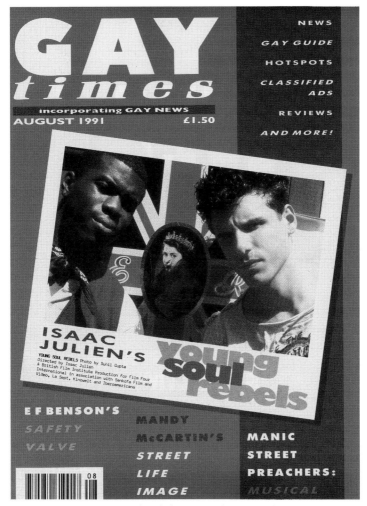

Young Soul Rebels (Isaac Julien, 1991)

I also want to show the facade of black masculinity. I want to go beneath that. I am showing behind this mask, this image, that black men are vulnerable . . . As far as I am concerned all the black characters in *Young Soul Rebels* were there in 1977. I knew them. What I have tried to do in the film is give them some kind of integrity and construct them as believable characters in their own right rather than being characters that represent different political points of view.[20]

Unfortunately, though Julien picked up the Critics' Prize at the 1991 Cannes Film Festival, it was not the blockbuster that everyone expected. Peter Burton offered the following explanation in *Gay Times*:

Perhaps the main fault of the movie is the ill-conceived screenplay (Paul Hallam, Derrick Saldaan McClintock, Isaac Julien) which sets a murder story and an inter-racial romance (black dj; and white punk) against the background of Betty Windsor's Silver Jubilee celebrations ... The murder plot was clearly never fully thought through and serves best as a goad to the various relationships which are more central to the film. Surprisingly, as it is the creation of a gay man, the relationship ... is entirely lacking in reality or erotic tension.[21]

Since *Young Soul Rebels*, black lesbians and gays have all but vanished in mainstream film and television, with just a few exceptions. In the 1990s the BBC's comedy hit *Absolutely Fabulous* included an occasional (marginal) role for Gary Beadle as Oliver, the lover of Edina Monsoon's ex-husband Justin. Says Oscar Watson, a capacity builder for black arts in south east London, '*Ab Fab* was fun, not a social document. I didn't think Oliver was a negative character. He was a joke, a running gag. I didn't feel insulted by him.' [22] Perhaps if Jennifer Saunders had expanded the role of Oliver, he might have become the best-known black lesbian or gay character on British television. However, since this did not happen, the title has to go to hairdresser Della Alexander (Michelle Joseph). She first appeared in the cast of BBC1's soap *EastEnders* in March, 1994 – and stayed for about a year.

At first, Della was going to be the new love interest for Steve Elliot (Mark Monero), but started a relationship with Binnie Roberts (Sophie Langham) instead. Their kissing scene caused fewer ripples than anticipated, probably because viewers had seen it all before. A year earlier Channel 4's soap *Brookside* had taken all the media flak with Beth and Margaret. But perhaps this also had something to do with the fact that Della and Binnie were unconvincing characters, even if they had been liberated from the worst aspects of television's previous stereotypical view of lesbians, a point emphasized by Tilly McAuley, television critic for the lesbian lifestyle magazine *Diva*:

Suddenly, lesbianism is under the microscope in *EastEnders* (BBC1). My money was on Michelle Fowler but she's fallen for a menopausal male who still thinks it's the Seventies. Instead we have Della and Binnie, both newcomers to Albert Square. Perhaps their newness is where the problem lies, but I don't give a toss about either of them; my video is not programmed to catch every last lingering look and stolen kiss (as it was in the early days of Beth and Margaret); I wouldn't even mind if Della finally ran off with Steve. Both girls have more attitude than angst, and while this may be terrifically right-on, it doesn't make for compelling drama. No one can empathize with such two-dimensional characters; there is no chemistry in their scenes together, which are therefore hopelessly unerotic. I know *EastEnders* goes out before the 9 p.m. watershed but I've seen more sexual tension in an episode of *The Magic Roundabout* – and each line of dialogue sounds like it was vetted by the BBC's Committee for the Advancement of Politically Correct Ideology.[23]

Since it was launched in 1984, producers of ITV's police drama series *The Bill* have refused to include a gay or lesbian officer at Sun Hill police station. In 1995 the programme's (then) Executive Producer, Michael Chapman, declared: 'Homosexuality would be of no more interest to us than any other peculiar behaviour, and I can't think that having homosexuals hanging around the place is going to commend the programme usefully to the public.'[24] Five years later the show's six-part spin-off, *Burnside*, starring Christopher Ellison in his old *Bill* role as CID tough guy Frank Burnside, featured a mixed-race gay sidekick for the hardman cop:

> Justin Pierre, who plays DS Dave Summers, insists that the character is 'totally at ease' with his sexuality. 'Summers has a lot more sensitivity than Burnside,' says Pierre. 'He thinks before he does things and uses his charm and sensitivity to get results.'[25]

However, in spite of its pretensions to social relevance, *Burnside* was far more interested in action than exploring the relationship between Burnside and Summers. Said Harry Venning, television critic for *The Stage*: 'It remains to be seen whether Summers's sexuality is merely tacked-on tokenism (a gay Burnside – now that would be interesting), but the early signs are not encouraging.'[26]

DS Summers's appearance in *Burnside* came in the wake of Channel 4's controversial but ground-breaking gay drama series *Queer as Folk*, in which black gay men were conspicuous by their absence. Channel 4 more than compensated for this oversight by commissioning the black gay writer-director Rikki Beadle-Blair to create a new series. The result was *Metrosexuality* (2001), an energetic, helter-skelter, six-part 'urban drama series' about Kwame, a teenage heterosexual who just cannot understand why his two gay dads have split up. Kwame spends most of his time running around Notting Hill devising schemes to get them back together again. Beadle-Blair, who also played one of the dads, explained:

> I've always wanted to do kaleidoscopic pieces. That's what interests me. I've always had friends of different ages and colours. I've never done mono – mono-racial, mono-sexual – things. That's not the world I live in. My things have always been more free-wheeling than that. It's very 70s. It must be all the Bowie records I listened to.[27]

Though Channel 4 gave it the late-night 'graveyard' slot (11 p.m.), the fate of most of their black and/or gay programmes, *Metrosexuality* managed to find a large audience who enjoyed its fast and furious, bold and brash, wild and wacky style. Says Oscar Watson,

> I really enjoyed it. I like television that is active and makes you pay attention. The energy is great and the style new to mainstream television. The multiple plot strands often make it difficult to follow, but it is great seeing so many black gay characters on the screen![28]

NOTES

1 Lynne Reid Banks, *The L-Shaped Room* (London: Chatto and Windus, 1960), p. 46.

2 Bryan Forbes, letter to Stephen Bourne, 29 August 1995.

3 David Stuart Leslie, *Two Gentlemen Sharing* (London: Secker and Warburg, 1963), pp. 54–5.

4 Esther Anderson, *Cinema X*, Vol. 2, No. 3, 1969, pp. 40–1.

5 Alexander Walker, *Evening Standard*, 12 August 1971.

6 Richard Afton, *Evening News*, 16 March 1978.

7 Ned Sherrin, *A Small Thing: Like an Earthquake* (London: Weidenfeld and Nicolson, 1983), p. 208.

8 Richard Last, 'Sympathetic view of homosexuality', *Daily Telegraph*, 11 April 1979.

9 Keith Howes, 'Play for today?', *Gay News*, No. 165, 19 April–2 May 1979.

10 Robert Cushman, *Radio Times*, 28 April–4 May 1979.

11 Keith Howes, 'Some good advice', *Gay News*, No. 166, 3–16 May 1979.

12 Floella Benjamin, *Time Out*, 2–8 November 1979.

13 Louis Heaton, *Chic*, September 1986.

14 Cathy Tyson, interview with Saskia Baron, *City Limits*, 28 August–4 September 1986.

15 David Leland, letter to Stephen Bourne, 17 June 1986.

16 Keith Howes, *Broadcasting It: An Encyclopaedia of Homosexuality on Film, Radio and TV in the UK* (London: Cassell, 1993), p. 388.

17 Bernadine Evaristo, *Spare Rib*, September 1991.

18 Alexander Walker, *Evening Standard*, 22 August 1991.

19 Isaac Julien, interview with Stephen Bourne, London, 21 April 1987.

20 Isaac Julien, interview with Stephen Bourne, 'Putting the record straight', *Gay Times*, August 1991.

21 Peter Burton, *Gay Times*, April 1993.

22 Oscar Watson, interview with Stephen Bourne, London, 17 March 2001.

23 Tilly McAuley, *Diva*, August 1994.

24 Stephen Bourne, 'No PC at *The Bill*', *Capital Gay*, 16 September 1995.

25 *The Pink Paper*, 14 July 2000.

26 Harry Venning, *The Stage*, 13 July 2000.

27 Rikki Beadle-Blair, interview with David Smith, 'The man with kaleidoscope eyes', *Gay Times*, February 2001.

28 Watson, interview with Bourne.

FURTHER READING

Isaac Julien and Colin MacCabe, *Diary of a Young Soul Rebel* (London: British Film Institute, 1991.

17

Soaps

Doing the White Thing

When *Coronation Street* reached its fortieth birthday on 9 December 2000, there was one face missing from the birthday celebrations. It belonged to Thomas Baptiste who, on 7 January 1963, became the first black actor to appear in the programme. He played Johnny Alexander, a working-class bus conductor, who accused Len Fairclough of not paying his fare. Len complained to Johnny's inspector, Harry Hewitt, who was also Len's drinking pal, and Johnny was sacked. But afterwards Len admitted he had lied, and asked for Johnny to be reinstated. When Len and Harry visited Johnny at his home to tell him the good news, Johnny stuck to his principles, and told Len he didn't want his old job back. When Len asked him why, Johnny replied, 'Because I've just been down to the Labour Exchange and got a job where they trust you and where they don't have Peeping Toms spying on a man twenty-four hours a day!' Johnny and his wife, played by Barbara Assoon, were shown as a believable working-class couple who lived in cramped conditions with their two small children. However, even though the Alexanders didn't stay in the programme for very long, their appearances provided *Street* viewers with a rare glimpse of working-class African-Caribbean family life. It also showed a black man making a defiant stand against racism.

Thomas Baptiste came to this country from Guyana in the 1950s and has enjoyed a long and successful career in films such as *The Ipcress File* (1965), Lionel Ngakane's *Jemima and Johnny* (1966) and *Sunday, Bloody Sunday* (1971). On television he has given many memorable performances, including leading roles in *Fable* (BBC1, 1965) and *Play for Today: King* (BBC1, 1984), but he regrets his appearance in the *Street* has been forgotten:

Peter Adamson, Ivan Beavis, Barbara Assoon and Thomas Baptiste in *Coronation Street* (1963)

For about a year after I appeared in *Coronation Street* I was recognized all over the place for that part. What I feel sad about is when Granada celebrates the *Street*'s birthdays, I am forgotten. I am not remembered in its history, in the books they publish, or in its celebrations, yet I was the first black actor to appear in the programme. It's like I never existed, and that is a corruption of history.[1]

In spite of Baptiste's appearance, for years *Coronation Street* ignored the existence of black people. In his autobiography, published in 1981, H. V. Kershaw, the *Street*'s first script editor, and later a producer and contract writer on the programme, explained why:

It has long been a rule that all our coloured characters should be seen to be fully and happily integrated into the community. Which explains why one issue has, apparently, been shirked – namely, that successive producers have been loath to bring a coloured family into the *Street* itself. If this were to be done producers and writers would be forced by the very nature of the show to allow integration to develop at its own pace and to air a mixed bag of opinions on immigration and racialism. I am not alone in believing that such subjects are far too important simply to form one of many themes in a popular drama serial. What is more, in keeping faith with our existing characters, we would again be forced to put unhelpful comment into the mouths of fictional men and women who command a wide following among the serial's millions of viewers, with potentially dangerous effect. It is far easier to inflame the extremists with fictional support for their beliefs than to awaken the consciences of the uncaring with fictional moralities and it would be quite wrong for an entertainment programme to run such risks and accept such responsibility.[2]

In 2000, *Coronation Street* archivist Daran Little revealed in his commemorative book *40 Years of Coronation Street* that, in 1967, when writer Jack Rosenthal became the *Street*'s new producer, he planned some ambitious new storylines, 'Great plans were afoot to alter the face of the programme ... new characters were planned who could play more issue-led stories, including plans for the programme's first black family.'[3] But nothing came of this. However, Little did make a brief acknowledgement of Baptiste's appearance in 1963, but unfortunately misspelled the actor's name.

In the thirty years between Baptiste's appearance and Angela Griffin's debut as hairdresser Fiona Middleton in 1993, only a handful of black characters have appeared in *Coronation Street*, usually in roles so small that, if you blinked, you missed them! In 1966 Cleo Sylvestre played raincoat factory worker Cilla Christie in six episodes. In 1974 Alan Igbon was seen as the army pal of Bet Lynch's illegitimate soldier son who has been killed in Northern Ireland. Also in 1974 Emily and Ernest Bishop fostered two black children, Vernon and Lucy Foyle (Paul Steven Blidgeon and Andrea Blidgeon). Emily became very attached to the children and in one of the *Street*'s most emotional scenes she had to return them to their father, Winston (Volney Harris), when he came out of hospital. In 1975 Diana Queesikay appeared in two episodes as nightclub singer Sophie Edwards, and in 1983 Tony Marshall appeared as teenager Ray Valentine, an apprentice to Len Fairclough in the builder's yard. Also in 1983 the McGregor brothers, one white, one black, who later resurfaced in their own sitcom, attended Eddie Yeats's engagement party in the Rover's Return.

Perhaps the best-remembered black character from this early period is Janice Stubbs, the waitress from Dawson's Café, who in 1978 wrecked Deirdre's first marriage to Ray Langton. Angela Bruce, who played Janice, later recalled how the introduction of such a storyline had caused uneasiness:

Leslie Duxbury wrote ten episodes for me to come in and threaten the marriage of Deirdre and Ray Langton. For the Street this was a revolution. In its 25 year history, black people had never featured. There was one historic moment when a black person threw a dart at the Rover's, but he never said a word. At first the producer Bill Podmore did not want to have me. He said he was worried about racial prejudice, that the viewers might switch off and that the part could easily be done by a white woman. It took months to persuade him, and even when he agreed he wanted me to have bodyguards in case of any adverse reaction. I hoped that I had broken a barrier and this would open the door for other good roles for black actors. But they have since closed up and black people do not really feature.[4]

So far the longest stint has been enjoyed by Lisa Lewis who played Shirley Armitage, one of Mike Baldwin's factory workers, from 1983 to 1989. For several years she remained practically silent, with just a few lines here and there, quietly munching a barm cake in the background while Ivy, Elsie or Vera took centre stage. For Lewis, a role in the *Street* was an exciting breakthrough in her acting career, though she was always aware her participation in the storylines might never develop: 'I'm not afraid of being typecast as Shirley because she's such a nice, versatile character. But I think she's unlikely to develop into a bigger part.'[5]

In 1988 Shirley was given more prominence in the series when she became the girlfriend of Curly Watts, much to the disapproval of his parents and her mother. The young couple set up home together in the flat above Alf Roberts's corner shop, and there were occasional appearances by Shirley's formidable mother, played by Mona Hammond, who later joined the cast of *EastEnders* as Blossom Jackson. However, in 1989 Shirley and Curly's relationship was cut short when Lisa Lewis left the programme to have a baby. Said Juliet Robeson in *The Weekly Journal*:

> Shirley worked at Baldwin's factory for some years quietly in the background before she came out of herself and into her own strong, interesting character. She was neither politically aggressively 'black' nor cautiously 'positive' white. She totally belonged to the Street's community, doing Bingo with Vera, as well as probably getting her extensions done by a cousin down the road. Shirley was a success, totally believable. Like most characters in 'Corrie', an issue didn't touch her, particularly the race one, until that is, she tried to get the flat over Alf's shop, and was dealt out of it. Then after moving in with Curly she enjoyed a full but brief 'relationship' which touched briefly the problem of encountering his parents and their inherent racism. Her character worked well, her colour rarely discussed except when relevant. In short, she was absorbed nicely into the Street's storyline.[6]

Angela Griffin joined the cast of *Coronation Street* on 5 March 1993. By 1997, with the financial help of her brother Lee, she had become a successful young businesswoman, taking over the hair salon from Denise Osbourne. In some respects this young, attractive black woman promoted a 'positive' image. However, by 1997, she still hadn't been seen with a black boyfriend, welcomed a black woman into her salon or been seen popping into The Kabin to buy a copy of *Pride* from Rita Sullivan. Though her black father and white mother made a brief appearance at the opening of the salon a year earlier, it was only for one episode. In 1996 an explanation was offered when a *Coronation Street* spokeswoman, interviewed by the *Caribbean Times*, had this to say: 'We are colour blind when it comes to selecting actors for different roles. Fiona, the black hairdresser, got the role for talents, not her colour. We do not consider racial factors when we are appointing.'[7] However, in less than a year, the scriptwriters of *Coronation Street* had a change of heart. In fact, it took them thirty-four years to acknowledge the existence of racism, and in doing so they helped make a one-dimensional character become believable. It happened when Fiona and Alan McKenna (Glen Hugill), a white police officer, fell in love. In an episode shown on 21 March 1997, Fiona discovers that Alan has not invited her to a police 'bash'. 'It's not because I'm black, is it?' she asked. Suddenly the character of Fiona took on a new dimension. She became real and interesting. In the next episode Alan tried to apologize, but Fiona stood her ground. 'I'm a black girl,' she said, adding that Alan's colleagues at the local nick would laugh at him if they saw her with him. The 'difficult' situation was resolved when Alan asked Fiona to marry him, though the relationship ended in tears, and Fiona left the Street in 1998. So *Coronation Street* finally came full circle from its early days when Thomas Baptiste appeared as Johnny Alexander and stood up to Len Fairclough's bigotry.

Thomas Baptiste was not the first black actor to appear in a British television soap. In 1959 Gloria Simpson played a nurse in *Emergency – Ward 10*, ITV's first long-running soap opera (1957–67). The series also provided occasional roles for black actors like Trinidad's Frank Singuineau, who, in 1961, made an appearance as a patient. Later that year Jamaica's Clifton Jones became a regular member of the cast as Dr Jeremiah Sanders. Jones stayed with the series for nearly a year. In 1962 Earl Cameron was featured in several episodes as Lucky Jones, described in the *TV Times* as 'a Jamaican carpenter brought in with his arm almost severed'. But the black character who made the biggest impact in the series was Louise Mahler, an African doctor from a wealthy family, played by the Jamaican actress Joan Hooley.

Joan Hooley with John White and John Carlisle in *Emergency – Ward 10 (1964)*

When Joan auditioned for *Emergency – Ward 10*, she found herself thrown into an embarrassing situation:

> They wanted a black actress for the part and several of us auditioned, including Carmen Munroe and Leonie Forbes. At the audition we had to kiss a white actor, John Carlisle. He played Dr Large in the series, and the actress who kissed him most passionately was given the part! That was quite an embarrassing thing to do.[8]

Joan made her first appearance on 20 March 1964 and, within several months, she became the centre of attention in a controversial storyline involving a romance between Dr Mahler and a white doctor, Giles Farmer (John White). Problems arose when the script required Louise and Giles to kiss in a bedroom:

> The kiss between Louise and Giles was quite controversial because when they originally wrote the script we were supposed to be in my bedroom, and I was supposed to be wearing my slip. We were going to embrace and kiss, but the powers that be decided that it was too risqué for a family programme. It would not have been risqué if a white actress had been

playing my role. It was controversial because I was black, and John was white. So they changed the whole setting from the bedroom to the hospital garden. Our television kiss in the bedroom was banned! In the end we did kiss, but the script had to be drastically altered.[9]

The day after the scene was shown, the *Daily Express* published a photograph of Louise and Giles kissing, and informed its readers 'not a viewer rang up to complain'. Off screen, Joan was married to a white man, and says that they 'fell about laughing' at the ban and the media attention the television kiss attracted. However, by the end of 1964 the romance had ended, and Louise was killed off. She made her final appearance on 8 December: 'The scriptwriters had great difficulty in keeping our romance going. Our dialogue was often quite stilted, and lacked credibility. In the end they decided to end the relationship, and kill off Louise. She returned to Africa and was bitten by a snake!'[10]

The BBC took a little longer to introduce a black character into a television soap. A few months after Joan Hooley began making regular appearances in *Emergency – Ward 10*, Trinidadian Horace James joined the cast of *Compact*, the BBC's top television soap. Set in the offices of a popular women's magazine, *Compact* was launched on 2 January 1962. It had been conceived by writer Hazel Adair as she waited to deliver an article to *Woman's Own*. Hazel developed the idea with Peter Ling, with whom she created another hugely successful soap, *Crossroads*, two years later. Horace made his first appearance as photographer Jeff Armandez in *Compact* on 17 August 1964. Altogether, James made twenty-six appearances in *Compact*, leaving the cast on 13 October. Sadly, none of these were recorded.

Hooley and James's roles in *Emergency – Ward 10* and *Compact* are early examples of integrated casting, then still in its infancy in American television. At this time, their roles were breakthroughs, for no other black actors had played continuing roles in popular television series, especially for the BBC. So what was the reason for casting Horace James in *Compact*? Hazel Adair remembers:

Peter Ling and myself wrote it in the storyline that there should be a black photographer in *Compact*, but we did not actually sit in on the casting sessions. We made a point of not referring in any way to his colour, but just took it as a matter of course that he was an excellent photographer and that is why he had the job. There was not a great deal of viewer reaction to this casting. There was far more about another storyline we did about a mixed-race girl marrying a white man. This did occasion a storm of protest, including a lot of hate mail to the actress concerned, who was of Spanish extraction. We were not influenced by the American soaps, but rather the fact of portraying contemporary life where black people were beginning to take more important roles in all areas of society.[11]

In January 1970, four years after playing a factory worker in *Coronation Street*, Cleo Sylvestre joined the cast of the daytime soap *Crossroads*:

> I remember my first line came right at the end of the episode. I walked into the motel with my suitcase, went up to the reception, and said, 'Could I speak to Mrs Richardson, please?' The receptionist said, 'Yes. Who shall I say wants her?' And I replied, 'Tell her it's her daughter, Melanie,' and then the theme tune started over the end credits. Can you imagine, in 1970, a young black woman appearing in a popular soap and announcing she's the daughter of the star of the programme? In the next episode it was revealed I was her *foster* daughter who had been studying in France, though Meg had never mentioned her existence to anyone![12]

Crossroads had been launched by ATV in 1964. Set in King's Oak, a fictitious village in the Midlands, the series was built around Meg Richardson (Noele Gordon), the owner of a motel. Originally scheduled to run for just six weeks, *Crossroads* became a firm favourite with viewers, and rivalled *Coronation Street* as Britain's most popular soap. For almost twenty-five years, until it was axed in 1988, *Crossroads* was ridiculed for its bad acting and wobbly sets. The butt of endless jokes, the series carried on regardless. Of course, few of the critics who belittled the series bothered to acknowledge that *Crossroads* was one of the first soaps to address social issues and include a regular role for a black character. Cleo was asked to join the cast after its producer, Reg Watson, had seen her in the BBC drama-documentary *Some Women* in 1969:

> Cleo is one of my favourite actresses from my years producing *Crossroads* and, if she hadn't agreed to play the part of Melanie Harper, I wouldn't have gone ahead with it. I knew she would make Melanie a charismatic character (which was essential) and I don't doubt that people still fondly remember her as Melanie. I also remember that she brought a lot of laughter to us behind the scenes at the studio. I was sorry she decided not to continue.[13]

With her lively personality, Cleo became a favourite with viewers and she has nothing but happy memories of working on the programme. She feels that Watson's decision to cast her may have had something to do with the rise in anti-black feeling in Britain, especially after Enoch Powell made his 'Rivers of Blood' speech in 1968:

> The series was ridiculed but, as far as I was concerned, it did a tremendous

amount of good just having an ordinary character in there who happened to be black. It is important to remember this happened around the time Enoch Powell was making all those terrible 'Rivers of Blood' speeches, and British television audiences needed to see someone like Melanie every week. She was someone they could identify with. I remember feeling apprehensive about appearing on television every week. Powell caused a great deal of racial tension and I was worried people in the street would recognize me, and be hostile towards me. But when I went into Birmingham fans of the show would stop me and ask about *Crossroads*. They loved the programme, and obviously liked Melanie. I never had any trouble.

It was a very happy period, though the pressure of making five episodes a week was tremendous. It was like weekly repertory in television. Noele Gordon was lovely. She went out of her way to be helpful. I left the series after Reg Watson came to me one day in the spring and said, 'Cleo, we've got a storyline for you in November,' and I suddenly thought, 'no, I'm not going to stay.' I wanted to get out and return to my first love, the theatre.[14]

In 1974 Equity's Coloured Artists' Committee monitored British television, and in the report of their findings, *Coloured Artists on British Television*, published in August 1974, they criticized the lack of black representation in soaps. Their findings clearly failed to influence the makers of *Coronation Street*. However, three months after the publication of the report, a black family was introduced in *Crossroads*. In November 1974 Trevor Butler signed a contract with ATV to appear in *Crossroads* for twenty weeks as Winston James, a juvenile delinquent who runs away from home. Noele Gordon remembered:

Our story had a teenager, born and bred in Birmingham, whose parents originally came from Jamaica. He had never known any other country but Britain, and clashed with his somewhat Victorian father who looked back with nostalgia to the way of life he left behind in his own country. The father, steeped in the tradition of his own background, just couldn't accept that he now had an English son who wanted to live the English way of life. This is a problem very prevalent among Britain's immigrant parents.[15]

The conflict with his father, Cameron James, played by Lee Davis, was eventually resolved, thus ending that particular storyline and, sadly, the characters. Elizabeth Adare also appeared in the cast as Winston's protective sister, Linda, who worked at the motel.

Crossroads was the first British drama series to integrate a black family into its regular cast, even if their stay was short-lived. However, the appearances of Melanie Harper and the James family were not isolated cases, as Dorothy Hobson pointed out in 1982:

Crossroads has been anxious to reflect the cultural and ethnic groups in the area and has had a number of black and Asian families and characters in its storylines. Currently it has the character of Mac, the black garage mechanic who is working at the motel garage and becoming increasingly more important in storylines.[16]

Carl Andrews joined the cast of *Crossroads* as Joe 'Mac' MacDonald in 1978 and played the role until 1986. In the early days he had a romance with Trina, played by the Jamaican actress Merdelle Jordine. They subsequently married and had a baby. Says Christine Geraghty:

Given British soaps' lack of regular black characters, *Crossroads'* use of Mac was something of a landmark. He was not so heavily marginalized as Dominique [in *Dynasty*] and much was made of the 'ordinary' way in which he cared for his wife, Tina [*sic*], and the baby, and the grief he felt when his marriage broke up. Nevertheless, like Dominique, Mac tended to be on the fringe of main plotlines concerning the garage, content to be a mechanic while others jostled for positions of greater power. At the same time, stories about Mac's dealings with white characters tended, on examination, to be about them – their liberalism, their thoughtlessness – rather than him. In these stories, Mac was a cipher for something strange but tolerated in the community, a black hole which absorbed the attitudes of others towards him ... In such a situation, the black character as an individual disappears under the responsibility of carrying the 'race' issue and is used largely to demonstrate the notional tolerance of the largely white community.[17]

In 1987 actress Dorothy Brown, who played sports instructress Lorraine Baker, revealed to the press that she had been sacked. A new producer, Bill Smethurst, joined the team and made many sweeping, unpopular changes. Dorothy expressed her disapproval of the change in direction in an interview in *The Voice*: 'I don't agree with what he is doing. I don't think it will work. There are no black characters left, and I doubt that there will be any more. If things go badly, he'll be sacked as well.'[18] Just over a year later, on 4 April 1988, as Dorothy predicted, Smethurst lost his job when *Crossroads* was axed after twenty-four years. Like a phoenix rising from the ashes it made a welcome return on 5 March 2001 with a racially integrated cast that included kitchen hand Minty (Peter Dalton).

One other black actress who appeared in *Crossroads* – towards the end of its run – was Sharon Rosita, who briefly appeared in one episode as a temporary kitchen hand. This was the same actress who had previously been seen as Kate Moses in Channel 4's top soap, *Brookside*. Down-to-earth, bubbly Kate shared a house with her white friends, Sandra Maghie and Pat Hancock, and worked as a nurse in the local hospital. In a dramatic storyline, Kate was pestered by a stalker who, obsessed with his mother, blamed Kate for her death. The storyline reached a climax when he took the trio hostage in a siege of their house in 1985. Kate helped her two friends to escape, but was killed by the psychotic gunman. Her funeral included the first appearance of her family. We had never seen Kate with them, except in death. She had always been a black character without any contact with other black people. After Kate's death, one could only feel a sense of loss, as well as frustration, that a good actress had been wasted.

For over a year, Sharon Rosita played the likeable, friendly Kate, but during that time the scriptwriters failed to do anything with her. During her stay in *Brookside*, she never become a major character, or as interesting as some of her neighbours, such as Sheila and Bobby Grant. Christine Geraghty has described Kate as a 'classic example' of the 'singleton strategy':

> Little attention was paid to her private life and unlike Sandra she was not involved in stories dealing with her work as a nurse. In the main, she was a foil to the more dramatic lives of her friends and comforted Sandra and made tea for Pat during their various crises. Given Kate's marginal position, it was somehow appropriate that she should be the one of the three to die in the siege even though the death was based on contingencies other than her ethnic origin.[19]

For over a year, Kate remained a 'token black' who, once installed in *Brookside*, was given little to do except stand on the sidelines. Such has been the fate of many black characters in British soaps. Today, while most television soaps have black characters, as yet, none of them are being given any real dramatic scope, or a black cultural context. Most of the time they are dull and one-dimensional. Actor Treva Etienne feels that producers often employ black actors just to fill quotas, or so they can be seen to be 'doing their bit': 'Once you're in that situation, the producers don't know how to deal with having a black actor in the scenario. So we get a black actor walking around, playing the part, but never really feeling involved or part of the overall action.'[20]

This has happened time and time again in BBC1's *EastEnders*, (launched on 19 February 1985), even though its first producer, Julia Smith, was quoted as saying: 'Our East End setting was chosen for the diversity of its past – the strong 'culture' it has, and the multi-racial community that has developed.' Since it began, *EastEnders*' mix of social realism and melodrama has been consistently popular with the British public. But its black characters have rarely been as interesting as their white counterparts, or been given any storylines of substance.

When the series began, the original cast included Tony Carpenter (Oscar James) and his teenage son Kelvin (Paul J. Medford). Subsequently, Sally Sagoe joined the cast as Tony's wife Hannah, and Judith Jacob (in 1987) took the part of social worker Carmel. However, none of these characters stayed very long, and most disappeared amid controversy. Before he left the series in May 1987, Oscar James complained that the BBC didn't promote the black characters as much as the white characters. Viewers were more likely to tune in to watch the antics of Dirty Den, his wife Angie and bad boy Nick Cotton than the Carpenter family or Carmel:

> the powers that be do not think I am interesting enough. Is it because I am a member of an ethnic minority? How often do you see Paul J. Medford being publicised? ... It's as though the BBC are playing us down. I can't believe the white majority of the public are against blacks being stars. They don't give a damn.[21]

After his arrival in *EastEnders* at the beginning of 1994, Alan Jackson (Howard Anthony) became the butt of many jokes in the black community, and the criticisms are justified. When he arrived in Walford, he shared some of the characteristics of his *Brookside* counterpart, Mick Johnson (Louis Emerick). They were portrayed as good, reliable, hard-working fathers, and as well-integrated members of their communities. This was a noticeable departure from the pimp/villain stereotypes viewers had become used to, including Carmel's dodgy brother Darren. However, Alan's goodness made him terribly boring, and his extramarital affair with 'bad' Frankie was totally implausible.

Another problem with *EastEnders* is its constant waste of talented black actors. For example, who was Alan's mother, Blossom Jackson? What Caribbean island did she come from? What church did she go to? Why did we never see her talking to any other black women of her age group in Walford? After arriving in Walford in 1994 she became the invisible woman of Albert Square. The scriptwriters gave her little to do except serve in the café and say one line: 'You want another cup of coffee?' During her stay in *EastEnders*, Blossom Jackson should have become the Ena Sharples of Walford, a fiesty matriarch, scrapping with Peggy Mitchell or Pauline Fowler in Albert Square. Her scenes with grandson Alan lacked the humour, tension and passion of Peggy and Grant. Surely Alan's relationship with bad girl Frankie would have been enough to push Blossom over the edge?

When she joined the series, the scriptwriters should have taken a close look at the career of Mona Hammond, the actress who played Blossom.

RADA-trained, she is one of our most versatile actresses, having acted on stage in Shakespeare and Oscar Wilde. Since the 1960s Mona has appeared on television in many dramas and sitcoms. Her most memorable roles have included the Nurse in *Romeo and Juliet* for BBC2's *Shakespeare Shorts* (1996) and Adrian Lester's mother in *Storm Damage* (2000). She deserved much better from the writers and producers of *EastEnders* for, at the end of the day, it is they who have to take responsibility for wasting the talents of black actors. This feeling is shared by Joan Hooley, who played Josie McFarlane in the series at the end of the 1990s:

> There is still this tokenism in television where black characters are concerned ... She says she feels demoralized by her 18-month run in *EastEnders*: 'I think they could have done better for me. I mean, there were so many big stories happening when I was in. I sort of sat back and waited and thought, well, Tiffany's dead now and Bianca and Grant have gone and then there's this big murder story and all that and I waited and waited and bugger all happened.[22]

Things did look up in 1978 when BBC2 launched *Empire Road*, a five-part drama series which was later (inaccurately) described as Britain's first 'black soap'. It was created by the Guyanese writer, Michael Abbensetts, who was responsible for all the scripts:

> My intention with *Empire Road* was to produce something which didn't show black people as only being 'The Drug Dealer' or 'The Criminal'. Also, it's important for black people to be able to turn on the TV to see something of their lives that they can be proud of ... *Empire Road* was the only one of its kind ... There should be more black writers.[23]

The BBC even employed a black director, Horace Ové, for one episode and it had three superb actors – Norman Beaton, Corinne Skinner-Carter and Joseph Marcell – heading the cast. A second, ten-part series, was commissioned and shown in 1979 and the series should have continued running into the 1980s. Indeed, if the BBC had wanted it, *Empire Road* could have become Britain's first black soap opera, but someone pulled the plug. Norman Beaton was devastated:

> *Empire Road* was given a lot of media coverage. It was hailed as the Black *Coronation Street*. Enormous expectations were raised within the black community ... The series was well-received by the press ... Michael [Abbensetts] was invited to do another ten episodes for transmission the next year ... The [second] series was screened at a later hour and got higher viewing figures than the first series had done. In spite of that it was taken off. I have never been given a satisfactory explanation as to why this

extraordinary decision was reached. It was getting a larger audience. It had bigger audiences than some of the other programmes that were transmitted on BBC2. More important than this, however, was the fact that it was the only indigenous drama series on television catering to the specific needs of the Afro-Caribbean community ... Yet *Empire Road* was abandoned. To many of us it was a grossly insensitive decision.[24]

NOTES

1 Thomas Baptiste, interview with Stephen Bourne, London, 8 July 1991.
2 H. V. Kershaw, *The Street Where I Live* (London: Book Club Associates, 1981), p. 170–1.
3 Daran Little, *40 Years of Coronation Street* (London: Granada Media, 2000), p. 45.
4 Angela Bruce, interview with Tony Sewell, *The Voice*, 21 February 1987.
5 Lisa Lewis, interview with Judi Goodwin, *TV Times*, 1–7 December 1984.
6 Juliet Robeson, 'Why the Street is doing the white thing', *The Weekly Journal*, 22 October 1992.
7 *Caribbean Times*, 29 August 1996.
8 Joan Hooley, interview with Stephen Bourne, London, 23 July 1991.
9 *Ibid.*
10 *Ibid.*
11 Hazel Adair, letter to Stephen Bourne, 30 October 1996.
12 Cleo Sylvestre, interview with Stephen Bourne, London, 3 April 1989.
13 Reg Watson, letter to Stephen Bourne, 29 August 1989.
14 Sylvestre, interview with Bourne.
15 Noele Gordon, *My Life at Crossroads* (London: W. H. Allen, 1975), pp. 151–2.
16 Dorothy Hobson, *Crossroads: The Drama of a Soap Opera* (London: Methuen, 1982), pp. 38–9.
17 Christine Geraghty, *Women and Soap Opera: A Study of Prime Time Soaps* (Cambridge: Polity Press, 1991), p. 142.
18 Dorothy Brown, *The Voice*, 21 February 1987.
19 Geraghty, *Women and Soap Opera*, pp.142–3.
20 Treva Etienne, interview with Omega Douglas, *The Voice*, 29 October 1996.
21 Oscar James, *Sun*, 15 November 1987.
22 Joan Hooley, 'Life begins at 60', *The Stage*, 18 May 2000.
23 Michael Abbensetts, interview with Lorraine Griffiths, *Weekend Voice*, 22–23 August, 1987.
24 Norman Beaton, *Beaton but Unbowed: An Autobiography* (London: Methuen, 1986), p. 214.

SOAP FACTFILE

First black actor to appear in a soap: Frank Singuineau as a patient called George Nathaniel Wilberforce Lewis in *Emergency – Ward 10* (ATV, 1961).

First black actress to appear in a soap: Gloria Simpson as a nurse in *Emergency – Ward 10* (ATV, 1959).

First black actors to have continuing roles in a soap: Clifton Jones as Dr Jeremiah Sanders in *Emergency – Ward 10* (ATV, 1961–2) and Horace James as magazine photographer Jeff Armandez in *Compact* (BBC1, 1964).

First black actresses to have continuing roles in a soap: Joan Hooley as Dr Louise Mahler in *Emergency – Ward 10* (ATV, 1964) and Cleo Sylvestre as Meg Richardson's foster daughter Melanie Harper in *Crossroads* (ATV, 1970–71).

The first black family in a soap should have been seen in *Coronation Street* in 1967, but Granada dropped the idea, so this honour falls to the James family in *Crossroads* (ATV, 1974–5), played by Trevor Butler (Winston), Elizabeth Adare (his sister Linda) and Lee Davis (their father Cameron).

First black lesbian in a soap: hairdresser Della Alexander (Michelle Joseph) in *EastEnders* (BBC1, 1994–5).

First black gay in a soap: none at the time of writing.

First black married couple to appear in a soap: bus conductor Johnny Alexander and his wife (Thomas Baptiste and Barbara Assoon) in *Coronation Street* (Granada, 1963).

First black children to appear in a soap: Paul Steven Blidgeon and Andrea Blidgeon as Vernon and Lucy Foyle, Emily and Ernest Bishop's foster children, in *Coronation Street* (Granada, 1974).

Longest-serving black actors in a soap: Carl Andrews as garage mechanic Joe 'Mac' MacDonald in *Crossroads* (ATV/Carlton, 1978–86) and Louis Emerick as Mick Johnson in *Brookside* (Channel 4, 1989–2001).

Longest-serving black actresses in a soap: Lisa Lewis as factory worker Shirley Armitage in *Coronation Street* (Granada, 1983–9) and Angela Griffin as hairdresser Fiona Middleton in *Coronation Street* (Granada, 1993–8).

18

Newton I. Aduaka and *Rage*

Newton I. Aduaka was born in south-eastern Nigeria in 1966 and moved to Lagos from war-torn Biafra in 1970. Arriving in Britain in 1985, he studied at the London International Film School where he wrote, produced and directed the short *Voices Behind the Wall*. After graduating in 1990 he worked as a sound recordist while writing screenplays and contributing to a literary magazine. He then made some independent short films, with *On the Edge* winning several awards as it played at over forty festivals. *Rage* is Aduaka's first feature film, made by Granite FilmWorks, the company he formed in 1996 with Maria-Elena L'Abbate.

Rage explores the lives of three youths in contemporary London where cultures, class, race and sexuality intermingle and influence each other freely, and adopted American street style is the fashion of the day. The three teenagers are mixed-race Jamie (aka 'Rage'), a rebellious rapper played by Fraser Ayres, Godwin ('G'), an introverted black gay pianist, played by Shaun Parkes, and white Thomas ('T'), a forlorn DJ in search of a cause, played by John Pickard.

First shown at the 1999 London Film Festival, it was picked up by a distributor, Metrodome, who then failed to promote it. Consequently, *Rage* has had a limited theatrical release in Britain, though it has played with great success at many international film festivals. In 2001 Newton received an award as Best Director of a First Feature at the Pan African Film Festival in Los Angeles, and soon afterwards he was honoured with the Oumarou Ganda Prize for Director of a First Feature at FESPACO, the Pan-African Film Festival of Ouagadougou.

Newton I. Aduaka was interviewed by Stephen Bourne in London on 9 March 2001.

SB: When did you get involved in film?
NA: I got passionate about film, and went to film school at nineteen, and left at twenty-two. So I had the protection of the film school, and the

whole thing about the black struggle to make films didn't hit me until I was about twenty-four or twenty-five. I don't let myself be stifled by this feeling that, if you're black, the world is against you, which it is, because I've always believed there are cracks and – as soon as you see a crack – you sneak through! If you are observant enough you will slip through.

SB: There have been different kinds of black film-makers in Britain, and directors like Isaac Julien are more experimental in their approach. His 1991 feature, *Young Soul Rebels*, was intended to be the second-coming of *My Beautiful Laundrette*, and it wasn't. What were your expectations of it?

NA: I'd just left film school and Isaac's film was the first black feature to come out while I was here, and I must say I was disappointed. A lot of money had been put into it and it didn't translate on to the screen. It didn't come together as powerfully as I had hoped. Then I heard about the struggles Isaac had faced to keep certain things in the film, and the battles that he had. John Akomfrah faced the same thing when he made his last film, *Speak Like a Child*. It wasn't theatrically released. Very sad.

I loved Isaac's *Looking for Langston*. I thought it was a very powerful film. It was from his heart. It was a totally passionate film. Beautiful cinematography. It had detail. It was amazing and I was totally blown away by it.

SB: What constraints have you experienced?

NA: I wouldn't work for Channel 4, because I cannot deal with their script editors. I don't mind briefing them, but most of these guys have an idea in the head about the film they want you to make. I don't mind briefing them, but they must leave me alone to do the work. That's what I do. I'm a film-maker. I'd say, 'You're an executive. I wouldn't tell you how to run your business.'

I went through the experience with two television series: *Capital Lives*, which was commissioned by Carlton, and the BBC's *Crucial Tales*, which was made by Lenny Henry's company. I had a lot of problems working with them. I came up with scripts, but I had to keep going to meetings with script editors, and they'd say this works, this doesn't work. But I write organically; I can't write to any formulas. They tried to get me to write something they have in their minds, and I ended up wondering why they didn't write the scripts, because they didn't want my input. I didn't know what I was supposed to be doing at those meetings. So I walked away. Both script editors were white.

For Carlton I had written some dialogue which had characters speaking partly Nigerian, partly English, as a Nigerian couple would speak, but the script editor said this would be totally inaccessible to a British audience. I responded by saying 'Don't you think the British audience wants to see something refreshing? A true perspective of being an African in London?'

SB: I live in a tower block in south-east London and I have Nigerian neighbours, and we get used to each others' speech patterns. If you listen you can understand. It's about communication. And if script editors are saying you can't have that on television, then we're in a sorry state.

NA: It was a sad situation to be in, and I walked away from Carlton's *Capital Lives* project because I'd gone through four weeks of nightmare, trying to explain myself, trying to tell them about people who live in this country. The sad thing was that *Capital Lives* was supposed to be about people's experiences of living in London. I had the same experience with the BBC and *Crucial Tales*, and I did try to speak to Lenny Henry about it. It was just so frustrating, I swore I would never work with those kinds of script editors again.

SB: Where did the idea for *Rage* come from?

NA: It comes from a lot of things. Bits of it are about me growing up in Lagos as a teenager when I had a band in high school. We got into a lot of trouble with our parents because we were skiving off school. After I came to England I hung around for about a year, doing odd jobs, and then I discovered cinema and took it from there.

But in *Rage* I wanted to tell this story about teenagers who have this belief and passion to do music and I set it around hip-hop because I wanted to deal with the idea of the phenomenon of hip-hop, which is very

Shaun Parkes, Fraser Ayres and John Pickard in *Rage* (1999)

185

current across the world. I was in Burkino Faso in Africa the other day and I could hear hip-hop from Senegal, Guinea and Nigeria playing all over the place. But I wanted to look at it in a very critical way, question how much they take this American culture and make it their own.

And also I wanted to deal with multiculturalism by casting a black kid, a white kid and a mixed-race kid in a real-life setting, and I chose Peckham.

SB: Peckham is about cultural diversity. The media portray Peckham as a black area, but it isn't, and never has been. It's mixed.

NA: I lived in Peckham for four years ...

SB: I've lived there all my life ...

NA: Peckham has everyone from everywhere ...

SB: But it was like that when I grew up in the 1960s. When Damilola Taylor was found murdered on the North Peckham Estate last year, in the media frenzy that followed, this white woman, about the same age as me, wrote a story in the *Daily Mail*, and she lied. She claimed Damilola's school, Oliver Goldsmith, was an all-white school in the 1960s, but it wasn't. I was there, it was racially mixed, and I have photographs to prove it!

NA: I lived on the North Peckham Estate for four years, and that was my first experience of living in London.

SB: The North Peckham Estate has been neglected for too long.

NA: That's what it is. Total neglect. And it felt right to make *Rage* there.

SB: Can you remember what your image of London was, before you arrived?

NA: It was one of possibilities. And then I saw how depressed my surroundings were and my ideas changed very quickly. And then I started to experience racism, which was something I wasn't used to. At first it was little things. You hear people talk. Then you become aware of people disliking you. I'd get on a bus, and a white woman would grab her bag. And you realize what that means. But I also found racism in Kellys, the Caribbean club. There was this thing between young Africans and Caribbeans. Life's a funny thing, because someone always has to be the underdog. So, for me, it was a very strange situation to suddenly find myself a second-class citizen.

But then I found cinema, and I went to the International Film School, and spent as much time there as possible, watching as many films as I could, because I didn't have the film knowledge before. I developed this voracious appetite for cinema, and I loved being around people who knew about cinema.

SB: Was this interest technical?

NA: Oh, yeah. Technical. I tried to work on as many film school productions as possible.

SB: But were you encouraged to watch films?

NA: Oh, yeah. Hitchcock. Eisenstein. *Citizen Kane*. John Ford. The standard thing. Very limited. But after school we attended a film club.

SB: Were there any particular film-makers you found interesting?

NA: Well, the thing I loved about film school, above everything else, was being with fellow students from all over the world, and it was they who introduced me to old Russian cinema, Greek, Mexican, South American, South African cinema. My knowledge of cinema came from friends and colleagues. It was a great time.

So *Rage* came from all of this. The story is about three kids just hanging out together and their desperation to make music.

SB: One of the things I really like about *Rage* is the way it turns things around. For instance, Marcus, the old Rastafarian intellectual, gives Jamie a book, and you think it's a book about Black Power, or Malcolm X, but at the end of the film we discover it's a sex novel he has written himself! Then there's the gun. The audience believes it's a real gun because it's in the possession of a young black man from Peckham. But it turns out to be a lighter!

There were other things, such as the relationship between Jamie and his white mother. I could understand why there is tension between them. She doesn't understand his need to ask questions about her relationship with his father, and his cultural heritage.

NA: I was asking a question. Why can't life be as simple as this woman dreams about?

SB: I thought you were criticizing her. Saying that if you are white and have a mixed-race child, you should have some knowledge of that child's cultural heritage, and history.

NA: There's two things. I believe in love and for me love is a good excuse for a lot of things. It's the most powerful force in the world. When she fell in love with Jamie's father she wasn't aware of certain things.

SB: You're right. How can we blame her for being born in a country that doesn't educate her about black history?

NA: Exactly. There are black kids who don't know anything about black history. There are black men and women who have gone through the school system here and know nothing about their history because they're not taught anything. If you didn't go out and search for it, you wouldn't know anything.

SB: The chances are that if she'd gone to a school that taught her about the culturally diverse history of this country, she may have been able to teach Jamie something. But our schools only teach kids about traditional British history. So they learn about Queen Victoria. Then they're lied to. They're told only white Londoners lived through the 1940 Blitz.

NA: But I also see the point of view from Jamie's eyes, and I wanted to explore the basis of the argument between these two people. I wanted to tell two sides of the story, because people buy into a thought and, if you're charismatic enough, like Hitler or Enoch Powell, people will believe you. That's where fascism comes from. So the mother cannot offer Jamie a quick fix, and he has to go out into the world and define himself.

SB: But the ending is very hopeful, because you feel Jamie is doing that.

NA: Exactly. He's doing that. He's thinking, and expressing himself in his final rap. You have to tell the world who you are, because if people keep telling you who you are, you're gonna keep swinging like a yo-yo. You have to decide who you are, and live by it, and say to the world, 'This is who I am. Like me or don't like me. This is who I am.'

SB: All my life people keep saying to me, you do this, you do that, but you're white. You write this book about black history, but you're white. It annoys me. So you're right. In the end I had to decide who I was, and I live by it. For instance, I say to those people, 'Not all white people come from all-white families.' I'm not from an all-white family. I had an aunt who was black, and I was informed by her. I was raised in a culturally diverse community and my work, my thinking, my outlook, is informed by all of this. But in life some people have to ask you these questions. If you made a documentary about Julie Andrews, people would ask, 'But Newton. Why are you making a film about Julie Andrews?' But the probability is you may have grown up watching films like *The Sound of Music*.

NA: That's right. As a child I saw *The Sound of Music* ten times. I saw *Sesame Street* growing up. They informed me. It's part of who I am. It's given me a broader outlook on life. You watch certain things, and they're telling you something. But if I had been isolated from it, I would have a narrow-minded point of view.

SB: I want to talk about your portrayal of the police officers in *Rage*. Anyone who has lived in Peckham will know there have been tensions between the black community and the police. Even I, as a young white male, was stopped and searched in Peckham in 1980. At that time, the boys in blue used to stop and search anything that moved, except, perhaps, little old ladies with shopping trolleys. So we have all been touched by this. But instead of complaining about the situation, I decided to take control, and in 1992 I became involved in community liaison work with the police in south-east London. So, though I still have some reservations about the police, since the inquiry into Stephen Lawrence's murder, they have tried to shift, and I felt your portrayal of the police wasn't balanced. Yes, you were right to show a police officer being racist, because that kind of behaviour still exists, in spite of what has happened in the last few years.

But I'm curious to know why you didn't show the other policeman challenging the racist officer.

NA: In that scene, the younger officer is very nervous in the presence of the old dinosaur officer. He doesn't agree with what is happening. When Jamie says to the dinosaur, 'I'm not gonna listen to your shit' and walks away, the younger officer says something like 'You don't want trouble, move on.' It's there, but it's not overt. Also, we planned the film before the publication of the Stephen Lawrence report, so it's about what was happening just before that. I didn't want to portray a good cop and a bad cop, either. I like things that are grey. But I am aware that some younger officers are more sensitive.

SB: Where has the support for *Rage* come from?

NA: From the people, from the audience. In Britain, the London Film Festival screened it in 1999. The Black Filmmaker International Film Festival in 2000. It's been to the Ritzy in Brixton and Peckham Premiere. Now it's doing well in film festivals around the world. So far this year [2001] I've taken *Rage* to festivals in Toronto, Los Angeles, Burkino Faso, Milan and India.

SB: I had enthusiastic feedback from friends who live in Peckham who saw it when it played at the Premiere. But when I looked it up in the *South London Press* cinema listings, it had been taken off! I was so disappointed, because I wanted to see it with a local audience.

NA: That's unfortunate. Audiences who have seen it have been great. Fantastic. Everywhere I go audiences have engaged with the film. They want to talk about it.

SB: But these are debates that should be happening here. It's sad that it hasn't happened.

NA: Metrodome pretty much messed up the film. They didn't know how to reach the audience. They categorized the film as a black film, they categorized me as a black film-maker, and then gave it a small release. But *Rage* is about cultural diversity. It's broader than a black film. Any young person will connect with this story. Metrodome gave it poor publicity, no visibility on the street, and what happened was the film died at the box office. I will never forgive Metrodome for that.

SB: But why did they pick it up in the first place?

NA: To make some money through video and television sales. We were learning as we went along. You never know what people's agendas are. So we went to Metrodome, told them they had sabotaged my film, and asked them to return the film. They said, 'Fine, you can have it.' We've approached the Film Council, asked for £13,000, which is nothing, and with their help we're planning to re-release the film. We're planning an internet campaign, a street campaign, for £13,000. Films like *The Full*

Monty and *East Is East* had £3 million spent on publicity. Crazy money. So of course they're going to be successful.

One thing I always said to myself is, 'I didn't want to be part of the statistics of black films in this country that have failed,' but now I understand why they do. It's not the film-makers or the films, it's in the minds of the people who market these films. They do not know how to get to the market.

SB: It's similar to the situation I found myself in with the first edition of *Black in the British Frame*. When it came out in 1998 I expected lots of coverage and reviews in the mainstream, in the broadsheets. But nothing happened. No mention in the *Guardian* or the *Independent*. No interview on Radio 4. Nothing. I realized that, if I had written a book called *Diary of Jackie Brown* and included exclusive interviews with Quentin Tarantino, Samuel L. Jackson and Pam Grier, I'd have been reviewed in everything: *Sight and Sound*, *Time Out*, *Empire*. But nothing happened. I felt excluded because I am not African-American, and my book is not about African-American cinema. But I didn't sit back and let that exclusion destroy me. I found other ways to promote my book.

NA: At the Film Council someone said, 'I really like you as a director, and I'd really like us to do something together.' But he didn't understand what *Rage* was about. And I thought to myself, is it the film that you find offensive? And I bet if he asked me to direct something for them, it would be something really mundane.

SB: Because of the title, people are going to think *Rage* is an angry film. Because it's about a young mixed-race guy from Peckham, they'll expect the film to be about guns and yardies. But it isn't that, and that's what I liked most about the film. It isn't predictable, and anyone with any sensitivity can see that *Rage* has universal appeal. You've made a film for everyone. And this is what we're up against in this country. People in control who dictate who sees what.

NA: That's what has hijacked a lot of interesting films.

SB: How did the gay character, Godwin, come into the film?

NA: Godwin's role was cut back. In the cut version, every time you see him in the jazz club, there's a young white man sitting there and Godwin looks at him from time to time. In the uncut version there was interaction and dialogue between the gay couple, and a key sequence where Godwin kisses the young man. A whole gay subplot existed.

SB: So what happened to the gay sequences?

NA: Metrodome said, 'We can't have the gay subplot in the film. We cannot market a film with a gay subplot to the teenage audience. Get rid of it.' I said, 'Look, you knew about the subplot when you picked up the film, and now I've signed the contract you're telling me you don't want the subplot in it.' I said, 'Screw you', and for a week I was depressed. Totally shattered, because I wanted to have a gay relationship in the film, and deal with the issue of a gay man in the black community. After talking about this to Tom Charity in *Time Out*, Metrodome started receiving anonymous phone calls, accusing them of being homophobic! I was so happy!

SB: But aren't young black audiences more prepared for this than they were ten years ago?

NA: Sad to say, it isn't true. I showed the uncut *Rage* at the Ritzy in Brixton. It was a free screening for fourteen-to nineteen-year-olds from local schools and colleges. The cinema was packed, and the audience was lively, they liked the film, but every time the gay couple appeared, there was silence. Then when the kiss happened, there was uproar. And in the question-and-answer session afterwards, they wanted to know why I had put gays in the film. They didn't like it. But I always show the uncut version, with the gay subplot, and kiss, at film festivals around the world.

I have no right to judge anyone. I want to make other films like *Rage* that are non-judgemental. To highlight the problems we have in human nature, of man's injustice and hypocrisy to others. I want to deal with this, and fight this, in cinema. That is my chosen field.

We have to get out of this state of mind where we think this island and its narrow-minded executives who run the film industry is all there is. They have a British Empire mentality. There's a world out there.

SB: There's another Empire mentality and that's the *Empire* magazine mentality that gives Vinnie Jones an award for Best British Film Actor! I witnessed this embarrassing spectacle on television the same week I saw *Rage*, and I said to myself, 'This is what the British film industry has come to. Ignoring your film, and honouring Vinnie Jones!'

NA: It's a disgrace. It is the most shameful situation that any country can find itself in. I can find you an actor, or a kid in the street, who can act better than Vinnie Jones.

19

Black in the British Frame
A Film and Television Drama Survey
1936–2001

The purpose of this chapter is to highlight some of the most important film and television dramas, produced since the 1930s, which have been located in Britain. Film titles are followed by director and year of release. Television titles are followed by channel and year of transmission. Due to lack of space, it has been impossible to include long-running television drama series such as *Casualty*, *London's Burning*, *The Bill* and *Playing the Field*. Special attention has been given to the work of black writers and directors. This chapter also includes a tribute to the actor Norman Beaton (1934–94) who was the most influential and highly regarded black British actor of his time.

In the late 1930s Paul Robeson was one of Britain's most popular screen actors (see Chapter 3) and two of his most interesting films were located in London and South Wales. In *Song of Freedom* (J. Elder Wills, 1936) he played a London-born dock worker who dreams of visiting Africa. Said Graham Greene in the *Spectator* (25 September 1936):

Apart from Mr Robeson's magnificent singing of inferior songs, I find it hard to say in what the charm of this imperfect picture lies. The direction is distinguished but not above reproach, the story is sentimental and absurd, and yet a sense stays in the memory of an unsophisticated mind fumbling on the edge of simple and popular poetry. The best scenes are the dockland scenes, the men returning from work, black and white in an easy companionship free from any colour bar, the public house interiors, dark faces pausing at tenement windows to listen to Zinga's songs, a sense of nostalgia. There are plenty of faults even here, sentiment too close to sentimentality, a touch of 'quaintness' and patronage, but one is made aware all the time of what Mann calls 'the gnawing surreptitious hankering for the bliss of the commonplace', the general exile of our class as well as the particular exile of the African. But everything goes badly wrong when Zinga reaches Africa.

In *The Proud Valley* (Pen Tennyson, 1940), Robeson's role as David Goliath, a miner in South Wales was much admired. The film has been described by Peter Stead as

> a curious mixture of realism and stereotype, of radicalism and soap opera, of innocence and sharpness. It is a sentimental, lyrical and, of course, musical tribute to the working class made essentially by outsiders who attempted to convert a political and industrial drama into a warm folk-tale. There is no trade-unionism on show and all the bright ideas came not from any organization but from David Goliath's young friend Emlyn, but the miners are real people, we do see them producing leaders and choosing delegates, and by the end of the film there is a sense that the men themselves and their community constitute a real and perhaps irresistible force.[1]

The Man in Grey (Leslie Arliss, 1943), a popular Gainsborough costume drama set in Regency England, included a young black page called Toby in the supporting cast. He was played by Harry Scott, the son of Harry Scott of Scott and Whaley fame (see Chapter 1). Toby's appearance in the film offered a rare glimpse of a black servant in Britain in the early 1800s. He is devoted to Clarissa (Phyllis Calvert), who is befriended by Hesther (Margaret Lockwood), a scheming, ambitious adventuress. 'Good' Clarissa is fond of Toby, and treats him with kindness, whereas 'bad' Hesther shows contempt for him, calling him an 'urchin' and 'a slave's brat'.

Great Expectations (David Lean, 1946) includes a tracking shot that reveals Magwitch (Finlay Currie) and other prisoners in the dock as they are about to be sentenced by the judge. Prominent in this scene is an unidentified black extra as a defiant-looking prisoner. It is one of the most powerful images in the film and an extremely rare example of an adaptation of a Charles Dickens novel that acknowledges the black presence in Victorian England. Black extras were subsequently included in screen adaptations of *Oliver Twist* (David Lean, 1948) and *The Pickwick Papers* (Noel Langley, 1952), however, to date, no speaking roles have ever been given to black actors in film or television adaptations of Dickens's literary classics. Admittedly, Dickens did not include black characters in his novels, but this does not mean that black actors could not play some of his characters. Many thousands of black people were living and working in Victorian England, and this should be reflected on the screen more often.

Pool of London (Basil Dearden, 1951) featured Bermudian Earl Cameron (see Chapter 11) as a Jamaican seaman who comes ashore for a weekend, and befriends a white woman (Susan Shaw). For the first time since Paul Robeson in *The Proud Valley*, a serious attempt was made to present a black character in a British film as an ordinary human being and not a stereotype. In her review of the film in the *Observer* (26 February 1951), C. A. Lejeune said:

> One thing, however, comes shining out of *Pool of London*, and that is the performance of Earl Cameron. In a film in which the jumpy construction gives no player enough time to develop or sustain a character, he makes full use of every glancing minute. It is very difficult indeed for a white person to estimate accurately the acting talents of a man of colour, for everything he does is charged with a certain air of emotional mystery, but I can say with truth that Mr Cameron's touching performance remains for me the best memory of *Pool of London*, and left me with deeper thoughts about the colour problem than I have ever had before.

A Man from the Sun (BBC, 1956) was British television's first attempt at dramatizing the lives of Caribbean settlers in post-war Britain (see Chapter 12). *Hot Summer Night* (ABC, 1959), Ted Willis's explosive anti-racist stage drama, was adapted for television's popular *Armchair Theatre* series (see Chapter 13).

Tiger Bay (J. Lee Thompson, 1959), starring Hayley Mills, was filmed on location in Bute Town (known as 'Tiger Bay'), situated close to the Cardiff docks in South Wales, where a racially mixed community had existed for over seventy years. In J. Lee Thompson's film, Bute Town became little more than an exotic backdrop for a thriller that told the story of a displaced white child from London, who witnesses a murder and then befriends the killer. In spite of its location, no black residents appear in the tenement building where the child lives with her aunt and uncle. However, Thompson does include the first black wedding seen in a British film, and *Tiger Bay* was important to some members of the local African-Welsh community, who welcomed a filmed record of their neighbourhood before post-war redevelopment raised it to the ground. However, one resident complained to the *Spectator* (31 October 1958): 'When people see the story of this film they are going to think that Bute Road and Loudoun Square, what they call Tiger Bay, is where a man can pick up a girl easily. They'll think all coloured people have loose morals. Think we play dice down here all day.'

Sapphire (Basil Dearden, 1959) was made shortly after the 1958 Notting Hill race riots and confronted cinema audiences – for the first time –

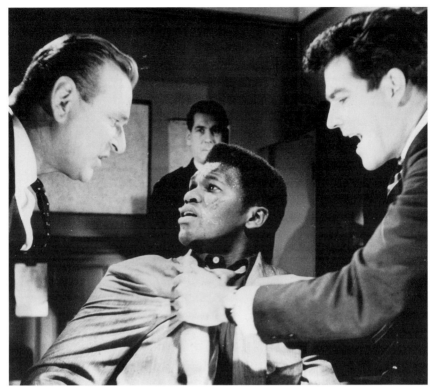

Nigel Patrick, Harry Baird and Michael Craig in *Sapphire* (1959)

with the problem of racism in post-war Britain. Though *Sapphire* won the British Academy Award for Best British Film (other nominees included *Look Back in Anger* and *Tiger Bay*), critic Nina Hibbin was unimpressed with the liberal tone of the film. In her review in the *Daily Worker* (9 May 1959) she declared:

> You can't fight the colour bar merely by telling people it exists. You have to attack it, with passion and conviction. Commit yourself up to the hilt. Otherwise you're in danger of fanning the flames. A case in point is *Sapphire*. More's the pity – because it is an extraordinarily good mystery drama, intelligent, sympathetic, full of local atmosphere, deeply rooted in the London scene. But I have an uneasy feeling that it will do more harm than good . . . the prejudices are presented 'fairly', from all angles. A colour-baiter among the audience could well find himself in complete sympathy with the racialism on the screen. Meant as an objective exposure, it is perilously near to becoming a justification. In an effort not to be over-romantic about the Negro people, too many of them have been put on the shady side of life . . . the method used is trying to put out a fire with petrol.

Flame in the Streets (Roy Ward Baker, 1961) was the screen version of Ted Willis's *Hot Summer Night*. However, it was generally felt that the film was inferior to the stage and television versions. Even so, John Mills gave an outstanding performance as the working-class trade unionist who is forced to put his 'liberal' beliefs to the test, while West Africa's Johnny Sekka (in the role created by Lloyd Reckord) and Earl Cameron gave excellent support. Said Ted Willis:

> I was proud of the play. It was the first West End production to deal with racism. It was considered scandalous for 1958, especially the black and white kiss, but the reviews were good. I set the play during the oppressive heat of summer, an 'irritation', but when they made the film, Rank chose to set the story in winter, against my wishes. So the sense of claustrophobia and oppression is missing from the film. Rank filmed it in Technicolor and aimed it at the American market. I was against this. I felt it should look like other 'social realist' films at that time, which were made in black and white. I wanted Cy Grant to play the role created by Lloyd Reckord, but the director, Roy Ward Baker, insisted on Johnny Sekka, who I didn't think was right for the part. After I had submitted the script, I had very little to do with the rest of the production.[2]

A Taste of Honey (Tony Richardson, 1961) was based on Shelagh Delaney's critically acclaimed stage play. It's a poetic and often funny observation of a working-class Salford schoolgirl, played by Rita Tushingham, who has a brief encounter with a young black Liverpudlian sailor, played by Paul Danquah. Said Gary Null in *Black Hollywood* (1975):

> Instead of stuffing their black character into a tightly fitting role as a symbol of heroism, villainy, or anything else, they simply gave him room to breathe. The character, a young black sailor, is shown as a rather ordinary person involved in everyday life, a man who, just like everyone else, is capable of helping, hurting, and making mistakes.[3]

When the film's director, Tony Richardson, was in the planning stage, a Hollywood producer made him an offer he flatly refused. 'I have just one suggestion to make,' said the producer. 'This girl who's been made pregnant by the Negro – now don't worry, I don't wanna change that, that's good offbeat drama. But let's give the film an upbeat ending. Let her have a miscarriage.' *A Taste of Honey* won four British Academy Awards, including Best British Film and Best Screenplay of a British Film. The following year, *The L-Shaped Room* (Bryan Forbes, 1962) included another ground-breaking black character, the gay jazz musician Johnny, played by Brock Peters (see Chapter 16).

Ten Bob in Winter (Lloyd Reckord, 1963), a short, twelve-minute comedy of manners, is now acknowledged as the first film drama made by a black film-maker in Britain (see Chapter 13). 'A Place of Safety' (BBC1, 1964) was a gripping episode in the popular police drama series *Z Cars*. John Hopkins has described this as 'the most completely realized episode that I wrote'. Johnny Sekka gave an outstanding performance as the tormented Sadik who loses control, attacks a bailiff and barricades himself into a room with his family. Hopkins does not shy away from exposing the racist attitudes of the police. When Chief Inspector Barlow (Stratford Johns) succeeds in tricking Sadik, and arresting him, he maintains, 'Treat them like animals, you get animals to deal with. Treat them like normal human beings, they won't know what you're talking about, but you've got more chance – getting them to do what they're told.' *Fable* (BBC1, 1965) was also written by John Hopkins, this time for the BBC's controversial but innovative *Wednesday Play* drama series. Here, apartheid is reversed so that white people find themselves oppressed, second-class citizens under black control. Black actors in the cast included Thomas Baptiste, Barbara Assoon, Dan Jackson, Carmen Munroe and Bari Jonson. Hopkins had this to say:

> Everyone knew we were working for a very conservative Board of Governors at the time. I can only assume that the Governors didn't see it . . . when I was about sixteen I saw a news trailer in the cinema of the first images coming out of Belsen . . . it was the beginning of my concern for people who are victimised and violated . . . And it's there in *Fable*.[4]

Jemima and Johnny (Lionel Ngakane, 1966), set in London's Notting Hill in the aftermath of the 1958 race riots, explored the friendship between a black girl and a white boy in a racially mixed neighbourhood (see Chapter 13).

To Sir, with Love (James Clavell, 1967) was based on E. R. Braithwaite's autobiographical novel, first published in 1959, about a Guyanese teacher working in a tough school in London's East End. It starred the Oscar-winning Hollywood superstar Sidney Poitier, in glorious Technicolor, with an eye on the American box office, where it became the eighth highest-grossing film of 1967. But it should have been made in the early 1960s, in black and white, at the height of the vogue for 'kitchen-sink' drama. Trinidadian Errol John (see Chapter 12) would have been perfect for the leading role. A potentially interesting character, the mixed-race pupil Seales (Anthony Villaroel), is marginalized. Said Nina Hibbin in the *Morning Star* (9 September 1967): 'By over-simplifying social and racial attitudes of seventeen years ago and attributing them to youngsters who, at that time, hadn't even been born, James Clavell has made a nonsense film.'

197

Rainbow City (BBC1, 1967) was the first drama series on British television to star a black actor (see Chapter 12). Errol John played a Jamaican lawyer living and working in Birmingham. The regular cast included Gemma Jones as his wife, and Trinidadian Horace James, who also contributed to some of the scripts. Other black actors who appeared in the series included Carmen Munroe, Calvin Lockhart, Charles Hyatt and Barbara Assoon. Lloyd Reckord and Leonie Forbes were featured in episodes filmed on location in Jamaica.

Leo the Last (John Boorman, 1969) starred Italy's Marcello Mastroianni as an emigré European prince who lives in a crumbling mansion in London's Notting Hill. Gradually, he emerges from his self-indulgent, unreal world to find himself living in a working-class black community. Calvin Lockhart gave a memorable performance as man-of-the-people Roscoe, who tries to improve his community. Glenna Forster Jones played his girlfriend, Salambo, who is saved from a life of prostitution by Leo. John Boorman won the director's prize at the 1970 Cannes Film Festival, and the supporting cast included Ram John Holder. In the *Observer* (24 May 1970) Holder defended the film 'for and on behalf of the black actors' in the film:

> After returning from the Cannes Film Festival where the British entry *Leo the Last* was repeatedly hailed as a masterpiece I couldn't believe my eyes when I read Penelope Mortimer's non-review (10 May). If *Leo the Last* is patronising to blacks and poor people, I assure you we can use more of that kind of patronage. In the words of Albert Johnson, leading black American critic at Cannes, *Leo the Last* is beautiful, powerful and tragically real. We also consider it a clear Boormanesque articulation of the desperate need for a more equalitarian and just society.

Two months later Jan Dawson, writing in the *Listener* (23 July 1970), had this to say: 'Perhaps his compatriots will one day forgive Boorman for using a political situation to create not a pamphlet but a contemporary myth – witty, surreal, inexplicit, and surely the best British film since the war.'

Pressure (Horace Ové, 1975) is acknowledged as the first feature film drama to be made by a black film-maker in Britain: Trinidadian Horace Ové. It exposed some of the harsh realities of being young, black and dispossessed in Britain in the 1970s. Ové collaborated on the screenplay with a fellow Trinidadian, the novelist Samuel Selvon. Ové explained:

> I didn't make the film sitting in my room: I went out with Samuel Selvon and researched it. I was aware of the political situation, I know what's going

down. So when it was made, and people started saying, 'That's not true,' I knew that either they didn't know what they were talking about, or they didn't want to admit to things. *Pressure* has had a lot of pressure. It's a touchy film, about something that's happening here.[5]

Herbert Norville played the central role of Tony, a black school-leaver who finds himself alienated from his family after racism prevents him from getting a job. A fine supporting cast included Oscar James as his politically active brother and Lucita Lijertwood as his long-suffering mother. One of the best performances came from the veteran Trinidadian character actor Frank Singuineau, who played Tony's disillusioned father. For years regarded as the 'father of black actors' in Britain, Singuineau began his stage career in 1948, and started acting in films in 1953. His many screen credits included *Peeping Tom* (1959), *Seance on a Wet Afternoon* (1964) and *The Pumpkin Eater* (1964). He made his final film appearance in *An American Werewolf in London* (1981). However, no entry can be found for him in the most recent edition of *Halliwell's Who's Who in the Movies* (HarperCollins, 1999). Frank Singuineau died in London in 1992.

At the time *Pressure* was released there were very few black film critics working in Britain. An exception was Akua Rugg, who praised the film in *Race Today* (December 1975):

Ové is a pioneer, in that he is attempting, for the first time, to use the medium of film to reveal the inner soul of the black condition in Britain . . . Perhaps the greatest pleasure of the film was being able to watch black actors allowed the freedom to interpret their roles with authenticity and accuracy.

Akua Rugg also praised *Black Joy* (Anthony Simmons, 1977), one of the first mainstream British films to star African-Caribbean actors. In *Race Today* (January 1978) she said:

Much has been made of the fact that the film is not political, and merely provides an hour of good, dirty fun. The residents of Brixton are shown cussing, fighting, bedding down and messing each other over with monotonous regularity. Reggae and soul music provide a contrast to the drab physical environment of a decaying inner city area . . . A film which, in the main, depicts blacks as making the best of a bad job, rather than seeking alternatives, is a political statement in itself.

In *Black Joy*, gullible Benjamin Jones (Trevor Thomas) arrives in London from Guyana, where he finds himself at the mercy of 'Artful Dodger' Devon (Paul J. Medford) and Dave King (Norman Beaton), one of Brixton's busiest hustlers and con men. Beaton's engaging, charismatic performance in this upbeat, uninhibited comedy drama deservedly earned him an award from the Variety Club of Great Britain for Best Film Actor:

> Much to Jamal Ali's dismay the political thrust of his stage play was more or less jettisoned to conform with the director's view of what he wanted to say in the film. . . . I was invited to the Variety Club of Great Britain luncheon at the Savoy Hotel where I was put at a top table with Sir Alec Guinness. When I heard my name called as Film Actor of 1977, it was the most wonderful moment in my life. I had disproved the claim 'They can't act, there are no black actors'.[6]

Black Christmas (BBC2, 1977) is a compelling study of a 'family at war' by the Guyanese dramatist Michael Abbensetts, and one of the best television dramas of the 1970s. Carmen Munroe (see Chapter 14) played Gertrude, an African-Caribbean matriarch who is determined that her family will enjoy Christmas, but who is defeated as her living-room turns into a battlefield. It was Munroe's finest hour on television and she should have been nominated for a BAFTA. A fine supporting cast included Norman Beaton, Shope Shodeinde, Janet Bartley and Stefan Kalipha. It was directed by Stephen Frears. Nancy Banks-Smith described the play in the *Guardian* as 'Very funny and sorrowful. A brilliant bit of pain.'

Launched in 1978, *Grange Hill* (BBC1) is still, after more than twenty years, one of British television's most ground-breaking, realistic and sometimes controversial dramas. Set in a London comprehensive school, the original cast included Terry Sue Patt as Benny Green, and the tradition of using a culturally diverse cast has continued to this day.

In the *Daily Mirror* (13 December 1980), Hilary Kingsley described *The Sailor's Return* (Jack Gold, 1978) as

> destined for the cinema when it was made three years ago. But probably because it featured no rape, monsters from the deep nor a star in the Clint Eastwood league, it was demoted to the small screen. The Victorian story of love and racial hatred brought us a staggering performance by newcomer Shope Shodeinde as the confused yet dignified African girl . . . beautiful to look at. It wins my vote for play of the year.

After writing *Black Christmas*, Michael Abbensetts scripted two series (fifteen episodes) of *Empire Road* (BBC2, 1978–9) (see Chapter 17), a drama about Birmingham's black and Asian communities. Norman Beaton gave a terrific performance as Everton Bennett, known as 'the godfather', a businessman who owns a terrace of houses and runs the local Soul food grocery store. The regular cast also included Corinne Skinner-Carter (see Appendix III) as his wife, Wayne Laryea as his son and Joseph

Marcell as his brother-in-law Walter Isaacs. In episode seven, 'D.I.V.O.R.C.E.' (4 October 1979), Everton reflected on twenty years in Britain, and movingly conveyed to Walter Isaacs his unhappiness and disillusionment with the 'Mother Country'. 'Tell me Walter, have you ever been happy here?' he asked. '*Really* happy? Come closer. I have a secret to tell you. We're not welcome here.' Parminder Vir later described this as

> a moving and revealing episode which cut deep into the theme of white hostility as it is experienced by the blacks themselves. It exposes the raw hopeless hurt felt by the victims of the continuous racial jokes ... it is important for ethnic minorities to be involved in the creative and consultative process of programme making. If this is not done more often then programmes will continue to be made in the name of black people which are both patronising and hypocritical.[7]

In 1979 black television drama in Britain continued to come of age when Horace Ové (who also directed) and Jim Hawkins collaborated on the screenplay of *A Hole in Babylon*, shown in BBC1's ground-breaking *Play for Today* series. This powerful drama was based on events leading up to the 1975 Spaghetti House siege in London. It investigated the motivations of the three protagonists, superbly played by T-Bone Wilson, Archie Pool and Trevor Thomas. Said Ové:

> The political mood at the time was that nobody wanted to admit what was going on ... that black people were fighting for their rights under a very racist situation and that they were finding ways and means of demonstrating their feelings ... Despite requests from American TV and university film distributors to show *A Hole in Babylon* in the US, the BBC bluntly refused the rights to do so. One BBC sales executive said: 'We are not going to sell a film abroad about a group of black hooligans'.[8]

In *Babylon* (Franco Rosso, 1980), Blue (Brinsley Forde) finds himself under extreme pressure as he attempts to win a sound-system contest. Director Franco Rosso made realistic use of the streets of south London for one of the first mainstream films to draw attention to the new black 'subculture' emerging in Britain at that time. Said *Time Out* (23–29 May 1985):

> Caught a little awkwardly between drama-doc and melodrama, but otherwise a powerful and pretty intelligent account of the problems facing young unemployed blacks in Britain today ... what distinguishes the film as a whole is the way it sharply depicts the details of its characters' lives: the

importance of reggae, the gulf between parents and offspring, and a precise sense of location and community. And Aswad's Forde is excellent as Blue.

However, at the time of the film's release, Molara Ogundipe-Leslie in the *Guardian* (7 January 1981) drew attention to the problem of white film-makers tackling black subjects:

> If there are funds for the making of such films as *Babylon*, should they not be awarded to black film-makers? Or, could non-black film-makers work more closely at the conceptual level with black artists and intellectuals who know their people better and who can define their own reality more truthfully? This is not to argue that culture runs in the genes but to say that it is necessary to know a people's emotional life from within to produce authentic works of art about such people. And the barriers are not racial: they are cultural, psychological, and emotional.

For *Babylon*, Franco Rosso received the 1981 *Evening Standard* British Film Award for Most Promising Film-Maker.

Though progress had been made in television dramas like *Black Christmas*, *Empire Road* and *A Hole in Babylon* towards the end of the 1970s, the start of the 1980s witnessed a contender for one of the worst television dramas ever made. *Wolcott* (ATV, 1981) may have boasted the first appearance of a black police officer on British television, but it failed to deliver the goods. Elvis Payne, who played a mugger, later condemned the production, and in doing so expressed the frustrations of a new generation of black actors:

> It's a terrible, terrible programme about a black CID detective. They say it's not racist but it is. The black cop is the hero but the series shows blacks in the way the reactionary racist media puts them over – all those ideas about blacks being degenerate and animalistic. In fact, I play a mugger of all things! I've talked to a lot of black people on the set about it and we all say we wouldn't have done it if we'd seen the script. It's a bad programme and black people shouldn't stand for it. If someone could get their hands on those tapes! It's not as if black people have access to the media to produce a counter argument to it. It would be a good thing if it made blacks conscious of how the media ignores them most of the time and when it does deal with them it does it in such a way that it is an insult to them.[9]

Burning an Illusion (Menelik Shabazz, 1981) was the first British film to give a black woman a voice of any kind. As seen through the eyes of Pat Williams (Cassie McFarlane), the film explores the social relationships between young men and women in Britain's African-Caribbean community. Its writer/director Menelik Shabazz sensitively charted Pat's growing awareness of herself as a woman, and of her black identity. Said Akua Rugg in *Race Today* (December 1981–January 1982):

> Shabazz has concocted a molotov cocktail of a movie, using the most common-place of plots – boy meets girl – to explode a number of ideas on race, sex and class struggle … Underneath the lush, surface bloom of the film … is a revealing account of the refusal of young blacks to be treated as victims in this society.

Cassie McFarlane, who received the 1982 *Evening Standard* British Film Award for Most Promising Newcomer, headed an exciting young cast that also included Victor Romero Evans, Beverley Martin, Angela Wynter, Malcolm Fredericks, Chris Tummings, Trevor Laird and Brian Bovell.

On television, *King* (1984), written by Barrie Keefe and shown in BBC1's *Play for Today* series, provided Thomas Baptiste with one of his most memorable roles. He played Mr King, who has had a good life in England, and is looking forward to retirement in Jamaica. But a celebration with his daughters, played by Josette Simon and Ella Wilder, does not go as expected.

Black writers continued to work for television at this time. In Caryl Phillips's *The Record* (1984), shown in Channel 4's *Bacchanal* series, Joanne Campbell played Rita, a teenager who wants to become a pop singer, but is opposed by her tyrannical father (Rudolph Walker), who believes that pop singers are all either 'prostitutes or drug addicts'. With death-defying courage, Rita ignores him. Said Louis Heaton in *The Voice* (7 July 1984): 'Director Horace Ové handles his material with a great deal of sensitivity, never quite allowing the characters to fall into stereotype or cliche.' The cast also included Carmen Munroe and Sonya Saul.

Mustapha Matura's dramatic monologue *Nice* (1984), shown in Channel 4's *Here and Now on Four* series, provided Norman Beaton with one of his best roles. He played a hapless inmate of one of Her Majesty's prisons and relates his tragicomic story to camera. This is one of Beaton's finest performances and he should have been nominated for a BAFTA (that year's nominees included three actors from *The Jewel in the Crown* and George Cole in *Minder*). Mustapha Matura also devised *Black Silk* (1985) with Rudy Narayan, an eight-part series for BBC2 about a black barrister. Rudolph Walker played the barrister, Larry Scott, and he felt let down when the BBC decided not to commission a second series: 'I was obviously very disappointed. Everyone I spoke to had very high praise for the series. I don't know why the BBC didn't do another series.'[10] The regular cast also included Kika Markham, Mona Hammond and Suzette Llewellyn. Various episodes were written by black writers, including Tunde Ikoli, Mustapha Matura and Edgar White. Said Matura:

> I wanted him [Larry Scott] to be more rootsy, more involved in the community, than he eventually turned out. I find he's too well dressed, and I wanted him to be more of a rebel, who didn't speak the Queen's English all the time. I see Larry Scott as someone educated in the West Indies who came to Britain to study law, being more West Indian than British. The ensuing result is that the character comes out less interesting, and less complex than he would otherwise have been. When things start to go through the television process that seems to happen. There are people involved in television who are scared of going outside the tiny reality they know.[11]

Two contrasting films about the black British experience, *The Passion of Remembrance* and *Playing Away* were premiered in the 1986 London Film Festival. *The Passion of Remembrance* was the first fiction feature to be produced in Britain by a black film and video workshop. It was made by Sankofa whose members – Maureen Blackwood, Isaac Julien, Martina Attille and Nadine Marsh Edwards – came from several London film colleges, and set up as a group in 1983 to consolidate their previous work in film and video. Their aim was to produce a range of images of the black subject, and to explore perspectives new to British film and television. Martina Attille told Isiling Mack Nataf in *Spare Rib* (December 1986):

> People have found the structure quite new and experimental ... what the film is saying politically comes out of us, the Black communities we come from. You're working with a medium which has quite a long history in, say, the Caribbean. Living in England, growing up in England, you know you've been involved in that history, whether it's been one of exploitation or not.... So, in a way it's saying we actually do have access and we should make claims on this society.

In *Playing Away*, written by Caryl Phillips and directed by Horace Ové, a cricket team from Brixton in south London accepts an invitation to play a 'friendly' match in a rural, gentrified Suffolk village as part of its 'Third World Week'. Norman Beaton gave one of his best performances as the team captain who is trying to decide whether or not to return to the Caribbean. The cast also included Robert Urquhart, Brian Bovell, Gary Beadle, Suzette Llewellyn, Trevor Thomas, Stefan Kalipha, Joseph Marcell, Jim Findley, Ram John Holder and Archie Pool. When *Playing Away* was shown on Channel 4 the following year, Horace Ové told Kathy Watson in *Weekend Voice* (5–9 November 1987):

Norman Beaton and Nicholas Farrell in *Playing Away* (1986)

People don't talk to black film-makers about technique. They talk about politics. But I don't think black people have to only make films about politics. White people can make films about anything or anyone, of any race. There are different audiences within the black community. Some black people love *No Problem* [Channel 4 sitcom]. Others think it's degrading and prefer documentaries. And they should have that choice. Take Spike Lee's *She's Gotta Have It*. That broke away from what people expect black people to make films about.

Channel 4 continued to commission original work from black dramatists in 1987. In Michael Abbensetts's *Big George Is Dead*, Boogie (Norman Beaton) is the chief mourner at Big George's funeral, but he's angry and confused when Tony (Rudolph Walker), once his best friend, arrives from Trinidad after a fourteen-year absence. In Tunde Ikoli's *Elphida*, Angela Wynter gave an outstanding performance as a young wife and mother who plans to restart her education when her youngest child goes to nursery, only for the nursery to close down. On top of this, her parents are contemplating divorce, and want her to act as a go-between. *Elphida* also explored Elphida's memories of St Lucia and adapting to life in Britain. Ikoli also directed, and Wynter was supported by a great cast that included Gary McDonald as her intolerant husband and Rudolph Walker and Corinne Skinner-Carter as her battling parents.

After working on *The Passion of Remembrance* with Sankofa, Martina Attille wrote and directed *Dreaming Rivers* (1988), a compelling, evocative and nostalgic thirty-minute drama which explored the displacement of Caribbean migrants through the eyes of Miss T., a dying woman, beautifully played by Corinne Skinner-Carter. Through the reminiscing of her three children, we revisit this woman's shattered existence.

In *For Queen and Country* (Martin Stellman, 1988), Denzel Washington was imported from America to play Reuben, a disillusioned Falklands' war hero. After leaving the British army (because they refused to give him promotion), Reuben returns home to Peckham in south-east London to confront more racism, and an urban war. The screenplay, by Martin Stellman and Trix Worrell, was based on fact, but Washington failed miserably in his attempt to adopt a south London accent, though he succeeded in conveying Reuben's sense of isolation and alienation. The film was described by its makers as an 'urban Western' and some sequences indeed looked as if they had come straight out of a Clint Eastwood spaghetti Western. At times it felt as if the film should have been called *Gunfight at the OK Peckham*! Therefore, it was hardly surprising to find that Irwin Eversley, the ex-paratrooper whose story was used as the basis for the screenplay, refused to be associated with the publicity campaign for the film.

Washington was cast over a number of qualified black British actors, including Gary McDonald, who told *Caribbean Times* (17–23 February 1989): 'I was supposed to be doing that film. I worked on it for about four weeks and joined the territorial army so that I could actually become the part.' In the end, Gary lost the part because the Americans were putting up most of the money and they wanted an actor their audience could recognize. 'I was gutted. If a black actor from this country had been used it would really help get things moving for us here.'

Horace Ové directed *When Love Dies* (1990), shown in Channel 4's *4 Play* series. A witty and poignant look at family life, family secrets and the way in which families manage to survive, the superb cast included Josette

Simon, Brian Bovell, Norman Beaton and Mona Hammond. Writer Mike Phillips adapted BBC2's three-part thriller *Blood Rights* (1990) from his novel. Brian Bovell was excellent in the leading role of a journalist who is hired by a prominent MP to find his missing daughter. Said Phillips:

> The way in which the story was constructed by television made it a fairly average domestic thriller. This obscured the strengths of the original conception of the story and the relevance of the myth … I saw that myth as the situation of the black community – this is our heritage, we're partly fathered by this country, we return to claim a heritage, and we're denied.[12]

Until the 1990s black women writers were unheard of in television drama, with just two exceptions: Sylvia Wynter, who co-authored *The Big Pride* (1961) with her husband, Jan Carew (see Chapter 6), and Nigeria's Buchi Emecheta, who wrote 'The Ju-Ju Landlord' for Granada's *Crown Court* series in 1976. This was immediately followed by Emecheta's *A Kind of Marriage* for BBC2's *Centre Play: Commonwealth Season*. In 1991 the Jamaican dub poet and storyteller Jean 'Binta' Breeze wrote the screenplay for *Hallelujah Anyhow*, shown in BBC2's *Screen Two* series. This examination of evangelical religion and sexual politics in London's Caribbean community featured Dona Croll. Breeze told Claudette Williams in *Spare Rib* (December–January, 1990–1): 'I am not interested in white people and their reaction to us. Our responsibility is to ourselves. If we are constantly worried about the society, its mental warp, and stereotyping, then we have a problem looking at our own truths.'

In the early 1990s black film-makers continued to break new ground. *Young Soul Rebels* (Isaac Julien, 1991), set during the Queen's Silver Jubilee celebrations in 1977, explored the relationship between a young black man and a young white man (see Chapter 16). The film also looked at definitions of Britishness through punk culture, racial conflict and changes in sexual attitudes. *Who Needs a Heart* (1991), written and directed by John Akomfrah, looked at 'Black Power' by investigating the life and times of Michael X – urban bandit, mystic, Black Power leader. The film focused on the life of this contradictory and emblematic figure by dramatizing the context and background to 'race politics' in 1960s Britain. *We the Ragamuffin* (Julian Henriques, 1992), an enjoyable musical drama set around a group of real 'ragamuffins', was more realistic than *For Queen and Country* in its portrayal of life on a council estate in Peckham, south-east London. Said Lorraine Griffiths in *The Weekly Journal* (5 November 1992):

> *We the Ragamuffin* bravely attempts new innovations … Interweaving a

gritty realism with the fantasy of the musical genre, the film is as humorous as it is elucidating. Like a mirror image of the community itself, *Ragamuffin* carries the simple message: music is a powerful and social force.

Black Poppies (BBC2, 1992) was a television version of a stage production premiered at the National Theatre Studio by a group of black actors who had interviewed a number of black people serving in the armed forces, including survivors of the Second World War. The actors recounted their stories and experiences. Filmed on the Broadwater Farm estate, *Black Poppies* was shortlisted for the Commission for Racial Equality's (CRE) 1992 'Race in the Media' award for Best Television Drama.

Funky Black Shorts (BBC2, 1994) was a series of six ten-minute dramas celebrating black writing, including *The Godsend*, written and directed by Lenny Henry, in which a male nanny (Treva Etienne) revolutionizes a disorganized family home. Others in the series included *A Chance to Dance*, written and directed by Kolton Lee, with Victor Romero Evans; and *Home and Away*, written and directed by Danny Thompson. *Flight of the Swan* (1994), shown in Channel 4's *Short and Curlies* series, was a twelve-minute study of Obe, a young Nigerian girl (Hilja Lindsey-Parkinson), who leaves her village for the cold, harsh landscape of England. In an alien world she discovers ballet and falls in love with its grace and beauty – but her ambition to become a 'black swan' is rejected. This memorable film was written and directed by Ngozi Onwurah. Also shown in Channel 4's *Short and Curlies* series was Maureen Blackwood's *Home Away From Home* (1994), in which Miriam, who lives with her four children in a cluttered suburban house, dreams of a return to her rural African home.

The Concrete Garden (1994), director Alrick Riley's short (twenty-three mins) graduation film at the National Film and Television School, was a moving study of a young Jamaican girl's traumatic experiences on arriving in Britain in the 1950s. At the Chicago International Children's Film Festival, *The Concrete Garden* received the Best Short Film Award that 'best represents the United Nations Declaration of the Rights of the Child'. Alrick Riley has since worked as a director in television, including two top-rated drama series: BBC1's *Playing the Field* and BBC2's BAFTA award-winning *The Cops*. He is one of the few black directors to find work in mainstream television. In an interview in *Untold* (March–April 2000) he said: 'People ask more questions when you're black. They wonder why you want to do a project that might not have a black angle. But if you keep pushing eventually they'll recognise that good filmmaking doesn't have an awful lot to do with your colour.'

In *One Sunday Morning* (Manu Kurewa, 1994), a twenty-minute short that was also produced at the National Film and Television School, Mordecai (Oke Wambu) and Margaret (Lauretta Nkwocha), recently arrived in London from Nigeria, are told that Mordecai's visa has not been extended. They try to carry on with their lives under the shadow of deportation, but family tensions begin to surface. Another outstanding short film made in 1994 was Danny Thompson's *Fathers, Sons and Holy Ghosts*, in which a young African-Caribbean man learns to be a father while he is still coming to terms with being a son. The cast included Lennie James and Oscar James.

On 13 December 1994 Norman Beaton died at the age of sixty in his birthplace, Guyana, collapsing in a friend's arms hours after going home to die. He had been one of Britain's leading actors since the 1970s. Apart from a distinguished stage career, for his performance in *Black Joy* he was named Best Film Actor by the Variety Club of Great Britain, the first black British actor to be honoured with a film award. Nine years later he starred in *Playing Away*, giving an outstanding performance as the quiet but determined captain of an all-black cricket team. Among his most memorable television successes were *The Fosters* (London Weekend Television, 1976–7); *Black Christmas* (BBC2, 1977); *Empire Road* (BBC2, 1978–9); *Nice* (Channel 4, 1984); *Big George Is Dead* (Channel 4, 1987); and *Little Napoleons* (Channel 4, 1993). In spite of his brilliant work as a dramatic actor, perhaps Beaton will be best remembered for his role as the manic barbershop owner in the long-running sitcom *Desmond's*. Created by a young black writer called Trix Worrell, *Desmond's* ran from 1989 to 1994 on Channel 4. The show was described as an African-Caribbean equivalent of America's *The Cosby Show* and, as a result of its popularity in America, in 1991 African-American television star Bill Cosby invited Beaton to make a couple of guest appearances in *The Cosby Show*. Beaton readily accepted a role as a cricket-loving doctor, and Cosby was so taken by the actor that he wore Beaton's gift of a *Desmond's* baseball cap in the show. Shortly after he died, Channel 4 aired *Shooting Stars* in their *Black Christmas* season, which contains a memorable appearance by Beaton reading a sonnet by Shakespeare. Towards the end of his life, Beaton reflected on his career:

> My own view is that what you've seen me in are the only roles that are available for black men in this country, and they don't really reflect our views, our understanding of life, our intelligence, or where we are coming from. In that respect I would say that Caryl Phillips' scenario for *Playing Away* did get around that particular hurdle. It lived up to nearly all the expectations that black people ought to be living up to . . . But what I find

difficult to come to terms with is the absence of a heroic figure like Paul Robeson in all the work I've done. There is no writer on that scale, or in those grand, magnificent terms for film and television about a black figure who we all admire or aspire to be like. And I don't know when our people are going to actually start saying 'We are terrific!' and start writing something wonderful about just being us.[13]

After Beaton died, actress Carmen Munroe, who worked with the actor on many occasions, and played his wife in *Desmond's*, told *The Voice* (20 December 1994):

> He put his whole life and soul into any part he was asked to play and never spared himself. He worked at his craft and produced brilliance. His particular blend of comic energy and professional application will be missed most keenly in the future when excellence is sought.

Sidney's Chair (Roberto Bangura, 1995), an enjoyable 21-minute short produced at the National Film and Television School, was set in Stepney in the East End of London in 1967. It told the story of Ricci Owobe (Ricci Beevas), a mixed-race twelve-year-old who learns that Hollywood superstar Sidney Poitier is filming *To Sir, with Love* in his neighbourhood. After sneaking on to the set, and receiving racist abuse from the technicians, he steals Sidney's chair. But Ricci's adventure doesn't quite turn out as planned.

Ngozi Onwurah's controversial first feature, *Welcome II The Terrordome* (1995), brought into focus techno-musical influences from the popular culture of the African diaspora. Linking the themes of slavery and urban conflict, it took a ritualized look back to the future. Onwurah told Tom Charity in *Time Out* (13–20 January 1995):

> 'What I'm frightened about is what happens to our humanity. The greatest strength of black people is that we kept our soul, and that might have to be the sacrifice. Being of mixed race, I'm asked all the time, directly or indirectly, who I am. And whereas black people often give me the choice, white people never do: I'm always black.' She sounds almost weary. 'I'm sure the film will be seen as a political monologue from beginning to end, but as a first feature I'm glad I made it extreme. If you start off playing safe as a director, you've got nowhere to go. I'm very proud it's been made . . . even if half my nice friends won't speak to me again!'

Blazed (1995), shown in Channel 4's *Battered Britain* season, was a fast-moving drama that took its audience on a journey to the hearts and minds of black youth in one of the toughest inner-city areas of Coventry. The film-makers worked with an all-black cast of twelve youngsters, aged between fourteen and sixteen, to create a drama which reflected their environment.

Secrets and Lies (1996) was conceived and directed by Mike Leigh and featured Marianne Jean-Baptiste as a young black woman who has been fostered, and then discovers her mother is white. Jean-Baptiste's memorable performance earned her Best Supporting Actress nominations in America's Golden Globe and Oscar awards ceremonies, as well as a BAFTA nomination. Onyekachi Wambu expressed his reservations about the film in *The Voice* (11 June 1996):

> But despite generally liking the film, I nevertheless had huge problems. When most Black people arrived in Britain, we did not arrive as strangers. Some of us were coming 'home' to the 'mother country', drawing on a 400-year relationship with the British which was mainly painful and brutal. The ignorance, hostility and fear which confronted us on our arrival, despite the centuries-old relationship, was one of the most astonishing things to hit the 'Windrush generation'. This fear and ignorance continues to haunt Britain still, and one catches hints of it, even in *Secrets*. Hortense goes forward to meet her White family – but in order to do this she has to go alone. We see no pictures of her Black foster parents, her two brothers are seen once arguing with each other but never talk to her.

The Final Passage (Channel 4, 1996) was a two-part adaptation by Caryl Phillips from his award-winning novel which charted a family's move from a small Caribbean island to England in the 1950s. This was the first time a British television drama had focused on the experiences of post-war Caribbean settlers since John Elliot's *A Man from the Sun* in 1956 (see Chapter 12). Newcomers Natasha Estelle Williams and Michael Cherrie were cast as the young couple who come to the 'mother country'. Carmen Munroe and Oscar James were particularly memorable in supporting roles. Phillips told *Time Out* (3–10 July 1996):

> It suddenly occurred to me that all the people of my parents' generation who came over to Britain then were either dying or going back. That the majority of British black people have no relationship with the Caribbean except as a place where their parents are from, and that nobody has actually bothered to tell the truth about that era.

On 18 October 1996, BBC2 launched a ten-part drama series called *Brothers and Sisters*. Described as a 'drama with a comic touch about the congregation at a northern gospel church', it has been labelled in some quarters as a 'black soap'. Unlike its predecessor, *Empire Road*, the series

Natasha Estelle Williams and Michael Cherrie in *The Final Passage* (Channel 4, 1996)

suffered from terrible scripts, and a cast of actors who looked as if they'd rather be 'resting'. Bobby Joseph summed this up in *The Voice* (18 November 1996):

> This 'gritty' Black soap has the makings of a good show but is let down by the execution of the various plot lines, ham-fisted dialogue and the actors' lack of ummm . . . er . . . timing! Did anyone notice they all lost their accents within two minutes of speaking?

The series returned for a second, eight-week run on 28 October 1998, but Carol Magdalene complained in *Black Film Bulletin* (Winter 1999) that the series

> did not address its supposed black audience. Aquilla had lost her edge. The only gay black character had disappeared, an issue providing ample

opportunity to explore its particular take, character and texture within the black communities. The sense of inter-generational differences and conflicts – again, very relevant to the black communities – were lost … Petronella did, however, remain a breath of familiarity, predominantly due to Sandra Bee's performance.

Crucial Tales (1996), produced by Lenny Henry's company Crucial Films for BBC2, was a series of four thirty-minute dramas that showcased black and Asian writers and directors. The series included *Revolver*, written and directed by Avril E. Russell; *Spiders and Flies*, directed by Danny Thompson; and *I Bring You Frankincense*, written by Jonti and directed by Ngozi Onwurah. Jonti told *The Voice* (12 November 1996):

> I'm not a fan of minority programming. It's a typical BBC move to create a little niche for us and think that's that. All the stories are mainstream enough to be part of normal programming. We make up a big enough population in this country and I want to be represented, not isolated.

Crucial Tales received the Commission for Racial Equality's 1996 'Race in the Media' award for Best Television Drama.

Constance (Cyril Nri, 1997) was an award-winning, eleven-minute short in which an African-Caribbean woman (an excellent performance by Dona Croll) serves meals to prisoners at the local police station. One day she meets a prisoner she believes is the son she abandoned thirty years ago. Cyril Nri, who has worked as an actor for many years, received several awards for *Constance*, including one from the BBC for Most Promising Director.

The Full Monty (Peter Cattaneo, 1997) became one of the biggest money-making British films of all time, and it came as no surprise when BAFTA nominated it for eleven awards. Three of those went to the performances of Robert Carlyle, Mark Addy and Tom Wilkinson. When the winners were announced, it was great to see Robert Carlyle and Tom Wilkinson win, but where was Paul Barber, the one black member of the cast, in the line-up? This had nothing to do with Barber, best known for playing Denzel in BBC television's popular sitcom *Only Fools and Horses*. On the contrary, you only have to read the film script to understand why his name failed to figure among the nominations. His character, next to those of his co-stars, seemed almost two-dimensional. He is relegated to the sidelines. It is inconceivable that Barber's African-American peers – Morgan Freeman, Samuel L. Jackson, Will Smith and Denzel Washington – would ever consider playing such a character, especially one called 'Mr Horse'. All in all, it was a sorry state of affairs when the only black movie stars we could offer the world in 1997 were 'Mr Horse' and Scary Spice from *Spice World*. *American films, by contrast, were offering a range of black characters in mainstream movies such as Men in Black, Amistad, Jackie Brown and Sphere.* We were further down the ladder than we thought. Yet had Barber played a more rounded character in *The Full Monty*, the chances are BAFTA would still have ignored him. Since 1952, only three black actors have won BAFTAS, all of them African-Americans – Sidney Poitier, Whoopi Goldberg and Samuel L. Jackson.

The original idea for *The Full Monty* came from a black writer, Paul Bucknor, who was credited as the film's co-producer. In an interview with Carl Daniels in *Black Film Bulletin* (Summer/Autumn 1997), he explained:

> It was my idea. I developed a film about male sexuality. I knew straight away that it was good. The hairs on the back of my neck stood up … It didn't change at all in the broad sense. The structure is identical to my story. Some details changed. Instead of it being multi-racial – there are now five white guys and one black guy … I made a deal that I would co-produce the film. To make the deal I had to give up creative control. I decided to because I had a lot to learn … I wanted a type of film that would not be condescending to the general public. That was my selling point. Not like these middle-class film-makers who make films about the working-class, but they don't feel it. I am a black British man. I come from a poor working class background. So all the characters in *The Full Monty* are characters from a similar background to me … I would have included at least one other non-white character. That's what I was arguing for all the way through. But the thing is, because I gave up control, I couldn't push too hard because I would have been excluded. And what was important for me was to get the hands-on experience. I made the deal with that understanding. Business is always a compromise … as a result I am not on the posters and advertising … I should have insisted on an original story credit, but I didn't. Now lawyers are talking.

The Girl with Brains in Her Feet (1998), the first feature made by Roberto Bangura, the director of the acclaimed short *Sidney's Chair* (1995), told the story of 'Jack', a teenage girl from a mixed-race family, with ambitions to be a great runner. The film was described by Liese Spencer in *Sight and Sound* (June 1998) as

> Somewhere between a racy episode of *Grange Hill* and a '70s photo-story from a teen magazine … [the film] is a rites-of-passage movie with a breezy, low-budget feel. Deftly written by Jo Hodges, the film follows teenager Jack (Joanna Ward) as she comes of age among the redbrick, working class estates of Leicester.

A Respectable Trade (BBC1, 1998) was an impressive four-part drama series about the trading of African slaves through Bristol in the late 1700s. This was adapted by Philippa Gregory from her novel and received the CRE's 1998 'Race in the Media' award for Best Television Drama. An outstanding cast included Ariyon Bakare as the educated, sensitive but defiant slave Mehuru, and Hugh Quarshie as the freed slave Caesar Peters, who introduces Mehuru to the abolitionist movement. The character of Mehuru owed much to Olaudah Equiano, the Nigerian who, in the 1700s, published an autobiography to help forward the cause of the abolition of slavery.

In 1998 the BBC's ambitious *Windrush* season (May–August) marked fifty years of the African-Caribbean community's contribution to post-war Britain. The season included *Still Here*, a memorable series of short dramatic monologues: *Serpent's Tooth* (27 July), written and directed by Kolton Lee, with George Harris; *The House of Usher* (3 August), written by Carol Russell, directed by Avril E. Russell, with Sandra Bee; *Just So Much a Body Can Take* (10 August), written by Patricia Cumper, directed by Avril E. Russell, with Claire Benedict; *The Record Collection* (17 August), written by Michael Abbensetts, directed by Kole Onile-Ere, with Oscar James; *No Nation* (24 August), written by Carlton Dixon, directed by Kole Onile-Ere, with Nicholas Pinnock; and *The Arrival of Brighteye* (25 August), written by Jean 'Binta' Breeze, directed by Kolton Lee. *Still Here* was produced by Paulette Randall.

In *Babymother* (Julian Henriques, 1998), Anita (Anjela Lauren Smith), mother of two, yearns to become a local dancehall diva. She is encouraged by her 'rude girl' friends, Sharon and Yvette, but her family and the children's father are unsupportive. This semi-surreal reggae musical, packed with attitude, ambition and outrageous outfits, was described by Stuart Hall in *Sight and Sound* (September 1998) as 'an engaging black British extravaganza. Anita, Sharon and Yvette make the Spice Girls look like convent fifth-formers at a Sunday afternoon tea party.' In spite of mixed reviews, *Babymother* was popular with young audiences, though no blockbuster. The producer of the film, Parminder Vir, explained why more black films aren't made in Britain:

> I think it is to do with institutional racism. It is to do with the people who make decisions. They are a like minded lot. There isn't diversity among the decision-makers … What other reason is there – our stories are undervalued. And they can't say we don't have good story tellers, we do. If you look at British literature, amongst the top ten writers are Asian, Afro-Caribbean and African writers. Ben Okri, Salman Rushdie, Hanif Kureishi, Caryl Phillips – you can't deny anymore that we don't have the capacity to

tell stories. We have the capacity to translate those stories into screenplays. But I believe the shift has to be at that institutional level.[14]

Colour Blind (Carlton, 1998) was a three-part television adaptation of a novel by Catherine Cookson, set in Tyneside between the two world wars. Soap opera from start to finish, and aimed directly at a mainstream audience, it told the story of Rose Angela, the mixed race daughter of an Irish Catholic and a black merchant seaman. Though flawed (see Appendix IV), it was good to see a black actress, Carmen Ejogo, take the lead in a populist romantic drama in a peak viewing slot.

In complete contrast to *Colour Blind*, *The Murder of Stephen Lawrence* (Granada, 1999) was a dramatization of the events leading up to the murder of black teenager Stephen Lawrence in 1993, and the subsequent bungled investigation by the police. From the sudden, brutal murder by a gang of south London racists, through to the opening of the inquiry into the conduct of the case, its writer/director Paul Greengrass employed a fast-fading, semi-documentary style to powerful effect. There were low-key, totally believable performances from the entire cast, including Marianne Jean-Baptiste and Hugh Quarshie as Stephen's parents, Doreen and Neville Lawrence. Jean-Baptiste told Brian Dessau in *Time Out* (17–24 February 1999):

> All you can hope is that the film will open people's eyes to what happened and the extent the Lawrences were messed around. Institutionalised racism is a serious problem. You are not going to end it with a drama. It's a piss in the ocean. I'm not naive enough to think it will make major changes, but it will reach into people's homes and get them thinking about it.

The Murder of Stephen Lawrence received Best Television Drama awards from the CRE and BAFTA. However, though nominated for the Royal Television Society's Best Actress award, Jean-Baptiste was ignored by BAFTA. The following letter appeared in *The Voice*:

> It is a disgrace that BAFTA members have overlooked Marianne Jean-Baptiste's superb portrayal of Doreen Lawrence in ITV's *The Murder of Stephen Lawrence* in their Best Television Actress category. Since 1954, when the television acting awards were introduced, no black actor has ever been nominated and Ms Jean-Baptiste should have been the first. For too long, BAFTA has overlooked the work of fine actors such as Norman Beaton and Carmen Munroe. As for Maggie Smith being included in the line-up, she has been honoured more than any other actor (including Laurence Olivier) collecting fourteen nominations for film and television since 1958, and winning five.[15]

Michael Attwell, Chairman of the Television Committee, explained:

> I'm afraid that BAFTA is not able to control who is shortlisted for awards. These are voted for by the members and the broadcasters. The representation of black people on British television and their representation within BAFTA itself remain important issues for us. We try wherever we can to extend the range of people included in the awards ceremonies, so for instance this year we invited Lennox Lewis and Thierry Henry to present awards. Floella Benjamin is, as you know, a member of both Council and the Television Committee. She keeps this matter at the front of our minds – which is where it should be. We're not anything like as successful as dealing with it as we wish but we continue to try to address it.[16]

Notting Hill (Roger Michell, 1999) may be one of the most popular British films of all time, but it is also one of the most racist. In the opening sequence one of the stars of the film, Hugh Grant, lists the reasons why Notting Hill has become his 'favourite bit of London', but an important attraction is overlooked. It is the event for which Notting Hill has become famous since the early 1960s: the two days in August when the predominantly African-Caribbean neighbourhood celebrates carnival. Unsurprisingly, *Notting Hill* has been described as an 'insult' by Yasmin Alibhai-Brown. She accuses its makers, including screenwriter Richard Curtis, of 'whitening' the

> most famously Black area in London ... It is not that they don't see us, but that film-makers don't want us to litter up their olde worlde landscape. In this country 99 per cent of films are written by white, middle-class people. We have no Spike Lee yet or Denzel Washington because the much applauded British film industry has done nothing to make them happen.[17]

Notting Hill also angered a number of black British actors, including Lennie James:

> not enough fuss was made about the film *Notting Hill*. They must have sat down and had a conversation and said we are not going to have anything to do with the carnival. I don't care how much money they paid Julia Roberts. It ain't good enough to say that Richard Curtis doesn't know that many black people. Write the f★★king parts and we'll decide how black they are.[18]

Hope and Glory (BBC1, 1999–2000) starred Lenny Henry as Ian George, who takes over as headteacher of the notoriously underachieving Hope Park secondary school. Henry made a successful transition from comedy to drama in two series of *Hope and Glory*, though he had acted occasionally in television dramas before (*Alive and Kicking, The Man*). The first series was good, but the second series was outstanding. Lenny Henry, who seemed a bit wooden in the first series, excelled in the second. What was most memorable about the second series was Ian George's romance with a black woman, Clare Jensen (Suzette Llewellyn), the mother of one of his pupils. The fictional portrayal of black couples on British television is a rarity, and *Hope and Glory* broke new ground in this respect.

Driving Miss Crazy (1999), Treva Etienne's short film about a woman who gets stood up waiting for her date to arrive, was the second-prize winner at the Acapulco Black Film Festival and received the HBO (Home Box Office) award for Best Short Film. Etienne's many acting roles have included fireman Tony Sanderson in London Weekend Television's *London's Burning*. In a profile in *Untold* (March–April 2000) he said:

> For me as an actor becoming a director was a natural progression – watching how the cameras move and how the crew works to tell a story. Once people around you invest in your idea, all that fuels you ... British cinema is only just opening up to diversity with films like *East Is East*. Now we need to learn to come together, to share our wealth instead of keeping it all tied into ourselves. To young film-makers, my only advice is this, 'Don't let fear or history stop you and don't judge yourself by other people's measures of success or failure. The secret of success is to keep having a go.'

Rage (Newton I. Aduaka, 1999) explored the lives of three youths in contemporary London where cultures, class, race and sexuality intermingle and influence each other freely, and adopted American street style is the fashion of the day (see Chapter 18).

Pig Heart Boy (BBC1, 1999), winner of BAFTA's Best Children's Drama award, was adapted for television by Malorie Blackman from her novel. Since 1990 Blackman has written forty-nine children's books, but the number of black British novelists who have had their work adapted for the screen can be counted on the fingers of one hand. *Pig Heart Boy* was the provocative story of a black teenager who faces a terrible dilemma when he is diagnosed with a fatal heart condition, and given less than a year to live. His only hope of survival is an experimental heart transplant from a genetically modified pig. The series starred Marlon Yearwood as the teenager, Patrick Robinson, of *Casualty* fame, Mona Hammond and Clare Perkins. Apart from the BAFTA honour, *Pig Heart Boy* was also nominated for the CRE 'Race in the Media' award for Best Television Drama.

Blackman's previous work for children's television included BBC1's popular series *Whizziwig* and *Jevan*, a half-hour ghost story for ITV. Both productions featured major roles for young black actors. Until the launch of BBC1's *Grange Hill* in 1978, it was impossible to find black children portrayed in children's television fiction. An exception was Brinsley Forde in the comedy series *The Double Deckers* (1970). Now, thanks to writers like Blackman, all that has changed. She told Lincia Daniel in *Black Filmmaker* (Vol. 4, Issue 11, 2001):

> I think the major thing is to just keep pushing and just believe in the product. Believe in the possibility of the product and believe it will actually get done. I say to my daughter if you can't do something or if you fail at something that's fair enough so long as you had a good try. But what I don't want to hear is that you haven't even tried in the first place.

Native (BBC2, 2000) was shown in the *10x10: New Directors* slot and was a thoroughly engaging piece. Set in the 1960s, it told the story of an eleven-year-old African-Caribbean boy who finds himself caught between two cultures. *Native* was written by Rikki Beadle Blair, who went on to create and star in Channel 4's *Metrosexuality* (see Chapter 16).

Storm Damage (BBC2, 2000) came from the childhood memories of its writer, Lennie James. A hard-hitting drama, it starred Adrian Lester as Danny, a young teacher, who finds himself on the receiving end of a threat by an armed youth. Subsequently, he seeks to make sense of the youth's damaged life. *Storm Damage* also tells the story of Agnes Miller (Mona Hammond), who opens her house to, in the main, black, working-class teenagers and children, all of whom are victims in one way or another: the offspring of poverty, drug-addicted parents, inadequate housing and an ineffective education system. It is, at times, a very emotional drama, and attempts to show the effects of these very large forces on the lives of young, impressionable people. *Storm Damage* proved to be the best film or television drama written about the displacement and alienation of Britain's black working-class youth since Horace Ové's film *Pressure*.

Lennie James described Horace Ové in *Untold* (March–April 2000) as 'The godfather of Black British filmmaking', who

> gave me my first big job out of drama school, said if you get 60 or 70 per cent of what you envisioned into your final film, then you've won. On *Storm Damage*, I think we got more than 70 per cent. One of the things I learnt doing *Storm Damage* is, if you write something like that, a lot of energy goes into making the 'Yes or No' people understand why things in the script are important, because it's like a foreign language. They don't get nuances, why 'innit though' on its own is different to when it comes at the end of a sentence. Or why, if someone kisses their teeth to their parents or their friends, it's different. We always have to educate them. But it's worth

making that effort, because the film industry owes you nothing. There's nothing consistent, talent does not equal success, nothing is necessarily fair, it's a constant lottery and it's all about luck and divine intervention. The only thing you can hold onto and be sure of is yourself.

Mona Hammond, one of Britain's finest character actresses, gave an exceptional performance as the matriarchal carer who just tries to 'hold onto them, until they can hold on to themselves'. *Storm Damage* received the Royal Television Society award for Best Television Drama. At the Ethnic Multicultural Media Awards (Emma) ceremony on 23 May 2000, Adrian Lester was nominated for Best Actor for *Storm Damage*, but when he presented an award, he took the opportunity publicly to shame the British film director Guy Ritchie of *Lock, Stock and Two Smoking Barrels* fame. Ritchie had just told Neil Norman in *ES* magazine (19 May 2000) that

> There are no black actors around. The ones I've seen all speak Shakespeare beautifully but that's not the point. Now I see why they had to import Forest Whitaker to play a British soldier in *The Crying Game*. His accent was bloody awful.

Lennie James receiving the Royal Television Society award for *Storm Damage*

(2001)

On stage at the Emma Awards, Lester also tore up a copy of the interview in front of the audience, who cheered.

Ritchie upset a number of black actors, though not all of them agreed with Lester's comments. Vas Blackwood, who had appeared in *Lock, Stock and Two Smoking Barrels*, told Neil Norman in the *Evening Standard* (24 May 2000): 'It's all been blown out of proportion. Adrian Lester was bang out of order.' However, in the same article, Norman also interviewed writer Mike Phillips, who explained:

> I can understand why there is an uproar. I remember the days when black actors weren't cast because they couldn't speak standard English. Now that they have struggled to put themselves through drama school they are considered too well-spoken. You're buggered if you do and you're buggered if you don't. The question is not whether they're street-credible but whether they are good actors.

One year later, Lester stood by his comments when he told Lee Pinkerton in an interview in *The Voice* (12 March 2001):

> White actors out there now who have done Shakespeare, musicals, plays, they're not being judged on their accent, their colour, and that's what I object to. The problem with Guy Ritchie's statement is that he is now an example of what many British directors want to do. They're following his example, what he says. If he's gonna come up and say that, I think it needs a response. I thought that the Emma Awards was the best place to give that response.

NOTES

1 Peter Stead, *Film and the Working Class: The Feature Film in British and American Society* (London and New York: Routledge, 1989), p. 117.

2 Ted Willis, interview with Stephen Bourne, London, 8 March 1990.

3 Gary Null, *Black Hollywood* (New Jersey: Citadel Press, 1975), p. 185.

4 John Hopkins, in Jim Pines (ed.), *Black and White in Colour: Black People in British Television Since 1936* (London: British Film Institute, 1992), p. 97.

5 Horace Ové, interview with Clive Hodgson, *Film (BFFS)*, No. 64, August 1978.

6 Norman Beaton, *Beaton but Unbowed: An Autobiography* (London: Methuen, 1986), p. 199.

7 Parminder Vir, *Films and Plays from Pebble Mill: Ten Years of Regional Drama* (West Midlands Arts, 1980).

8 Horace Ové, in Pines (ed.), *Black and White in Colour*, pp. 126-7.

9 Elvis Payne, *Multiracial Education*, Vol. 9, No. 2, Spring 1981.

10 Rudolph Walker, in Pines (ed.), *Black and White in Colour*, p. 81.

11 Mustapha Matura, interview with Tony Dennis, *Focus*, November–December

1985.

12 Mike Phillips, in Pines (ed.), *Black and White in Colour*, p. 176.

13 Norman Beaton, in Pines (ed.), *Black and White in Colour*, pp. 118–9.

14 Parminder Vir, Kevin Arnold and Onyekachi Wambu (eds), *A Fuller Picture: The Commercial Impact of Six British Films with Black Themes in the 1990s* (London: Black Film Bulletin and British Film Institute, 1999), p. 33.

15 Stephen Bourne, *The Voice*, 1 May 2000.

16 Michael Attwell, letter to Stephen Bourne, 22 May 2000.

17 Yasmin Alibhai-Brown, *Who Do We Think We Are?: Imagining the New Britain* (London, Allen Lane/Penguin Press, 2000), p. 259.

18 Lennie James, 'Wot a double act', *Pride*, September 2000, p. 66.

Appendix I

'Coloured Artistes on the Screen' (1919)

In 1919 *The Kinematograph and Lantern Weekly* published an article entitled 'Coloured artistes on the screen'. This highlighted the popularity of some imported American comedies featuring black actors, and questioned several English 'celebrities' about the possibility of the emergence of black screen stars. Two respondents, Oscar Asche and Alice de Winton, felt that black actors had no chance of success. 'There is no possibility of success for negroes either on the stage or the film', said de Winton. Others either felt unable to express an opinion, or were optimistic. The final quote, from actress Ivy Duke, that only black actors should be allowed to portray black parts, was revolutionary at a time when most black roles were played by white actors in blackface:

The success of the new Ebony comedies, which are acted throughout by black actors and actresses, and which are being handled by United Kingdom Photoplays, has focussed a certain amount of attention on the possibility of negroes becoming popular screen artistes, and in more quarters than one the query has been propounded, 'Shall we have a black Mary Pickford or a black Charlie Chaplin?' Several well-known people having been asked the question, it may not be uninteresting to give the views of one or two.

George Bernard Shaw does not express any particular opinion as to the merits of negroes as film stars, but is very emphatic in his views as to the probability of their success in the legitimate. He thinks negroes act very well, and that their powers of physical expression are very effective on the stage.

Sir Harry Johnston, the well-known traveller, expresses the opinion that both negroes and negresses are born comedians, as well as being gifted naturally with powers of song and aptitude for elocution, for rhythmic pose – in short, for acting.

William Auber, the famous critic, says that not having seen negroes act, he can express no personal opinion, but adds, 'I have been told they are very clever.'

Gladys Cooper, the celebrated actress, says that she is unable to express any opinion, never having seen the work of negroes either on stage or screen.

Oscar Asche, writing from His Majesty's Theatre, says: 'I am one of the few who take no interest whatever in films except those portraying current events, so I cannot express any opinion about them. As regards your question as to whether a black man is capable of portraying characters of Shakespeare, Goldsmith, etc., in a way that will commend them to the general public, I think it is just as possible for a camel to pass through the needle's eye.'

Alice de Winton writes: 'Most emphatically no. I think there is no possibility of success for negroes either on the stage or the film.'

Miriam Sabbage, winner of the *Daily Mirror* beauty contest, says that negro humour does not appeal to her. Regarding film work, she thinks that results alone can show whether negroes will prove successful artistes.

Ivy Duke, the popular 'Lucky Cat' star, considers that a broad and impartial view should be taken. In her view, where a scenario writer or producer casts a part for a negro character, the only true delineation of that part must come from the natural born black.

(*The Kinematograph and Lantern Weekly*, 14 August 1919)

Appendix II

'The Eighth Wonder of the World':

The Paul Robeson Letters

I n May 1996 I published a letter in *Yours* magazine asking readers to share with me their memories of seeing Paul Robeson in British films and concerts from the 1930s to the 1950s. I was overwhelmed by the response. From May to September I received over one hundred replies from all over England, Scotland and Wales. My intention was to find out what impact Paul Robeson had had on ordinary people. I was touched by the generosity of the correspondents, some of whom sent me music sheets, concert programmes and newspaper clippings they had kept for years. One gentleman even tore Paul Robeson's autograph from his autograph book and sent it to me. This is now framed and displayed in my living-room. Another correspondent, who worked as a parlour-maid before the war, sent me a torn fragment of a photograph of Robeson she had kept for over fifty years. This was taken in the garden of her employer's home where Robeson had stayed as a guest in 1932. Robeson had a tremendous impact on the lives of the British public, and this collection draws together, for the first time, some of their memories of the man Mr C. McGrady of Cumbria describes as the 'eighth wonder of the world'.

In the 1930s Paul Robeson turned his back on concert halls with expensive seats. They generally attracted middle-class audiences. He wanted his music to reach the working class. In the autumn of 1937 Robeson's venues were such popular music halls and cinemas as the Kilburn Empire; Gaumont State, Kilburn; Trocadero, Elephant and Castle; and the Gaumont, Hammersmith. By performing at these venues he was able to reach the working classes, who understood the emotional depth of his folk songs and negro spirituals. Says Marie Seton in her biography of *Paul Robeson* (1958): 'Never before had a singer of Albert

Hall stature appeared on these stages for three performances daily. They would have considered it beneath their dignity. But to Robeson this was the way he could reach the British people.'

No one will ever take his place as a singer with that wonderful God-given voice. How lucky we are to have his records! My most beautiful memory is Paul Robeson in *King Solomon's Mines* singing 'Climbing up, climbing up, till I'm holding the clouds in my hand'. It always brings tears to my eyes when I play it. I was very lucky to see him in London in April 1949. He sang in the middle of this huge circle, like a boxing ring! When the audience asked him to sing 'Old Man River' he said, 'When I sing that song you will know it will be my very last song for tonight.' It was so wonderful to see him and hear him sing. It was an evening I will never forget.

Diana Beale, Reading

I was brought up in the Manchester area, and taken by my mother to the pictures to see Paul Robeson. She was a great fan, and an accomplished soprano, so she was pleased to hear such an outstanding voice. It was a voice that wrapped around you, warm and loving. We saw the same Paul Robeson films over and over again. *Sanders of the River* was my favourite. The 'River Song' haunts me, and I've never forgotten it. He appeared at a time when there were very few black actors. He was a commanding figure. He stood out, and was noticed. He was a fine actor as well as a singer. The people in the north of England are a loyal lot and they were sad when Paul Robeson was in trouble. They signed petitions. People in England didn't forget him. He had a super, one-in-a- million voice, and we are the poorer for not having it now.

Mrs Marjorie Bryan, Teignmouth, Devon

I saw Paul Robeson in 1937 or 1938 in Wolverhampton. One Sunday afternoon crowds of people waited to see the actor Tom Mix and his horse Trigger who were arriving to appear at Wolverhampton's Hippodrome. Also on stage that day was Paul Robeson. As we all waited, Robeson walked through the crowds. I said, 'Oh, it's Paul Robeson.' At this he turned and slightly acknowledged me. I shall never forget this. Incidently, Tom Mix went the back way, so we didn't see him.

Paul Robeson's songs were wonderful. He was a proud, strong man. His deep, mellow voice was wonderful to hear. Audiences loved him. As I write this I can still hear him sing and I am old now. I have yet to hear anyone as good as him.

Dorothy Bullen, Kidderminster, Worcester

My husband knew some people who were friends of Paul Robeson. In 1949 a box at the Royal Albert Hall was reserved for Robeson's friends and two spare seats were offered to us. The concert was well received. The Albert Hall was packed. The audience called for more, and more was given. Paul Robeson could sing a battle song that could nearly lift the roof off, yet a few minutes after, he could sing a gentle lullaby that would send any baby to sleep. Before 1939 I saw Paul Robeson in *Show Boat*, *Sanders of the River*, *King Solomon's Mines*, to name a few, all while I was living in Peckham. There were so many cinemas to choose from. My husband says you may have the enclosed programme.

Hilda Evett, Gravesend, Kent

In the programme for the 1949 concert at the Royal Albert Hall Paul Robeson's repertoire included 'Over the Mountains' (Old English, arr. Quilter), 'L'Amour de moi' (Old French, arr. Tiersot), 'Lord God of Abraham' (Elijah by Mendelssohn), 'After the Battle' (Mussorgsky), 'Hassidic Chant' (arr. Engel), 'The Orphan', 'Pride', 'The Silent Room' and an excerpt from Boris Godunov *(all Mussorgsky) and a selection of Negro folk songs ('I Got a Robe', 'Ezekial Saw de Wheel', 'Swing Low, Sweet Chariot', 'Great Gittin' Up in the Morning', arr. Lawrence Brown).*

In 1939 I visited relatives in Worthing and Paul Robeson gave a Sunday evening show in the theatre on the pier. He was accompanied by his pianist, Lawrence Brown. He sang spirituals and songs like 'My Curly-Headed Baby' and 'The Joy of Love'. The more we clapped, the more he sang. There was no effort in his singing and there were no histrionics. He just stood on the stage beaming between songs, and hardly took a bow. There was such a disarming modesty about the man. The long evening flew like ten minutes or so.

J. Flowers, Ely, Cambridge

I don't think I've ever heard such a powerful singing voice, and don't forget in the 1930s sound systems weren't so sophisticated as they are today. Those deep tones thrilled people. His films were probably the first to point out that black people were human beings. Today they wouldn't be considered very well done, but in those days they probably made some of us non-racist!

Mrs D. L. Garland, Cambridge

My sister and I were great admirers of Paul Robeson and saw all his films. His voice was unique, soothing and often sad. To our great joy he gave a concert at the Birmingham Town Hall. It was a long time ago and, although my sister and I went to all the celebrity concerts, Paul Robeson's singing and personality seemed to remain with us. There was a gentle melancholy that pervaded his personality. We both felt it was a great experience. The concert was before the war. We could only afford the cheapest seats – two shillings and sixpence – and they were at the back of the orchestra. We kept the programme of this concert but it was lost along with other belongings in a hasty move to Worcester after being bombed twice.

Anne Gay, King's Norton, Birmingham

I am eighty-two. I first saw Paul Robeson in *Sanders of the River*. I fell in love with him that day. I thought he was in Africa. Many years later I found out the film was made on the River Thames! I don't think there were fan clubs in those days. If there had been, I would have been the first to join. Paul Robeson had the most wonderful voice. Once you had heard him you would never forget him. He was handsome too and, I should think, a lovely person. That was the impression I had. As I said, I really did fall in love with him.

Mrs Gwendolen M. Gray, Melton Mowbray, Leicester

I was a fanatic then (1930s) and still am at the age of seventy-eight. I saw *all* the films but he was not allowed sufficient scope for his glorious singing voice which, like the man, was a classic. *Show Boat* has never been equalled with Paul singing 'Old Man River'. I am a little 'peeved' at the moment because my radio is permanently tuned to Classic FM and I have never heard Paul's voice and, as I say, the man, his voice, and his songs, are *all* classics, without equal. I think I could go on for ever but I will close with a sequel – I met and talked with Paul in a very unusual way.

I was travelling by train to London and, as I was passing one compartment, I looked in and saw Paul sitting in a corner, huddled in an overcoat and scarf, with men in the other corners, who were either escorts or bodyguards. I did not want to invade his privacy, but I *could not* pass by without meeting him, so I made gestures with my hands and he nodded that I could enter but I was clearly under surveillance. I introduced myself, and did most of the talking, by showing him my appreciation of his singing. Before I left him I asked him to sign his autograph in my Trade Union diary which I wanted for a disabled friend of mine who collected autographs.

Len Grayson, Sheffield

I have been a great admirer of Paul Robeson since my childhood and I have seen all his films. In the 1950s he made a personal appearance at the Savoy Cinema in Northampton and I had to go and see him with my husband and three sons, the youngest of whom is named after Paul. As each one was born, I wanted them named Paul, but not till the last one did I get my wish. Paul Robeson had such a marvellous voice, which I can hear now without putting a tape on. No other singer has had such an impact on me and my only regret is that, when he appeared at the Savoy, I didn't know that he was speaking to any of the audience who wished to meet him backstage. How I wish we hadn't hurried away.

Mrs Jean D. Higgerson, Northampton

People in Wales wanted him to open the Eisteddfod but some said he would want too much money, but when he was asked he shook his head and said all he wanted was a Welsh hymn book. He said Welsh hymns were the nearest thing to Negro spirituals. I heard this on the radio from actors and singers who, like me, adored the man. Paul Robeson was the eighth wonder of the world.

Mr C. McGrady, Barrow-in-Furness, Cumbria

I was a parlourmaid in 1938 working for Captain and Mrs May of Catisfield, near Fareham, Hampshire. One of the staff told me Paul Robeson had stayed at the house in 1932 when he was appearing at the King Theatre in Portsmouth. Captain May had to hire a bed from Knight and Lee of Southsea as Paul was about seven foot tall. Lawrence Brown, who played the piano for him, also stayed at the house. They stayed because Mrs May was very fond of Paul's singing. When Mrs May died a lot of papers and photos were thrown out and I just managed to save a photo of Captain May and Paul Robeson standing in the garden. I have carried it with all my bids and bobs all through my life. I always wanted something to remember this lovely singer. I enclose that photo. You are welcome to it. It's quite a few years old. Sorry it's a bit battered. I hope it will help.

I also remember Paul Robeson was a very good painter and did quite a lot of watercolours. These paintings were hung on Captain and Mrs May's drawing-room wall. I don't know what happened to them. I'm seventy-five years old now, but my memory is good.

Mrs Eva Mills, Gosport, Hampshire

I was born in south London. I loved the cinema – there was not much else to do. At the very small Palace in Southwark Park Road (it used to be called 'The Blue') there was a 'tuppenny rush' for the kids – two in a seat and peanuts crushing on the floor. Friday night was 'talent night' and how we laughed. The Trocadero Cinema at the Elephant and Castle was a treat. We queued for hours, snaking round the barriers – this is pre-war, of course.

I saw all of Paul Robeson's films. His warm personality and magnificent voice made an instantaneous impact. I also saw him 'live' at the Trocadero when he brought the house down (this was between two films). I have never forgotten this performance. He sang for at least an hour, all the favourites. 'Trees', 'Old Man River', 'Deep River', 'Lazybones'. This would be about 1935. 'The Canoe Song' from *Sanders of the River* was a great favourite, although I believe the film was not one of his own favourites. I enjoyed *The Proud Valley* although old films now seem to me to be very superficial and over-romanticized. They were good in their day, and some still stand out, of course.

Joyce Neville, Basingstoke, Hampshire

The first time I saw Paul Robeson in 'real life' was many years ago at the opening of the Gaumont State Cinema in Kilburn where he sang some of his songs, which will forever be in my ears. I was born in 1922 and I was a choirboy of about twelve to fourteen years. He came on stage on two occasions. First in evening dress, then a casual suit. His voice was very strong and clear and no microphone was needed. He sang with great meaning. Mr. Robeson asked the audience to join him for the choruses of some of his songs such as 'Old Man River', 'Canoe Song' and 'I Still Suits Me'. He was well and truly taken in by the ovations. He was clapped and cheered from a packed house. He was magic. There will never be another Paul Robeson in my lifetime. (I'm seventy-three not out.) He was certainly my pin-up boy and my favourite 'voice'.

Mr J. W. Newman, Brockley, London SE4

I found him a very likeable character and also at that time I had some of his records, but in 1934 I found myself working on one of his films. I was an electrician with the arc lamps and employed at the studio of Sound City Films at Shepperton in Middlesex, a few miles from my home. It was *Sanders of the River*. We had the River Ash running through the grounds of the area where all the action took place. The carpenters and plasterers built little huts along the river banks and it was all made to look like a little Africa. Of course, some of the shots took place in Africa. Zoltan Korda was the director and his brother Vincent was the art director. The black men came down every day from the film agency in London, and they were called the 'extras'. They were inclined to keep together. On the set they always did what was wanted by the director. We, the electricians, were far too busy to talk to them. We could not enter into conversation with people on the set because we were up in the gantry during filming. It was very enjoyable work, but monotonous. What struck me most was Paul Robeson, a man with such a powerful voice, with a microphone so close to his lips! On the set he seemed reserved. That was over sixty years ago.

Charles Packham, Addlestone, Surrey

I am a 69-year-old Welshman and my first fond memory of this great man was over fifty years ago when I was a lad and lived in the Welsh valleys. *The Proud Valley* was made in the next valley to us and Paul Robeson had lodgings in Cardiff when he made that film. His son came to Cardiff some years ago to see where his father had stayed. The thing that stands out most in my mind was being spellbound by this big, proud man when he sang with a rich and very powerful voice.

Cyril Perham, Shoeburyness, Essex

As a small boy in the 1930s I saw, with all my pals, *Sanders of the River*. Afterwards we made cardboard shields and borrowed our mum's broom handles to use as spears. Then we went charging through the streets banging our shields and crying like Paul Robeson as the warrior chief. He was our hero at that time. Strange we never thought anything about his colour. He was someone we looked up to as a man. When I was thirteen years old my headmaster, who worked with the choral society, asked me, and other boys and girls, to sell concert programmes at Eastbrook Hall in Bradford. At one concert Paul Robeson appeared with his pianist, Lawrence Brown. All the programme sellers handed in their autograph books to be signed by the two men. Paul Robeson was a boyhood hero and everything I have read about him since has not altered that memory.

James Priestly, West Riding, Yorkshire

I am sixty-seven years of age now so I was only a lad when my father took me to the cinema to see Paul Robeson. His rich and resonant voice made an impression on me which has lasted throughout my life, and I still say that his bass voice has a unique quality that has never been surpassed. When I saw *Song of Freedom* for the second time, when it was reissued just after the war, at the conclusion of the film some of the audience were singing the final song, 'Lonely Road', as they exited the cinema. As far as his acting goes, he just seemed to step effortlessly into a role. His muscular frame and expansive smile radiated friendliness.

About five years ago I was motoring in Wales and visited the Mumbles, near Swansea. While there, I visited the gent's toilet on the sea front which was below ground level and remarkable for being fully carpeted. Inside I heard a beautiful, deep voice singing 'Some Enchanted Evening' which reverberated round this hallowed underground temple. It turned out to be piped music of a Paul Robeson tape arranged by the cleaner of the public convenience. He had also provided the carpeting! He told me that he had met Paul Robeson when he sang in Wales, and had remained an avid fan of his.

Mr Frank Read, Littlehampton, West Sussex

In the 1930s he gave a concert at the Central Hall in Bristol. The seats were three to five guineas each, but Robeson said he would not appear unless the prices were reduced. So the seats were priced at three shillings and sixpence. I made some small cakes to sell to my friends at work to raise the three shillings and sixpence. When he appeared, the Central Hall was full to overflowing. His attraction was his magnificent bass voice and the many spirituals he sang. When I tell you I am eighty-six you will realize I am writing about a long time ago.

Mrs Violet Scutts, Salford, Bristol

In the 1930s I was the second youngest sibling in a Jewish family, living in Germany. When my father died in 1936 money became very tight as my mother had to raise three youngsters without any state help. So our only entertainment was the radio and I remember vividly listening to Paul Robeson singing his sentimental ballads as I lay in my elder sister's arm in a room lit only by the light of the street lamp outside the window.

In 1939 my younger brother and I were evacuated to a Christian family in England. Christmas that year was spent in a strange country with a strange family, speaking a strange language and celebrating a strange festival. When we sat down to Christmas dinner the radio was playing. Imagine my surprise when I heard a half-hour programme of Paul Robeson! All at once mixed feelings of home-sickness, nostalgia and renewal of broken bonds filled my young mind. It was a day never to be forgotten. I will always be grateful to him for helping me to cope with a traumatic time in my life.

Werner Simon, Emsworth, Hampshire

I admired Paul Robeson very much and loved his voice. When I was living in London in 1949 I went to see him at the Harringay Arena. He was wonderful and I waited outside at the end of the concert in the hope of seeing him in person. He came out and stopped near me to get into his car. I held my hand out and he shook it firmly. I swore I would never wash that hand again. I'm sixty-nine now and I have never forgotten the thrill of it.

Betty Smith, Lowestoft, Suffolk

I first became aware of this great person at the age of fourteen in 1936. He had the most wonderful voice that God ever gave to man. I went all over Bradford to see his films. I listened to every record and radio appearance that I could, just to hear him sing. At my place of employment the girls used to have pin-ups of Nelson Eddy, Allan Jones etc. But Paul Robeson was on my wall, outshining them all. I did get some leg-pulling but nothing deterred me from my adulation. When he came to Bradford I paid one shilling and sixpence to stand on the balcony – which I almost fell over in sheer delight!

Mrs Mary Smith, Bradford, West Yorkshire

As a child I saw *Sanders of the River*, *Song of Freedom* and *The Proud Valley*. Paul Robeson had a very commanding presence. I think many cinemagoers went to hear him sing rather than the simply awful dialogue and storylines of his films. As a child I was impressed by the sheer goodness of the man which shone through his screen roles. I cannot say how he rated as an actor because, looking back, I think the British films were very class orientated and everyone acted how they thought that 'class' of person would. Witness Lupino Lane's dreadful caricature of a cockney working man.

Mrs J. Stephenson, Rotherham, South Yorkshire

He was unforgettable in his films, enjoyed by all. That is where his charisma lay. We could enjoy the films and come away feeling the impact of a performance far deeper than mere entertainment. His physical presence, a commanding physique, conveyed a gentleness and dignity that invited trust. Add to this a magnificent voice, with such understanding and depth of feeling, and there you have an outstanding man of his age, not just a twinkling star.

Ruby Stuart, West Huntspill, Somerset

As a lad of thirteen in the 1930s I managed to get a job at the local cinema as a bill boy, posting bills advertising the films that were on the cinema each week. Instead of wages I was allowed to see all the Saturday matinees, and night-time shows. So as a lad I saw most of the films with not having to pay. Paul Robeson's films were a draw to me. I was fascinated by the African films. I would watch the African films more than the cowboys. Robeson's powerful, deep voice and the size of him made Africa seem such a powerful place. I would dream of the African jungle, crocodiles, other animals, the sound of the war drums and the chanting natives, rowing their canoes. I imagined every African was big and powerful like Paul Robeson. He had a great impact on me. While listening to his records I imagined Africa, and transferred myself to another world. Then war broke out.

I served in the RAF and, after two and a half years in England, I was picked to travel overseas, something every serviceman dreaded. We were not told where we were going for security reasons, but I was issued with a tropical kit: a tope, bush hat, mosquito boots, and six inoculations. After many weeks at sea we woke up one morning to discover a coastline full of palm trees. Yes, I had come to the land of my childhood dreams – Africa! Looking at it I had the same feeling I had as a lad when I watched Paul Robeson's films. To me it seemed so powerful. It was Africa, the place I had dreamed about as a lad. But, alas, it was not like the films. Terrific heat and diseases like malaria sapped our energy. After two years in the jungle I returned home to England in poorer health. We all suffered with one disease or another. They said the bullets may not get you, but the hazards of Africa will! How true. I lost many friends out there, buried in a field. I was glad, and lucky, to return home. To me, that was one of my dreams as a lad that never came true. I still admired Paul Robeson as a singer, but Africa was not for me.

I got on very well with the Africans, though. I came into contact with them every day in the two years I spent there. I helped them, and trained them for the RAF. They joined the West African Air Corps. They were keen to learn and we got on very well. I was delighted to teach them a trade. I got myself into trouble many times for defending them against prejudiced white servicemen. I saw myself as a visitor to Africa. It was *their* country, not mine.

Mr J. Thomson, Liverpool

I lived in Folkestone before the war and my mother and father took me to see Paul Robeson in a concert at the Leas Cliff Hall. I remember so well what a wonderful evening it was. The hall was packed and everyone enjoyed the superb voice of Paul Robeson. I had an added thrill as I had visited the Leas Cliff Hall during the morning. I was fourteen or fifteen years old. It was a warm, sunny day and, as I left the hall by the side door, I walked into Paul Robeson as he was coming into the hall! With some trepidation I asked him for his autograph which he charmingly gave to me. He was a wonderful looking man. So natural and gracious. Generous to his audience and I felt so angry that he was treated so badly in his own country after the war. His talent was exceptional. In my view there's never been another to equal him. The sad thing was that, when I left Folkestone in 1940, my autograph book was left behind.

Mrs Pat Tiddy, Bexhill-on-Sea, East Sussex

I saw him on stage at King George's Hall in Blackburn in 1939. He was absolutely magnificent. He looked larger in real life than he did on the screen. He stood on the stage, his hands clasped in front of him, and sang all the old favourites. Everyone sat enthralled and at the end he got a standing ovation. After the show my sister and I met Paul Robeson. We got his autograph. He was utterly charming and made us feel that we were the only ones that mattered.

Mrs H. Todd, Rishton, Nr Blackburn, Lancashire

In the 1950s I was living in Blackburn, Lancashire, and I was privileged to attend a concert given by Paul Robeson at the King George's Hall. It was an unforgettable evening. Never again will there be a singer of such quality. During each song you could have heard a pin drop. The audience was absolutely captivated by this magnificent man and his truly magical voice. When I take the old souvenir programme out I relive that wonderful evening.

Mrs Joan Topping, Poulton-le-Fylde, Lancashire

I had the great pleasure of seeing Paul Robeson in 1949 at the Royal Albert Hall. It was packed and what an ovation he received. A standing ovation at that. No one would let him speak. So he just stood on the stage, waving and clapping back to us.

Mrs D. Warner, Tulse Hill, London SW2

Appendix III

Staying Power

One of our best character actresses, Corinne Skinner-Carter, has appeared in several classic black British films including *Pressure*, *Burning an Illusion* and *Dreaming Rivers*. With her return to the big screen in *Babymother* she adds another memorable film to her list of credits. She talks to Stephen Bourne about her long and distinguished career, which has taken her from dancing with Geoffrey Holder's company to receiving Trinidad and Tobago's Scarlet Ibis Award for 'Outstanding and Meritorious Service'.

BFB: *Tell us about your background.*
Corinne: I was born in Port of Spain, Trinidad. My father, Harold Skinner, worked on the ships, and my mother, Iris, was a seamstress. In the early 1950s I joined Geoffrey Holder's dance company. My parents hated the fact that I wanted to be a dancer. They said no good would come of it. But soon after I left Trinidad they started putting up pictures of me from the newspapers in the house! I came to England in 1955 to train as a teacher. At that time the British education system offered the best qualifications. That's why a lot of our scholars came to England to study.
BFB: *What were your first impressions of England?*
Corinne: After arriving here, I travelled by train from Southampton to Paddington, and I hadn't seen so many flowers in all my life! There were flowers *everywhere* and it was beautiful. But I was shocked when I arrived at Paddington and discovered the porters were white! In Trinidad you never saw *white* porters! In those early months in London I held my breath all the time. I couldn't relax. I was so tense and worried.
BFB: *One of the most inspiring leaders in Britain's black community at that time was another Trinidadian, Claudia Jones. Can you tell us something about her and the first Carnival?*
Corinne: Claudia had been persecuted in America for her political beliefs. After settling in England, she launched the *West Indian Gazette* in Brixton. This was Britain's first major newspaper for black people. In 1958

Claudia decided to pull together a group of black people from the arts. She wanted to show everybody that we were here to stay, that there was harmony between blacks and whites, in spite of the Notting Hill riots. So Claudia co-ordinated the first West Indian Carnival in Britain with the help of people like Edric and Pearl Connor, Cy Grant, Pearl Prescod, Nadia Cattouse and myself. The first Carnival took place in St Pancras Town Hall, and it was *packed*! It was not until 1965, the year after Claudia died, that Carnival took to the streets of Notting Hill. After forty years, I am still involved.

BFB: *Tell us about some of your early film and television appearances.*

Corinne: As a dancer I appeared in films like *Fire Down Below*, which was made on location in Trinidad. Then I danced in *She* and the James Bond movie *Live and Let Die*. I spent six months in Rome on location for *Cleopatra*, and I was a belly dancer in the film version of *Up Pompeii* with Frankie Howerd. On television in the 1950s and 1960s I appeared in just about every programme that included Caribbean dance, as well as things like *Cool for Cats* and *The Benny Hill Show*. As an actress I was in *Dixon of Dock Green* and an early episode of *Dr Who*. I also played a nurse who attended to Stan Ogden in *Coronation Street*.

BFB: *Tell us about* In the Beautiful Caribbean *which was shown by the BBC in their* Play for Today *series in 1972.*

Corinne: That was Barry Reckord's beautiful play and I shall never forget it. I felt so proud and uplifted to be acting in something as special as this, a television drama by a Jamaican writer. If they'd told me to stand on my head, I would have done so! That's how thrilled I was to be in it. You see, in those days, when black actors appeared on television, we were often isolated from each other. With Barry's play, we were together, and we could relax. It was fantastic. Do you know that cast included some of the best Caribbean actors around at that time? We had Calvin Lockhart, Louise Bennett, Thomas Baptiste, Ram John Holder, Horace James, Joan-Ann Maynard, Mona Hammond, Charles Hyatt, Carmen Munroe and Frank Singuineau.

BFB: *Would it be true to say that you were like a family?*

Corinne: Oh, yes. We all knew each other, and supported each other. There was no jealousy or competition. And we kept those friendships going. Most of the friends I have today started from those early productions.

BFB: *That 'family' feeling must have continued in the drama series* Empire Road, *shown by the BBC in 1978–9, in which you co-starred with Norman Beaton?*

Corinne: Yes, it did. It was nice because Michael Abbensetts, who is Guyanese, wrote all the scripts, and we'd sit and talk to him. If something didn't seem right, we'd change it. Horace Ove, who is Trinidadian, directed one episode, the *best* episode, and Norman, also Guyanese, was a fantastic person to work with. He was very professional. We were very upset when the BBC axed *Empire Road*. The ratings were very good, but no official reason was given. Personally I felt the BBC didn't want a popular black drama series on television.

BFB: *Tell us about two other television plays you appeared in by black writers: Tunde Ikoli's* Elphida *[Channel 4, 1987] and Jean 'Binta' Breeze's* Hallelujah Anyhow *[BBC, 1991].*

Corinne: Tunde's script for *Elphida* was lovely, exploring tensions and conflicts in a black family. Angela Wynter played Elphida, a young wife and mother who wants to restart her education, and she was wonderful in it. Rudolph Walker and I played her parents who are contemplating divorce and want her to act as a go between. *Hallelujah Anyhow* was interesting because it explored the drama that went on behind the scenes of a group of gospel singers. I wish Tunde and Jean could write for television more often, but British television is afraid to take a chance on black writers and directors, unless it is a situation comedy like *Desmond's*. It is afraid the programme will not work, not draw an audience.

BFB: *Two ground-breaking films in which you acted were Horace Ové's* Pressure *[1975] and Menelik Shabazz's* Burning an Illusion *[1981].*

Corinne: Those two films were made by the British Film Institute and they never gave them a chance. They did not promote them properly, and yet those films were *so* good. For us it's frustrating because we do good work, and it's not promoted. Nothing happens. But working on those films was great, and the parts I played were satisfying. I enjoyed acting in those two films. I hope that *Babymother* will get the promotion it deserves, and be a commercial success. Without that it will be difficult for black film-makers to find work in the mainstream.

BFB: *One of your most memorable roles was Miss T. in Martina Attille's beautiful film* Dreaming Rivers *[1988].*

Corinne: *Dreaming Rivers* was my best thing. It was so nice doing that. Martina is a very good, precise director, and the results are there on the screen. Again, when we, black actors, writers, directors work together, we pull together. We have a better understanding of each other. Sometimes I feel uncomfortable with white directors. This wasn't the case years ago with people like Philip Saville, who directed *In the Beautiful Caribbean*. Some white directors and writers were more receptive and innovative in those days. Today the situation is very different. They haven't a clue about us. When I auditioned for a part in *Casualty* recently I wore my hair in small corkscrews. After I got the part, the make-up lady phoned me and said: 'They liked your dreadlocks. Can you keep them for the programme?'

BFB: *You recently took part in the* Windrush Gala Concert *reading Merle Collins's poem* Seduction. *You were absolutely wonderful in that.*

Corinne: Thank you. I was so happy to be asked to do that, and I was chuffed when a lot of the younger people in the concert came up to me and said how nice it was to be working with me.

BFB: *What is most striking about your acting career is the quality of your work, and the high standards you have set yourself. And yet you must have turned down a lot of rubbish.*

Corinne: I have always been very selective. If I am not happy with a script, I turn it down. But I have been fortunate. On coming to England in 1955, I trained as a teacher, so I haven't always had to rely solely on acting for my bread and butter.

Black Film Bulletin, Summer and Autumn 1998, Vol. 6, Issue 2/3.

On 14 November 2000 Corinne Skinner-Carter made her first appearance as Audrey Trueman, the mother of Dr Trueman (Nicholas R. Bailey), in BBC TV's EastEnders.

Appendix IV

Greater Expectations

Stephen Bourne asks why black actors are made invisible in historical dramas and adaptations of literary classics when people of African descent have been living in Britain since the 1500s.

Shakespeare in Love may have scooped Oscar and BAFTA awards for Best Picture, but for some it is historically inaccurate. A reader's letter published in *The Voice* in February complained that the British film industry promotes segregation: 'For some unknown reason, there are no black actors in the critically acclaimed new film about the Bard, *Shakespeare in Love*.' Some historians argue that the black presence in Elizabethan England was so small and insignificant that it is hardly worth acknowledging. However, by 1601, the black presence was large enough for Queen Elizabeth I to have made two attempts at deporting and repatriating her black citizens. She failed on both accounts, and from around 1555 to this day, there has been a black presence in Britain. As for Shakespeare, in the 1590s he befriended Luce Morgan, a beautiful and famous African courtesan who ran a brothel in Clerkenwell. Some historians believe that Shakespeare fell in love with her, and they have identified her as his Dark Lady of the Sonnets.

Luce Morgan may have inspired Shakespeare, but it took a long time for black actors to secure employment in this country. In Lancashire in the 1790s a black actress was cast as Polly in John Gay's *The Beggar's Opera*. In the 1800s the African-American Ira Aldridge became one of the most celebrated tragedians of the Victorian era. Since Aldridge's death in 1867, many black actors have made an impact in Britain but today, in spite of the talent available, the British film and television industries fail to offer a wide range of parts to our black actors. It is also rare to find Britain's pre-1948 *Windrush* black presence acknowledged in historical dramas, apart from an occasional glimpse of extras in the background. Recent examples include a sailor in ITV's *Hornblower* and a public schoolboy in *Nancherrow*. It is extremely rare to find black actors playing speaking roles in such productions and, too often, Britain's black past is made completely invisible.

One of the first British films to acknowledge Britain's early black presence was the popular Gainsborough costume melodrama *The Man in Grey* (1943). Set in Regency England, Margaret Lockwood starred as a scheming, ambitious adventuress. The servants in the film included a young black page called Toby, who gave a rare glimpse of black servant life in the early 1800s. Ten years later a film version of *The Beggar's Opera* – set in 1741 – starred Laurence Olivier as MacHeath the Highwayman and this included two exotically dressed black pages in the gambling house. Finally, in 1978, *The Sailor's Return* – set in Victorian England – starred Shope Shodeinde as an African princess and Tom Bell as her sailor husband facing opposition to their marriage in the West Country. Though the film was well-received after its premiere in the London Film Festival, a distributor could not be found to release it. Consequently it was sold to television.

In 1968, when Lionel Bart's musical *Oliver!*, based on Charles Dickens's novel *Oliver Twist*, was brought to the screen, Shirley Bassey was widely tipped for the role of Nancy. It was the film's director, Carol Reed, who wanted Bassey, but in the end he was defeated by the American backers who didn't want a black woman in the part. Thirty years later, it is still impossible to find a black actor cast in an adaptation of a Dickens novel. Television's most recent omission occurred in BBC2's adaptation of *Great Expectations* (1999). By the time *Great Expectations* was published in 1861, many thousands of black people were living and working in London. In fact, several early British film adaptations of Dickens's novels acknowledged this, with black extras appearing in David Lean's *Great Expectations* (1946) and *Oliver Twist* (1948). More recently BBC2's *Our Mutual Friend*, shown in March 1998, included a single black extra, but wouldn't it have been great if they'd cast a black actor in a speaking role?

However, in 1998, three television productions with historical settings *did* acknowledge Britain's pre-*Windrush* black presence and offered speaking roles to black actors. In April–May BBC1 screened *A Respectable Trade*, an impressive drama serial which explored the trading of African slaves through Bristol in the late 1700s. An outstanding cast included Ariyon Bakare and Hugh Quarshie. Later in the year, in November–December, BBC1's enjoyable six-part adaptation of William Makepeace Thackeray's *Vanity Fair* (first published in 1847–8) included a hilarious performance by Felix Dexter as the servant Samuel. In Dexter's capable hands, Samuel was not a one-dimensional stereotype. Instead he exposed the shallowness of his materialistic employers by asserting his superiority. ITV's *Catherine Cookson's Colour Blind* – shown in three parts throughout

December – was something else entirely. Television adaptations of Catherine Cookson's novels are often criticized for being formulaic, but no one can deny that these epic television melodramas are hugely popular with viewers. *Colour Blind* was probably the first to include important black characters and, to its credit, it didn't shy away from exposing racism in working-class England between the wars.

Opening in Tyneside in 1918, *Colour Blind* began with Bridget McQueen (Niamh Cusack) shocking her Irish Catholic family by marrying a black merchant seaman (Tony Armatrading). After their daughter, Rose Angela (Carmen Ejogo), leaves school, racism makes it difficult for her to hold down a job. At the end of the story, Rose Angela is reunited with her black father, and has fallen in love with a white artist. It's a tear-jerker of the first order, and as silly as anything penned by romantic fiction writers. But from start to finish it was aimed at a mass white audience. This is probably why the black heroine, Rose Angela, ends up in the arms of an educated white man who 'saves' her from her grim, working-class environment, and disappears with her into the sunset! However, in spite of its shortcomings, it was good to see a populist television drama in a peak viewing slot, confronting a mainstream television audience with black characters in a historical setting. Also, its Tyneside location showed that, in the past, black British citizens did not all live in London.

So would it have been too much to expect the BBC to cast Carmen Ejogo, the star of *Colour Blind*, as Estella in their 1999 adaptation of *Great Expectations*? No doubt Professors of English Literature would have fainted in horror, as would most of the white middle classes who resist any 'tampering' with 'their' literary 'classics'. To have a black extra in *Our Mutual Friend* is one thing, but a black Estella in *Great Expectations* would have been revolutionary. And yet, Estella's mother could have been black. After all, black women existed in all strata of society in London in the 1800s, including Mary Seacole, the famous Crimean nurse. And Estella, who was born into poverty, was accepted into English society because of Miss Havisham's wealth and patronage, not because she was white. Also, no one complained about black actresses playing Juliet and her Nurse in *Shakespeare Shorts* three years ago, a significant example of 'colour blind' casting. So why can't this happen with Dickens? Is it because television producers and directors are afraid of upsetting the 'literary establishment'?

While more and more historians are uncovering information about the lives of Britain's black population since the 1500s, such as Jeffrey Green in *Black Edwardians* and Susan Okokon in *Black Londoners 1880–1990*, younger generations are practising integrated casting in school plays. Some of our black youngsters will become professional actors, and may be cast as doctors and lawyers but, until there is a radical change in the thinking of producers, directors, casting directors and actor's agents, we're never going to see a black Estella in *Great Expectations*.

Black Film Bulletin, Spring 1999, Vol. 7, Issue 1.

Appendix V

Hidden Treasures

S tephen Bourne looks back at his involvement with *Black and White in Colour*, and wonders if the information the research team uncovered will ever see the light of day.

The role of television in popular culture – and the necessity of the preservation of its history – needs urgent recognition: in particular the African-Caribbean and Asian contribution which is still undervalued and poorly understood. Compared to America, Britain is way behind in documenting and making accessible the history of black people in television. As a result, the considerable differences in the respective histories are not widely realised. In post-war American television, racist caricatures like Amos and Andy were the norm, disappearing in the 1960s to make way for the – then – near-visionary integrated casting of series like *Star Trek* and *I Spy*. By contrast British television, after starting out with a very real – if casual and inconsistent – progressiveness, allowed it all to be almost completely eradicated in the late 1960s. It was no coincidence this happened immediately after Enoch Powell made his racist 'Rivers of Blood' speech, and the popularity of his fictional 'disciple', Alf Garnett, in BBC television's *Till Death Us Do Part*, was at its peak. So, aside from popular music and entertainment programming, viewers can hardly be blamed for thinking that a black presence on British television began in 1972 with the launch of Thames's reactionary sitcom *Love Thy Neighbour*.

British television has systematically failed black audiences. Only on very rare occasions has it seriously supported or cultivated African-Caribbean or Asian talent – in front of or behind the camera. However, some years ago, with proper funding and support, a black British television history vastly different from what we expected was unearthed. For two years, starting in January 1989, I was a member of the 'Race and Ethnicity' project team that rediscovered this 'hidden' history. First Michael Grade, then Controller of BBC1, and subsequently Will Wyatt, then BBC television's Deputy Managing Director, saw the potential of the research, and part-funded a long-term research programme with the British Film Institute (BFI). The project aimed, through archival research, to look at the involvement of African-Caribbean and Asian people in British television, both on and off the screen. So, with support from the British Film Institute and the BBC, we pieced together the history, resulting in, amongst other outcomes, *Black and White in Colour*, a two-part documentary first shown by the BBC in 1992.

There has been a black presence on the box since its beginnings but it is rarely, if at all, acknowledged in histories of television. When I joined the project I saw the work as a starting point, for there had been very little previous research on the subject. Certainly no one had looked at the pre-1970s history in any depth, and what little had been published tended to be sociological or theoretical. The research was divided into two: my colleague, Therese Daniels, documented factual programmes, while I concentrated on drama and entertainment (music, dance etc.). Our tasks included the compilation of a data-base of television programmes from the *Radio Times* (1936–89) and *TV Times* (1955–89). By scanning every page, we listed every programme we could find with African-American, African-Caribbean and Asian on-screen and off-screen involvement. Using this information we located, viewed and catalogued programmes from our television archives, and located and interviewed important on-screen and off-screen personnel.

The range and depth of programmes we found – especially from the 1950s and 1960s – was surprising. There were, it turned out, many more programmes featuring black people in the early years than we anticipated. Themes explored included decolonisation, the settlement of African-Caribbean people in post-war Britain, and mixed marriages. Racism was hardly absent – for example, the BBC's *Black and White Minstrel Show* ran from 1958 to 1978 – but it coexisted with the assignation of major roles to black actors in television plays and series such as Gordon Heath in *Othello* (1955), Eartha Kitt in *Mrs Patterson* (1956), Uriel Porter in *Dixon of Dock Green* ('The Black Noah') (1957), Cy Grant in *Home of the Brave* (1957), Lloyd Reckord in *Hot Summer Night* (1959), Earl Cameron in *A Fear of Strangers* (1964) and Errol John in *Rainbow City* (1967). In the early years, most Asian roles were portrayed by white actors in blackface. In 1964 the BBC's long-running *Kipling* series featured almost exclusively white actors 'blacked up' for Indian roles. But Zia Mohyeddin helped break this racist tradition when he was given leads in E. M. Forster's *A Passage to India* (1965) and Noel Coward's *Pretty Polly* (1967). Prominence was given to many black singers and entertainers too, from Winifred Atwell to Paul Robeson, but in most pre-1970s television programming, black people were quite clearly spoken about and referred to rather than directly addressed.

Before the existence of videotape (from the late 1960s), British television was transmitted live and could only be recorded if filmed on 35mm stock from the television screen. This process was known as telerecording. But due to the high cost and technical problems involved, telerecording was rarely used. Consequently, only a fraction of our television output from the early years has survived.

At first, our expectations of finding programmes were low. But due to the funding and support we received, we were able to unearth many fascinating dramas and documentaries which redefined our understanding of British television history. For instance, there were two compelling BBC documentaries: Jack Gold's memorable *West Indians* (1963) with a commentary by the Barbadian poet and writer George Lamming, and Philip Donnellan's poetic *The Colony* (1964), filmed on location in Birmingham's black community. There was also *Freedom Road – Songs of Negro Protest* (1964) in which Cleo Laine and Cy Grant performed protest songs from slavery to civil rights. In drama there was writer John Hopkins's hard-hitting and thought-provoking episode of *Z Cars* ('A Place of Safety') (1964) as well as *Fable*, his controversial *Wednesday Play* from 1965 in which he reversed apartheid and located it in Britain. Another highlight was rediscovering the BBC's telerecording of *A Man from the Sun*, a drama-documentary first shown in 1956. This was an attempt to explore the lives of African-Caribbean settlers in post-war Britain. It was transmitted live from a BBC studio with filmed inserts. In the light of the 1998 *Windrush* celebrations, *A Man from the Sun* has become even more historically significant and yet, because it is *television* it is not considered worthy of attention. Consequently *A Man from the Sun* is barely remembered or revived.

In the summer of 1992, the results of our research was given a high profile by the BFI and BBC. BBC2 broadcast the two-part *Black and White in Colour* documentary, directed by Isaac Julien. It was shown in a season of programmes celebrating the contribution which African-Caribbean and Asian people had made to British television. To coincide with the screenings the BFI published a collection of interviews from the *Black and White in Colour* programmes. For the National Film Theatre I programmed the first black British television retrospective, showcasing some of the many programmes we had rediscovered. In addition to these outcomes, a unique data-base was created with information about many thousands of British and American television programmes. The data-base was intended to provide a resource for scholarship and academic research about black participation in British television from 1936 to 1989. Researchers could find every type of programme from *Amos 'n' Andy* to *Z Cars*. However, it is not widely known that, since I left the project in

1991, in spite of my attempts to make it accessible, the *Black and White in Colour* data-base has been collecting dust at the British Film Institute. In 1994 I approached the BFI about gaining access to the data-base when I was writing my book *Black in the British Frame: Black People in British Film and Television 1896–1996*. However, after I was told by the BFI that this was 'impractical', because they hadn't found a 'home' for it, I had to undertake a great deal of time-consuming research and fact-checking, using alternative sources, repeating some of the work I had undertaken between 1989–91.

In 1997 my hopes were raised after I had a meeting with the BFI's then-Assistant Director, Jane Clarke. She assured me of her support in making accessible the data-base. In a letter to me dated 27 May 1997 Clarke described the data-base as 'a unique record of immense value to the British film and television industry'. However, in spite of Clarke's enthusiasm, nothing happened and the data-base continues to collect dust.

In addition to the data-base, students and researchers are not aware of the many black British television programmes the research team helped the BFI's National Film and Television Archive to acquire, all of which are available to view on the premises. In addition to the television programmes, the National Film and Television Archive also holds the videotapes of the forty unedited *Black and White in Colour* interviews, deposited after we completed work on the two-part documentary in 1991. Though I have tried, it has been impossible to promote the existence of this unique resource of black British history. For example, in 1997 the BFI rejected my proposal to publish a small catalogue of National Film and Television Archive holdings (including the forty interviews) of black British film and television.

Perhaps the most interesting of the archive 'holdings' – and one that, like *A Man from the Sun*, deserves greater recognition – is *The Big Pride*. In the 1950s, the Guyanese writer Jan Carew and his Jamaican wife, Sylvia Wynter, were part of a important generation of African-Caribbean poets and novelists who lived and worked here. In 1961 they were commissioned to adapt their BBC radio drama, *The University of Hunger*, for ITV's *Drama '61* series. Based on events that happened in Guyana in 1958, it tells the story of three men who break out of prison and try to escape, not only from their past, but the harsh reality of their lives. However, the recording that was made of this compelling drama, retitled *The Big Pride*, remained forgotten until I persuaded the National Film and Television Archive to acquire the worn, torn negative, restore it, and make a new viewing copy.

Very few examples of the early plays of African-Caribbean or Asian writers have survived in our television archives. Among those lost for ever are three by Trinidadian Errol John: *Moon on a Rainbow Shawl* (1960), *The Dawn* (1963) and *The Exiles* (1969). I acknowledge that the restoration and preservation of our television heritage is a difficult and costly business. But I know that, if I had focused on a cult television classic, I would have attracted immediate attention and support. If I had rediscovered a lost episode – or even a fragment – of *Dr Who*, I would have become a national hero! So I knew how important it was to encourage the National Film and Television Archive to save and preserve *The Big Pride*, even though it took me six years to persuade them! Consequently, in June 1997, thirty-six years after its first transmission, this hour-long television play was shown again. The packed cinema at the Museum of the Moving Image included its producer, Herbert Wise; several surviving cast members, such as Nadia Cattouse and Tommy Eytle; and – just ten minutes before the screening – Jan Carew arrived from America to introduce the event, to the surprise and delight of the audience.

Triumphs like this have made the struggle worthwhile. Meeting Jan Carew, and participating with him in the revival of his 'forgotten' television play in 1997, was one of the highlights of my life. But it is an absolute disgrace that the BFI and National Film and Television Archive have failed to acknowledge and promote the existence of a unique resource of black British history. Needless to say, I have found my own methods of promoting it, albeit on a small scale. I have given occasional talks at conferences and universities around the country. I have participated in Black History Month events. In 1998, Cassell (not BFI Publishing, who rejected it) published my book *Black in the British Frame*. Audiences and readers have responded enthusiastically to my work, and they have made me realise that, at the end of the day, it is *they* who matter. I know that I have been a thorn in the flesh of the BFI, but not without good reason.

(*Black Film Bulletin*, Autumn 1999, Vol. 7, Issue 3)

Bibliography

In addition to the Further Reading lists at the end of each chapter, readers may find the following of interest.

Hakim Adi, *The History of the African and Caribbean Communities in Britain* (Hove, East Sussex: Wayland, 1995).

Karen Alexander, 'Black British cinema in the 90s: going going gone', in Robert Murphy (ed.), *British Cinema of the 90s* (London: BFI Publishing, 2000).

Yasmin Alibhai-Brown, *Who Do We Think We Are? Imagining the New Britain* (London: Allen Lane/Penguin Press, 2000).

Kevin Arnold and Onyekachi Wambu (eds), *A Fuller Picture: The Commercial Impact of Six British Films with Black Themes in the 1990s* (London: Black Film Bulletin and British Film Institute, 1999).

Martin Banham, Errol Hill and George Woodyard (eds), *The Cambridge Guide to African and Caribbean Theatre* (Cambridge: Cambridge University Press, 1994).

Kenneth M. Cameron, *Africa on Film: Beyond Black and White* (New York: Continuum, 1994).

Phil Cohen and Carl Gardner (eds), *It Ain't Half Racist, Mum: Fighting Racism in the Media* (London: Comedia Series 10 and Campaign Against Racism in the Media, 1982).

Thomas Cripps, 'Meanwhile far away from the movie colony', in *Slow Fade to Black: The Negro in American Film, 1900–1942* (Oxford: Oxford University Press, 1977).

Therese Daniels, *Black and White in Colour* (London: BBC Education, 1992).

Therese Daniels, 'Programmes for black audiences', in Stuart Hood (ed.), *Behind the Screens: The Structure of British Television in the Nineties* (London: Lawrence and Wishart, 1994).

Treva Etienne, 'Colouring the face of British film and television', in Courttia Newland and Kadija Sesay (eds), *IC3: The Penguin Book of New Black Writing in Britain* (London: Hamish Hamilton, 2000).

Peter Fryer, *Staying Power: The History of Black People in Britain* (London: Pluto Press, 1984).

Roxy Harris and Sarah White (eds), *Changing Britannia: Life Experience with Britain* (London: New Beacon Books and George Padmore Institute, 1999).

John Hughes (ed.), *Who's Who of Black Achievers* (London: Ethnic Media Group, 1999).

Sarita Malik, 'Beyond the "Cinema of duty?" – the pleasures of hybridity: black British film of the 1980s and 1990s', in Andrew Higson (ed.), *Dissolving Views: Key Writings on British Cinema* (London: Cassell, 1996).

Harcourt Nicholls, 'Black British actors and the film industry 1935–1960', unpublished thesis, Middlesex Polytechnic, 1988.

Peter Noble, *The Negro in Films* (London: Skelton Robinson, 1948).

Kwesi Owusu (ed.), *Black British Culture and Society: A Text Reader* (London and New York: Routledge, 2000).

Jim Pines (ed.), *Black and White in Colour: Black People in British Television since 1936* (London: British Film Institute, 1992). Includes Stephen Bourne's interviews with, among others, Elisabeth Welch, Pauline Henriques, Pearl Connor, Lloyd Reckord, Carmen Munroe, Thomas Baptiste, Rudolph Walker, Joan Hooley, Cleo Sylvestre and Kenny Lynch.

Karen Ross, *Black and White Media: Black Images in Popular Film and Television* (Cambridge: Polity Press, 1996).

Akua Rugg, *Brickbats and Bouquets: Black Woman's Critique Literature Theatre Film* (London: Race Today Collective, 1984).

Untold, March–April 2000 issue. Includes Peter Akinti's interview with actor Leon Herbert; Uju Asika and Marc Boothe's article 'Black British cinema: the next wave'; and profiles of Nadine Marsh Edwards, John Akomfrah, Alrick Riley, Treva Etienne, Lennie James, Lazell Daley, Stella Nwimo, Stephen Phillip, Wayne Campbell and Newton I. Aduaka.

Index

Names

Films

Index

Television Programmes

255